D0712661

ONE MORE MISSION

A Journey from

Childhood to War

*To my new friend
Bill, Best wishes
with your new endeavors*

Jesse Pettey

Jesse Pettey

To order additional copies of this book, contact:
Xlibris Corporation
1-888-7-XLIBRIS
www.Xlibris.com
Orders@Xlibris.com

CONTENTS

r

PART II

DEDICATION

For editing various sections of this book, my thanks go to daughters Lana and Jan. Also to friends Gloria Caneen and Daniel Montgomery for their suggestions. To other members of my family I wish to acknowledge their encouragement and interest, for without their support, it is unlikely that I would have ever launched this project. I also thank my brother, Gordon, for helping me remember some forgotten events and for editing certain parts of the final draft.

I am grateful to former members of the 461st Bomb Group and to those volunteers who constructed and maintain a large amount of data in the 461st Bomb Group Association Internet Web Site. This information proved to be very useful to me while completing this volume of my autobiography.

I dedicate this autobiography to my wife June, my children Lana, Janet, Carrie, Mike, their spouses, and my grandchildren.

To June, I dedicate my special love and appreciation for her support while working on this book.

PREFACE

FOR SEVERAL YEARS, I had occasionally thought about writing my memoirs for my children, but because I was convinced that my life and my experiences were no more extraordinary than most of my generation had experienced, I procrastinated. As a youth, I had overheard family conversations about the "Depression", people jumping to their death from office windows, and lines of hungry people waiting for a bowl of soup, but since I had personally witnessed none of these events, I was largely unaware of the historical events unfolding around me. As a consequence, I assumed that my life had been rather uneventful. Although, older and a bit more mature when Japan attacked Pearl Harbor I registered for the military draft and volunteered for military service. Like other boys of my generation I postponed what I was doing at the time, went to war, returned home after a tour of combat, completed my education, and launched a career. The war had been boring at times, terrible exciting at other times but we who had survived without permanent injury rarely thought that we deserved more than a thanks in the form of a letter from the U.S. Government. Indeed, many even refused the offer to continue school at government expense. What was I to write about? The thought of writing my memoirs was therefore dismissed for many years until one day a daughter startled me by asking, "Who will write your life when you are gone?"

I began then to contemplate the extraordinary decades in which I had grown into manhood: the "Roaring Twenties," the "Great Depression" of the thirties, and "World War II" of the forties. I thought about my experiences leading up to that fateful day, December 7th, 1941, when Japan attacked the United States, my induction into the military service, my training and preparation for war, and the combat missions I flew as a combat bomber pilot. I finally realized that I had lived through some very pivotal years in world history and this era would no doubt be deemed even more consequential in the future. It was a time that forever changed the American people, the country, and the world, yet I was not yet fully convinced that I might have some interesting stories to tell. I believed that most young men of that time simply served their country in time of war and none were heroes.

While I continued to muse over the events of my life, I also remembered that I had sustained such a childlike belief in the immortality of my parents — that they would live forever — I had unwisely postponed asking them about their past. One day I found that not only had my parents left me, no other family members remained to answer my questions about them. Even as I write this, my generation is disappearing at an astonishing rate. It was a rather disconcerting experience for me to face reality one day and acknowledge that soon none of my generation would remain to tell subsequent generations about the manner in which we lived, our memories of the Great Depression, our World War II experiences, and about other momentous events that occurred during our lifetime. And so at last, I acquiesced and began recording my memoirs.

It is my desire and hope that this narrative will open a small window into the past, vicariously sharing with those who are interested, a glimpse, however small, of living in a small East Texas town during the depression and participating in a deadly world war. In the following pages I have attempted to chronicle some of my memories from birth until the time I was discharged from my World War II combat obligations.

The experiences I write about are engraved in my memory forever, but after many years, the precise words and conversations are mostly forgotten; therefore, the dialogue is founded on my memory of what the characters actually said or what they most likely said. Occasionally, I lapse into a vernacular, which has softened somewhat over the years but is still the colloquial speech used by native East Texans to this day. It is a true story and none of the incidents have been exaggerated or invented.

I am firmly convinced that each life is unique, as different as our fingerprints. Although our lives often merge for brief periods of time, each takes a distinct path throughout life and none observe an identical panorama. This book, then, is about panorama—a panorama I perceived—a view that I surveyed—a voyage that I made through my world as I saw it during my lifetime.

PART I

Growing Up In Nacogdoches, Texas

"From our ancestors come our names, but from our virtues
Our honors."—Unknown

THE PETTEYS ARRIVE IN NACOGDOCHES

O N SEPTEMBER 24TH, 1850, a group consisting of ten members of the Power family, one slave and several covered wagons departed New Market, Alabama en route to Texas.

Zachary Taylor had died that year, and Vice-President Millard Fillmore completed his term of office as President of the United States. California had been admitted to the Union as a free state allowing the frontier to extend to the Pacific Ocean and The Republic of Texas had been annexed five years earlier as a State of the Union. It would be another four years before the Republican Party would be founded.

The wagon master of the wagon train was a 48-year-old schoolteacher, Baptist Minister, and my great-great grandfather, Holloway L. Power. Accompanying him in the leading wagon was his wife, Elizabeth Meals Power. In another wagon rode my great grandfather, William Howard Pettey, his wife Sarah Power Pettey, daughter of the wagon master, and their three-year-old son, my grandfather, William Holloway Pettey. William Howard and three-year-old William Holloway were direct descendants of Hubert Patey/ Patty/ Petty who immigrated from England to Virginia sometime before 1665 where his name first appeared on a deed for 150 acres in the court records of Lancaster County, Virginia. His son Thomas was born sometime between the late 1670s or the early 1680s. Their descendants later migrated to Alabama by way of North Carolina and eventually to Texas; hence one may find many Petty/Pettey names in these states.

Holloway and Elizabeth Power owned a large comfortable home on their plantation near New Market. The plantation was so large that it was necessary to divide it into smaller parcels to sell it. Why would a successful man sell his home and move his family to Nacogdoches, Texas? To answer that question, one must refer to his prolific diary:

"AUGUST 5, 1850, TOOK MORE PILLS LAST NIGHT AND FEEL BETTER TODAY—I DREAMT LAST NIGHT THAT OVER THE LITTLE MISSOURI RIVER WAS THE PLACE TO FIND HEALTH. HOW GLADLY I WOULD GO THITHER FOR THE SAKE OF THAT BEST OF ALL GIFTS."

In 1833, Holloway had received a serious chest injury when he was crushed between a wagon and a cotton gin, a large building where farmers transported their cotton to be weighed, cleaned and pressed into bales. His ribs never mended correctly after the accident, causing him to suffer chest pains and various lung diseases. He became convinced that in order to improve his health, he must move to another part of the country. In letters to his sons, who had settled in Nacogdoches the previous year, he repeatedly inquired about doctors in Texas. After much deliberation, he decided to sell those items that he could not move with him and join his sons in Texas. The family spent the summer preparing for the move and on September 24th they departed New Market, Alabama.

Four days after leaving New Market, Holloway wrote in his diary:

"FELL SICK FROM FATIGUE AND BAD WEATHER. WEATHER VERY DRY."

A weary Power and Pettey family finally arrived in Nacogdoches 48 days later after sleeping in rain, traveling over rocky hills and flooding streams. They settled and for four generations raised their families and farmed their land around Nacogdoches. It is interesting to note that the Petteys never acquired and owned slaves. Although slaves would not be granted freedom for another 13 years, Holloway Power had already begun to develop an aversion to the practice and perhaps discouraged his family from purchasing additional slaves. He wrote in his diary in 1851:

> "CORRECTED A BLACK MAN FOR DISOBEDIENCE IN RUNNING ABOUT AT NIGHT. I FELT IT MY DUTY TO USE THE ROD, YET I DEPLORE THE NECESSITY, AND HEARTILY WISH ALL SUCH RELATIONS BETWEEN A MASTER AND SLAVE HAD BEEN DISPENSED WITH AT THE EARLY SETTLEMENT OF THE COUNTRY, BUT THE EVIL HAS NOW SPREAD UNTIL THERE IS NO REMEDY WITHIN HUMAN POWER."

For five generations, most of the Petteys and Powers remained in Nacogdoches and were buried at The Old North Church Cemetery north of town, but like other members of my generation, I moved away from Nacogdoches. I am not aware of any Pettey relatives remaining there, although several Powers' descendants continue to live in the area.

"William Holloway Pettey"

WILLIAM HOLLOWAY PETTEY

My grandfather, William Holloway Pettey, was born near New Market, Alabama, in 1847, the year that Brigham Young led a group of Mormons to a salt lake in Utah, later named Salt Lake City. James Knox Polk was President of the United States, and the gold rush was underway in California. My grandfather was three years of age when he departed New Market, Alabama, by wagon train in the company of his father and mother, William Howard and Sarah Power Pettey. Seven years after arriving in Nacogdoches, when he was 10 years old, his father died of an apparent heat stroke and was buried at North Church Cemetery. He would always blame his mother for the death of his father because, even after his father had complained of feeling ill, his mother had harried him to return and work in the fields where he collapsed and died a short time later.

William's resentment grew more intense when Sarah remarried. His dislike of his new stepfather and bitterness over his mother's remarriage prompted him to leave home and enlist in the Texas Confederate 4th Calvary. Perhaps this resentment, combined with other frustrations, contributed to the failure of his two marriages and separation from his children. He seemed to become more ill natured as he grew older and his family abandoned him. He lived alone in a home for Confederate Soldiers for several years and then in a small house provided by a friend until his death. He never visited our home; consequently I was not acquainted with him and saw him for the first time at his funeral.

From the information I have acquired from family members, it is reasonable to assume that despite my grandfather's intelligence and self-education, he was emotionally unstable. As a father, he would have been judged a poor role model for his children. According to stories told by them, he would curse his mother and God in their presence, blaming them for his problems. If true, it explains why they were afraid of him. It is remarkable that his children were able to escape serious emotional damage and live normal successful lives. My father and his siblings were apparently motivated at an early age to distance themselves from their father and fervently seek a different life style. Perhaps their negative experiences became a positive force that energized them to seek a better life than my grandfather could offer them. I would like to believe that he brought about some positive influence on their lives.

I have added the section about my grandfather to enable the reader to better understand the magnitude of the adversities my father was compelled to overcome in order to achieve any modest amount of success; however, in fairness to my grandfather, I must state that my information was obtained from his children, who were greatly influenced by my grandmother. As in all relationships, the beholder observes the unique conduct of an individual occurring at certain times and forms an opinion based on that behavior, while others may reach entirely different conclusions based on the activities of the same person occurring at different times. It is notable that his acquaintances and neighbors spoke well of him. Because my grandfather died while I was very young, I never had the opportunity to form my own opinion of his behavior.

Jesse E. Pettey Sr. & Maude Jefferies Pettey

JESSE E. PETTEY, SENIOR

My father was born May 29, 1897, on a farm a few miles west of Nacogdoches. His birth occurred one year after Henry Ford had driven his first automobile, six years before the Wright brothers flew their first airplane and four years before the radio was invented. He and my mother lived in one of the most eventful periods of history. My father grew up in the horse-and-buggy era, yet it was only a few years until the average family in America owned an automobile. He saw the first airplanes, heard the radio announcement of Lindberg's first non-stop flight across the Atlantic and the sinking of the Titanic. He read about the opening of the Panama Canal and the horrors of the First World War. He saw the first silent movies, witnessed through television the terrible atrocities of the Second World War, the Korean War, the Vietnam War, the blast-off of the first astronauts into space and their walk on the moon. During his lifetime, more advancement was made in civilization than had been made in all man's existence.

My father was born seventh of eight children. When they were strong enough to work, my grandfather demanded that they labor long hours, constantly reminding them that great riches lay ahead if they would only work harder. Living isolated and working long hours, the children had little time for school. My grandfather hoped, as did most farmers of the day, to keep his family working together as a family enterprise, but he was such a stern taskmaster that he unwittingly drove his family away from the farm when they were old enough to provide for themselves. My grandmother moved away soon after my father departed.

When he was 13, my father and a brother departed to live with an older sister where he completed the sixth grade and worked at odd jobs. Few children living on farms in those days attended school beyond the sixth grade. Later, at age 15, he applied for a job with Bell Telephone Company. By stating on his application that he was eighteen, he was subsequently hired as a lineman to maintain telephone lines. Lacking knowledge about electricity, it is remarkable that my father was not injured, but he learned by watching other linemen, asking questions, and in due course became a competent lineman. It is noteworthy that he not only escaped injury, he completed home-courses in electricity and later worked as an electrical engineer with Texas Power and Light Company. However, it was while working at Bell that he met and married my mother who also worked for Bell as a telephone operator. My father enjoyed saying, "When I first saw her; my heart stopped beating because she was so beautiful."

Telephone operators of the 1920s were, for the most part, young and single women who would ultimately leave their jobs when they married. Jobs for women were almost non-existent. Schools and Telephone companies were the largest employers of women and the prevailing belief was that a married female should be dependent upon her husband; that she must forfeit her job to another single and unsupported female. As a result, whenever a single female married, she usually quit or was fired. Every town or city needed switchboard operators to place and receive telephone calls.

The women operators sat facing a huge switchboard covered with many small openings designed to receive the end of a connecting cord when placed there by the operators. One end of the cord was connected to the switchboard while the free end was placed in an aperture connecting the switchboard to a caller that had lifted the cradle of his telephone. When the caller lifted a receiver or earpiece from its cradle, a light flashed over one of the openings signaled the operator that someone wished to call a number. She would then insert a cord into the aperture and say into her speaker, "Number please?" Some operators developed quite a unique pronunciation of the word "please" by raising the pitch of their voice so that it became "pluezze". The caller responded by telling her the number of the desired connection, usually a three-digit number in small towns. She would then place a connecting cord into an opening of the desired telephone number causing it to ring. Telephone operators wore earphone contraptions over their heads and a microphone mounted on their chests, allowing their hands to be free as they connected numerous cords to the desired openings. They could eavesdrop on any private conversation and were privy to many secrets of small towns. If information was needed about a resident of a city, one could do no better than to ask one of the local telephone operators.

Sometime after my birth, my father began working as a lineman for the Texas Power and Light Company. He wore spurs in order to climb light poles and maintain electric lines. Iron spurs were welded to two iron leg braces and attached with leather strips to the inside of both legs of a lineman. By forcing one sharpened spur at a time into a wooden light pole and holding onto the pole, a lineman could lift himself as if he were climbing a ladder. I recall seeing Dad almost run up a 30 foot pole in this manner. When the lineman was positioned beneath the electric lines, he would fasten a safety belt secured to his waist around the pole then comfortably and safely lean back to work on the lines above him. Occasionally a lineman's spurs would rip free from the wooden pole, but with his belt securely attached, he would only slide downward until he could again dig his spurs into the pole. On the other hand, most linemen liked to descend swiftly by deliberately dislodging both spurs and sliding down the pole with their safety belt still attached around the pole. Their rapid descent was slowed by digging both spurs into the pole every several feet, much like mountain climber rappelling down a mountainside. A good lineman could rappel down a pole in three or four leaps.

My father once described an event that occurred when he disturbed a nest of hornets located at the top of a light pole. He quickly determined that he could not descend the pole using his spurs before they would attack him; he therefore leaped backward, falling about thirty feet onto the ground. Both feet were broken but he escaped the hornets. His feet bothered him for many years.

While I was still a young boy, Dad was promoted to foreman of the line crew and never climbed poles again. The new job required him to supervise the linemen from the ground rather than climbing poles. It was often a stormy, icy, winter night when he was called to restore disrupted electrical power. Before leaving the house, he would ask me if I wanted to accompany him. I can proudly recall my father, guiding a spotlight mounted on his truck to provide light to the men working above on the power lines as he issued suggestions and instructions. As a young boy, these were exciting occasions and I was proud that my father was the "boss", but as I grew older my interest broadened to other activities and I no longer enjoyed accompanying the "boss".

These occasions were the few times that we shared together. Because he was a compulsive talker, he seldom encouraged me to talk about my interests, leading me to believe that he did not care about my activities. I now understand that it was not a lack of interest; he concentrated so intently about what he wanted to say that he never listened to me. It seemed that he was unaware of anything or anyone around him when he talked as if he were speaking to himself. It is not surprising, therefore, that I did not learn the art of conversation from him. In my immature judgment, I found it extremely difficult to overlook this fault and to admire his many other favorable characteristics.

While attending a business meeting on the Island of Cyprus many years later, I received a telephone call from a friend who was a doctor in Nacogdoches informing me that my father had broken his hip in an accident. He added that he had also developed pneumonia, and assured me that, at his age, it was critical. I immediately flew to Nacogdoches to care for him, because my stepmother was too elderly and in poor health to be his caretaker. After the death of my mother, my father, at age seventy married Thelma and had enjoyed sixteen years of marriage. A short time after I arrived, she broke her shoulder from a fall and was admitted to a hospital room only a short distance from my father's room. With no one to care for her at home, her brothers then placed her in a nursing home.

As I continued tending my father's needs at the hospital, I became aware that I was becoming more devoted to him each day. Perhaps my increasing devotion came about because of his weakened condition and inability to dominate the conversation. We, for the first time, were able to share silence together. Oh, that we could have learned early in life that sharing a moment of silence is often more important than incessant conversation.

On the night of his death, as I reflected over our life together and our inability to converse, it occurred to me how much I had always yearned to be able to communicate with him—to feel comfortable and comforted in his presence. I recorded the following thoughts that night:

> I Never Knew Him.
> I just know he was a good man.
> They all say what a fine person he was.
> Everyone seemed to know him;
> Everyone but me.
>
> I know he was a devout man,
> Many calls for help he answered.
> Everyone knew that he gave of himself;
> Everyone but me. . . .
>
> I know that when called at night,
> He left a warm bed to help.
> Everyone knew that he was a generous man;
> Everyone but me. . . .
>
> I know that he was proud of me.
> When I returned from war, a young officer with bride.
> Everyone knew that he talked of nothing else;
> Everyone but me. . . .
>
> I know we were separated by a generation of thought,
> And lived miles and miles apart;

everyone knew that he understood;
Everyone but me. . . .

I know he never wanted it that way.
Maybe he never knew just how to say,
But everyone knew that he loved me;
Everyone but me. . . .

I know that tonight he left me,
but somewhere we'll meet once more,
and I'll finally get to know him,
as I never knew him before.

November 21, 1983

MAUDE GRAYBILL JEFFRIES PETTEY

My mother was born in Willis, Texas, Montgomery County March 16, 1900. The 1900 U.S. census was taken when she was two months old and reveals that her family lived on a farm near Willis. The family consisted of her mother, father and three older sisters. Her father, William M. Jeffries was a farmer and to date I have been unable to unearth any information about him or my mother's early childhood. He died shortly after my mother was born, sometime between 1900 and 1902. I have been unable to find a death certificate, deeds, previous census or even where he is buried. The 1910 census reveals that my grandmother had married Albert Moore approximately two years after my mother was born. There was little information, such as birth and marriage certificates, assembled for the public in those days and most records were written in family bibles. Montgomery county was created from several other counties, and maintained few public records before 1900. A fire destroyed the 1890 census. Since so little is known about her from her childhood until my birth, I will write about my mother in future chapters as I remember her.

Author's birth place, Pillar Street.

JESSE E. PETTEY, JUNIOR

During the early morning of January 29, 1924, a baby boy was delivered to proud parents in an ancient house in Nacogdoches, Texas. The old house, built in the last century, appeared fragile with age and incapable of withstanding any additional ravages of time and perhaps it could not, for it no longer exists. It was located on Pillar Street, just around the corner from the Oak Grove Cemetery, where four signers of the Texas Declaration of Independence are buried: Thomas J. Rusk, Charles S. Taylor, John S. Roberts, and William Clark. The first Secretary of War of the Republic of Texas, a Texas Chief Justice, and two veterans of the Battle of San Jacinto are also interred there. Doctor W.I.M. Smith assisted the birth of the first son of Jesse Pettey Sr., then age twenty-six and Maude Graybill Jeffries Pettey, age twenty-three. It was a momentous time for my parents, and to celebrate my birth, they named me, Jesse E. Pettey Junior, in honor of my father. Many years later, while serving in the Army Air Corps, I never revealing that I was called Junior back home and introduced myself as Jess. I intensely disliked the name, Junior, but it was a frequently used name at that time.

Children born a few years on either side of 1920 became the "war generation" of World War II. Nearly all lived with ebullience and a disregard for the dangers ahead. Perhaps they understood that because of the war, many would be injured and would not live beyond their teens or early twenties. Helping their parents struggle through the depression, seeing deprivation around them, and later being subjected to military discipline combined to mature this generation at an early age. The depression also instilled an ethos of hard work, generosity, and honesty in them.

The unrestrained economic growth during the 1920s suddenly ended with the stock market crash of 1929, but until then, it was a decade of unparalleled prosperity. Vice-President Calvin Coolidge completed President Hardin's term of office at his death in 1923, inheriting a corrupt administration, but at the same time inheriting a period of speedy industrial growth, high profits, and a rising stock market. Upon his presidential election in 1924, he began to rid the administration of corruption and adopted a "hands off" policy of government called, "Coolidge Prosperity." The national debt was reduced, taxes were lowered time after time, and high employment from restricted immigration laws contributed to an overall rising standard of living for most Americans. Roads were built; houses equipped with plumbing and electricity; skyscrapers such as the Empire State Building in New York City were built; women gained suffrage with the 19th amendment, but another amendment, banning the sale of alcohol, fueled government corruption and crime in the larger cities. It was also a decade of advancements in aviation beginning with an around-the-world flight sponsored by the U.S. Army in 1924, the year of my birth. The same year Delta Air Lines was born as a crop dusting enterprise and three years later, Lindbergh flew nonstop to Europe in 1927.

Despite the national prosperity of the 1920s, poverty seemed to overcome the five thousand or so people residing in Nacogdoches County. At the time of my birth until the 1940s, Nacogdoches commerce consisted mostly of cotton farming, although some diversified their crops with corn, ribbon cane, watermelons and peanuts. Farmers were forced to sell their products at low prices and to buy their other products at high prices. Their problems only worsened during the next decade with the arrival of the Depression. Indeed, poverty was a way of life in the decades of the 1920s and 1930s in Nacogdoches.

EARLY MEMORIES

MY FIRST AWARENESS began at two years of age. I remember residing with my parents in a large house on West Main Street at the foot of Irion Hill. Main Street in Nacogdoches begins and ends with hills. Irion Hill, named after an early doctor, lies to the west of Nacogdoches, while to the east of the city, Main Street steeply ascends Orton Hill, another precipitous hill named after a former sheriff. The city nestles between the two hills, and, because of its location, the city has witnessed many automobile and truck accidents over the years as drivers, without brakes, plunged headlong into the city from the hills above. In addition to brakes being poorly constructed compared to brakes today, most roads were unpaved and poorly maintained.

My parents owned a Model T Ford with a canvas top. Model Ts were cheap, easy to repair, had only a few simple controls, and were slow. People would say, "All you need is a pair of pliers and a piece of bailing wire to keep a model T running." Once, while driving our Model T to a food store at the top of Irion Hill, my mother lost control of the car causing me to hurtle forward onto the dashboard and injure my forehead when the car suddenly stopped in a ditch. There were no safety belts at that time. Somehow, she managed to reach the store and seek help from the owner who wiped the blood from my face, applied a disinfectant, and placed a bandage over the wound. I, like most two-year-old children, fiercely resisted him screaming and crying until he said,

"You look like a grown man with that bandage".

Immediately I ceased my resistance and began to envision a grown man with a bandaged head. I was so proud of the bandage that I would not let my mother remove it for several days—maybe longer. It is said that we have no memories before the age of four unless we experience a traumatic event. This was indeed a traumatic experience and created a vivid memory of an event that occurred when I was two years old. It also provided a permanent scar on my forehead that, to this day, has been a constant reminder of the event.

. . .

It was 1927 when my father began constructing a house on an isolated road south of Nacogdoches. It was a short sandy road, replete with thick forests on both sides and a pristine, magical, wondrous road for a young boy to explore. I was free to roam about the countryside with few automobiles and strangers for my mother to worry about. The Locke family lived at the opposite end of the road from our house and had at one time owned all the property along the road. They named the street Jack Locke Street after their only son, Jack who was a few years older than I was. A room in the Locke home was set aside for Jack's hobbies and was filled with model airplanes he had built—an activity requiring patience and skills that I respected. It was a virtual museum of airplanes. Models were hung from the ceiling and aircraft paintings covering the walls; it attracted every boy within walking distance. Jack was the only child of a middle-aged couple who gave him everything he desired. Even so, he was shy, withdrawn, and alone most of the time until his life was tragically terminated at a young age in a tragic automobile accident.

My father constructed the first house to appear on Jack Locke Street but it was destroyed by fire only a few years after we moved into it. We were forced to move into a rented house located in the same neighborhood and conveniently near the destroyed house so that my father could reconstruct it when he was not carrying out the duties of his job. The house was expanded by adding a separate dining room and upgraded with beautiful hardwood floors. I was proud of the new home and considered it better than any other houses in the neighborhood or the homes of my friends. In the evenings, my musical friends and I would gather in our new home to emulate famous bands of the day by playing our whining, moaning musical instruments. Our unwelcome sounds were significantly amplified on tranquil evenings as they traveled great distances to distant neighbors lounging on their front porches seeking relief from the heat. I am sure most of them were puzzled or maybe even horrified when their calm, peaceful evenings were shattered by such peculair sounds.

It was in this house that I endured difficult pubescent years; yet, I also discovered modest talents and capabilities that would give me much pleasure later in life. The house on Jack Locke Street sheltered me at a time when I was learning the power of choice, of independence, of freedom, the beauty of music, the mysteries of nature and the exhilaration of living. While living there, I also discovered girls, experienced independence by leaving home, found jazz music, and became aware of the thrill of humble achievements. Living with good parents in this unadorned simple little house helped fortify me for future encounters with the harsh realities of life.

· · ·

My grandmother and step-grandfather lived in Huntsville, Texas with Uncle Brake and Aunt Daisy. My step-grandfather, Albert Moore, married my widowed grandmother when my mother was about two years of age and with the addition of his children, created a new family. Uncle Brake was employed as a guard at the state prison and lived within the walls of the prison. Because my grandfather was very ill, aunt Daisy nurtured and cared for him in her house. It was a thrilling experience for me to observe guards with guns, to see prisoners wearing prison uniforms nearby and to observe uniformed guards in towers holding guns as they watched over the inmates. Prisoners worked in adjacent fields, in my uncle's yard, and performed other small tasks around the house for him. The first time I saw him in his uniform, I thought he must surely have the best job in the world. My step-grandfather had a cancerous growth on the side of his nose, which I believe was melanoma but I doubt that a doctor had treated him since so little was known about cancer at that time. The disease was terminal, ending his life shortly after our last visit. My grandmother came to Nacogdoches soon after his death and resided in our home until she died in 1959, thirty-one years later. My mother buried her in Pine Crest Cemetery a few miles north of Huntsville, Texas. As a young boy, she was my baby-sitter, companion, surrogate mother, and a tough adversary over checkers. She enjoyed playing the game until I began complaining about her winning. She would then scold me for being a poor loser, put away the checkerboard, and present me a choice of promising to lose gracefully or discontinue the checker game. My fondness for the game would invariably cause me to choose the first alternate; I would promise to accept losing without complaining, at which time she would reopen the checker board and we would begin another game.

THE SATURDAY MOVIES OR PICTURE SHOW

THE SATURDAY AFTERNOON Picture Show, as it was called then, was regularly filled with squirmy overactive youngsters, for it was the best bargain in the county. It provided a low cost, safe baby-sitting function for mothers who needed a peaceful interval at home. A double feature movie lasted three to four hours, and cost fifteen cents. Popcorn cost another nickel (five cents), which I almost never possessed. My parents would say to me,

"A nickel will burn a hole in your pockets if you don't find a way to spend it."

But I had no fear of my pockets being burned; there were few nickels to be found. During the depression, nickels were rare as diamonds.

I regularly began attending the Saturday Picture Show when I was about six years old. My mother would drive me to the theater, and return for me when the movie ended. She had few things to worry about while I attended these Saturday afternoon rituals—I was safe. I would never leave the theater as long as there was an exciting movie to watch. There were no comparable places of interest in town, and even if I left the theater, it was impossible to become lost in such a small town. Pedophilia was unknown in 1930 in Nacogdoches.

The Saturday Picture Show was divided into segments that invariably ended with the hero caught in a perilous predicament: bound to a railroad track with a train bearing down upon him, or hanging from a cliff with a rope that was unraveling. The following Saturday movie would begin with the previous hazardous scene, but somehow the hero always managed to escape all dangers until near the end of the segment; he would then maneuver himself into another precarious situation just as the film ended with the captions, "To be Continued Next Week". No boy in town would voluntarily miss the next episode. I eagerly anticipated the different methods the hero might take to escape his latest dilemma and looked forward to the excitement the movie always generated the following Saturday.

Each Saturday afternoon, when the commercials were finished and the action began, I would bolt from my front row seat, along with the audience, to join the action of the movie characters. If the actors engaged in fist fighting, we would jump from our seats with clenched fists swinging at imagined opponents but if the villain was shot, we shouted our approval and applauded. Because we were near the action on the screen, the front row afforded the best seats in the theater and was sometimes worth a shuffle while claiming our seats.

The Saturday Afternoon Picture Show introduced me to Johnny Wiessmuler as "Tarzan of the Apes," Frank Buck as "The Great White Hunter", Flash Gordon "The Space Explorer", Tom Mix and other early cowboys as fierce Indian fighters, but it was the African movies that held me spellbound. I would attempt to reenact scenes from these movies in a forest across the street from our house, where plants grew from marsh-like earth with such profusion that it resembled an African rain forest. Not only did the forest provide an ideal setting for this enactment, but it also provided authentic grapevines for me to swing from treetop to treetop as I pretended to be Tarzan. Since I was smaller than Johnny Wiessmuler in size, I was content to only run from tree to tree holding a vine but with a bathing suit substituted for a loincloth, and a dull kitchen knife replacing Tarzan's knife, I was ready for mortal combat with any creature. It was essential, if I intended to become an expert Tarzan, that I learn the "Tarzan Cry"; a sound that proclaimed to all that he was king of the jungle. This distinctive wail-like call demanded a need for continual practice and it required a strong voice that could be heard for many miles around. Fortunately for my mother and father, we had few neighbors for me to disturb. While playing out my fantasies, there were no neighbors—only an abundance of lions to slay with my kitchen knife, bushmen to fight, huge snakes to wrestle. A problem sometimes arose when I entertained a guest who wanted to play the role of Tarzan. Because I had rehearsed the part so many times; because I was intimately familiar with the geography of the territory; because I knew where the terrors of the jungle lurked; because I knew how to call my ape, Cheetah, no one could be a better Tarzan. Another reason I think I did a creditable job acting the part of Tarzan, it was not easy to kill a lion with a dull kitchen knife.

As I grew older, my interest turned to cowboys. A cowboy hat, toy six-shooters and a bandanna were substituted for the bathing-suit-loincloth. Some of my favorite cowboy movie stars of those days were Tom Mix, Bob Steel, and Hoot Gibson. Each had unique characteristics that I memorized and imitated, but my best talents were reserved for Indian fighting. There were Indians behind every tree on Jack Locke Street, which fiercely resisted me, but with an unlimited supply of bullets, I eventually flushed them into the open where they could be dispatched. Indeed, the cowboy always defeated the poor Indians during those times and I never questioned any scene in the movies, however ludicrous they might seem. The prevailing scenario of that time portrayed the cowboy as an expert marksman who never failed to shoot down an Indian — an inept Indian who could never succeed hitting a white man. I found it easy to wipe out an entire tribe of Indians and could spend the entire day fighting them but invariably my mother called for me. How dare a mother call a cowboy hero home for lunch at a climacteric moment of an Indian war? I was never hungry or willing to cease firing at such times.

MOTHER AND LAUNDRY

WHEN WE MOVED into the house on Jack Locke Street, my mother continued to do the laundry in a black iron wash pot as she had always done. We did not own an electric washing machine until much later. She would build a fire under the wash pot every Monday morning and sort the laundry as she waited for the water to boil. When the water was boiling, she would add lye soap she had previously made from lye and lard. Lye is a product of leached wood ashes and when combined with lard and sodium, it forms a yellow caustic blob of soap. After adding soap, my mother would place soiled clothes in the boiling water with a large stick she would use to stir the clothes and lift them from the boiling water onto a clothesline. After cooling sufficiently to touch, she placed the hot clothes in a tub of cold rinse water and secured them to a clothesline to dry. My job was only to assist my mother hauling the dry clothes into the house. I was not yet tall enough to gather the dry clothes from the clothesline. Whether the clothes were adequately cleaned I am not sure, but I am most certain that they were sterilized. Germs could not withstand both the boiling water and the lye soap; the soap alone was strong enough to kill them. I remember my mother's red, chafed hands brought about from exposure to the strong soap. Observing my mother launder our clothes in this method leads me to believe that we wore not only sanitary, but also very durable clothes—anything less would have disintegrated.

. . .

During the 30s we acquired our first electric washing machine. It resembled a wash tub set on three legs but with rollers mounted on one side. Water was squeezed from wet clothes by compressing them between two rollers and turning the rollers with a hand-crank. An electrical powered agitator moved the clothes in water much like washing machines do today. As wet clothes were squeezed between the rollers, water spilled onto the floor compelling us to only use the machine outside the house. It would be several years before washing machines would contain electrically operated rollers and until then, my job was to turn the rollers by hand.

THE OLD ICE BOX AND CHURNING

BUTTER

PRIOR TO THE installation of electricity in most homes and the invention of electric refrigerators, a wooden cabinet appliance called an icebox was utilized to cool foods. Today one can only find these lovely old iceboxes in antique stores. They were constructed from skillfully stained wood, fitted with silver handles, and designed with an opening at the top to accommodate a block of ice. Cool air from the ice flowed downward into the food compartment and as the ice melted, water drained into a water container placed at the bottom of the icebox. During the hot summer months, the interior of the icebox was cooler than the warm air outside, but in the winter, my mother would place food outside the kitchen window where the air was cooler.

Images of a man carrying a block of ice on his shoulders, after knocking on the door before entering the kitchen to deposit the ice in our icebox, are yet vividly and clearly etched in my memory. He wore a piece of leather to protect his shoulder from the cold ice and a leather apron around his waist. Upon opening the top of the icebox, he would chip the ice with an ice pick worn on his belt in order to make it fit into the compartment. The interior of his ice truck parked outside was lined with a quilt-like material to insulate and protect the ice; although there was a continual stream of water dripping from the back of the truck as the ice melted. I delighted in crawling inside the cool ice truck seeking a small piece of ice to relieve the summer heat while he chipped ice inside the house and collected money from my mother.

Every city had its icehouse. The Nacogdoches Icehouse was built next to railroad tracks so that huge blocks of ice could be unloaded from the train directly into the icehouse. There it was chipped into 25 and 50 pound blocks of ice. The building displayed signs announcing: "25 LB. BLOCK OF ICE—10 CENTS", "50 LB. BLOCK OF ICE—20 CENTS", and "ICE COLD WATERMELONS—25 CENTS". The building sat alone adjacent to a large red graveled parking lot and contained a small door that when opened; allowed a block of ice to slide onto a large platform built onto the front of the structure. Several blocks of ice would be placed on an inclined track inside, which formed a chute leading to the small door. When the attendant opened the door from the outside, gravity would force a block of ice from the inclined chute onto the platform. Ice trucks and icehouses were not refrigerated in those days but were built with walls covered by a straw-like insulation covered with tin. The blocks of ice were somewhat preserved and their melting slowed. On a hot summer afternoon, I enjoyed standing near the platform and the ice house door so that when it was opened, a cool refreshing blast of icy air would gush forth covering me like a waterfall.

My father would drive to the ice house platform and ask an attendant draped in a rubber apron for a block of ice. The attendant would open the small door, allowing a block of ice to slide onto the platform, tie a piece of twine around the ice, grasp the block of ice with a pair of ice tongs, and place it near the edge of the platform. My father would then pay the attendant, lift the ice with the twine, and place it on the front bumper of his automobile. Car bumpers were built from solid steel, placed about one foot away from the body of the automobile and unlike car bumpers today, were durable and designed to protect the automobile. The empty space between the body of the car and the bumper was often used to transport any item that would fit, including a block of ice. During the drive home, as the ice melted, the edge of the bumper appeared to cut into the block of ice. The depth of the cut would depend on the length of time it had remained on the bumper; if left unattended too long, the ice block would be sliced into two blocks and fall to the ground.

My father purchased ice to be chipped into small pieces and placed in a wooden ice cream maker, to cool watermelons and sodas in a wash tub for various picnics, and to replace the ice in our icebox at home. Ice was usually delivered to our house where doors always remained unlocked. Since no one feared crime in those days, most delivery persons merely knocked to warn us that they were about to enter the house. Whenever my mother planned to be away, she would place money on the table for the iceman. If the sum of money was greater than the charge, he would leave change on the table. I cannot remember our house or automobile ever being locked. Keys were left overnight in the ignition of our automobile and keys to our house were nonexistent. It's more than likely that my father never possessed house keys because he never used them—indeed, in the midst of the depression, few people had valuable items that required protection; nevertheless, we were conditioned from childhood to respect the property of others. It was truly an age of trust.

. . .

My mother always made butter from the milk we obtained from our cows. She would strain the milk through a cloth to remove impurities and set aside a portion of the milk for churning in a large ceramic vase that held as much as five gallons of milk. An opening in the center of the lid of the vase allowed a long wooden handle to protrude that was attached to a paddle on the lower end. The operator lifted the handle and pushed the paddle down into the milk. The constant stirring caused the fat in the milk to congeal and create butter. I remember the sound, 'whosh, whosh, whosh', resonating throughout the house as my mother repeatedly lifted and pushed the paddle into the container of milk.

My mother used another smaller churn that held only a gallon of milk. It was a square clear glass container shaped like a box. A handle with gears was attached to the mouth of the jar so that when the hand-cranked handle was rotated, a paddle inside the jar agitated the milk and created butter. I was assigned the responsibility of making butter with the small churn and nominated CHIEF CHURNER.

THE STRENGTH OF A MOTHER

MY MOTHER SAT on the back porch shelling peas as I entertained myself by searching for things to do. Upon sighting a strange object on the wall above my mother, a bizarre idea suddenly flashed through my mind that I must climb something in order to inspect the target of my attention. It appeared to be a box containing several intriguing items made of glass, wiring, and copper fittings—most tantalizing to a young boy four years of age. Then, most electric meters were mounted inside an open box containing a switch for disconnecting the electric current and two exposed safety fuses. Ignored by my mother, I climbed onto the back of her chair and reached above to seize one of the fuses with one hand. Needing more support to climb further so that I could better observe the items in the box, I reached with the other hand to grasp the second fuse. Instantly an enormous hammer struck me as if I was a fly! I was lifted from the chair by the electrical current bolting through by body, convulsing my arms and facial muscles, while assaulting me with a burning pain I had never before or since known. Fortunately my mother knew what to do. She immediately tossed the pan of peas onto the porch, disconnected the electricity by opening the switch, and grasped me to her breast. During her panic, had she failed to disconnect the electricity before attempting to wrench me free from the fuses, both she and I might have been electrocuted.

My father worked most of his life around electricity, and although he respected it, he was not afraid of electricity. Many times I watched in horror as he tested a light socket by placing a finger inside the socket. If he felt a jolt of electricity, he was assured that the socket was "hot" and working correctly. My muscles, however, seem to have forever retained a memory of the experience on our back porch because I can yet feel a shock jolting through my hands when I recall the incident. As a consequence, I have retained a great respect, even a fear of electricity over the years. I will always be grateful to my mother who saved my life with her good judgment.

. . .

Several years later, my mother was driving along a road still wet from a recent shower, when we began to skid out of control. After the car turned 180 degrees and halted, she leaped outside, opened the rear door, seized my arm, and instantly lifted my brother and me out of the car as if we were weightless—all in the blink of an eye! I did not know before this event that she was so strong or could move so fast. I now understand how vigorously a mother can behave when her children are in danger.

AUNT MATTIE

My mother's sister lived on a farm outside Huntsville, Texas with her husband and three young children. I remember that my uncle had a constant cough—more than likely, caused by tuberculosis—which deprived him of the capacity to work. Because of his poor health and inability to work or buy land, his sole hope of survival was to grow food for his family on land that was owned by another farmer. Farmers earned little money, often none, during the depression but continued to own vast pieces of property that could not be sold. As a result, many land owners encouraged other less fortunate landless farmers to live and work on their surplus land for a small share of the crops. They were called "sharecroppers." Living in the midst of prosperity today, it is difficult to imagine the impoverishment of those sharecroppers. Often, they could scarcely produce sufficient food for their family let alone harvest a surplus to share with the owner. Farming methods were vastly inferior to those used today. Farmers depleted nutrients from the soil by repeatedly plowing the same soil year after year, thereby creating vast wastelands on which they strived in vain to make a living. When I was about five years old, my uncle died leaving my aunt without money, land or a home. The depression was just beginning, and there were few jobs available—none for a widow without skills and three small children. My father was fortunately employed in an industry unaffected by the depression and able to help her. Although he did not earn a large amount of money, his job was secure, and he doubtless felt a moral responsibility to help his sister-in-law. He soon found a house for her in Nacogdoches where he and my mother would be nearby if she needed assistance. It was a small, four-room house on several acres of land without running water, electricity, or sewerage. Moreover, cracks in the walls allowed cold wind to enter the house, yet it was not unlike most farmhouses of that time. It was a place that my aunt and cousins could seek refuge and make into a home. The elder son, Eugene, was strong and he was willing to work. Because he had learned to plow, he would in time become the main provider for the entire family. Somehow, my aunt managed to purchase a mule that provided power for plowing a small plot of ground, thereby allowing Eugene to provide vegetables for the family.

After they moved into the house, I would take advantage of every opportunity to spend a night with them. Aunt Mattie cooked with a wood burning stove and made splendid tasting food, notably biscuits. The house was heated by a wood burning stove producing tangy, pungent odors while a kerosene lamp with a dancing flame cast eerie moving shadows on the wall. My most enjoyable memories were the evenings. My cousins and I would sit on the floor beside the wood stove, while my aunt, using her fingers and hands, formed silhouettes of animals on a wall. Much to our delight, she brought them alive by moving her hands in a manner that caused the shadows to dance silently around the wall while she recited stories of their adventures. As we struggled to remain awake after going to bed, she would recount tales and adventures of her past life. My uncle had worked in various places in the U.S. before his illness, and their travels provided her with many stories of far away places. Aunt Mattie was a very good spinner of tales and captivated our attention by painting such realistic word pictures that we were spellbound as we silently slid into the oblivion of child-innocent sleep.

While Eugene plowed the earth during my visits, I would walk barefooted by his side in freshly plowed furrows captivated by the dark sweating mule and the plow cutting deep slippery wounds into the soil. The sweet smell of acrid damp earth ascended from the freshly opened ground and merged with the sour stench of the mule as my bare feet sank into the cool moist soil of the furrows. On the other hand, I also recall hesitantly walking barefooted through a field of prickly grass burrs, running on a blistering hot sandy road while desperately searching for a cool patch of grass, and cautiously stepping barefooted over jagged rocks on the approach to our favorite swimming hole. The delightful sensation of walking barefooted on soft cool soil after abandoning hot restrictive shoes on a summer day was well worth these few uncomfortable moments.

Eugene was the head of the family at twelve-years of age. He bore the responsibility of caring for his mother, two younger siblings, and doing the work of a grown man while attending school. From the time that I first remember him as a young boy shedding his adolescence to provide for his family, I regarded him as an adult. I admired him for his willingness to assume adult responsibilities and to this day he remains one of my favorite persons. He stands as yet another example of how a fulfilled and successful life may be attained without the accumulation of wealth.

. . .

Like flashing dancing angles of the dark, fireflies called lightning bugs in East Texas, winked their yellow-green lights at each other. During hot August nights the bugs were ubiquitous, as they flashed their lights from gnarled trees, ragged bushes, open fields, and the dark shadows of the woodlands. When I was a child there seemed to be an over abundance of these harmless little beacons of the forest; today they are rarely seen.

In one clinched fist, I held the final prey of the evening: a fiery pulsating lighten-bug. With the other hand I held a glass jar, containing perhaps twenty or more previously captured striped lightening-bugs. The flashing, whirling mass of bugs formed a maelstrom of light as they attempted to escape from their translucent prison.

"Mother look over here"! I shouted as I raised the glass jar over my head.

Most evenings my mother and grandma enjoyed an after-supper stroll along a dirt road near our house. I always ran ahead in order to capture bugs—anything that moved was a target. Although a few street lights cast a dim glow along the road, the forest on either side of the road provided a pitch-black backdrop and revealed innumerable lightening-like flickers of light. We were continuously surrounded by lightening-bugs signaling one another, like ships at sea, unfathomable messages from the darkness of the forest. I never witnessed a lightening bug flashing during the day. I never understood where they hide or what provokes their flashing beacons only after dark. I only know that I am content to let the memory of these charming fairy-like creatures remain a childhood mystery.

The streetlights also attracted many other insects. During hot arid summers, huge numbers of crickets and grasshoppers flourished. Attracted at night by the streetlights, they assembled into moving carpets of slithering, crawling insects on the ground where we walked. It was impossible to avoid stepping on them. I remember the loud buzzing, rasping noise produced by the masses of insects amid the crunching sounds as we stepped on them during our peaceful evening strolls.

My youthful nights resonated with insect and bird sounds. Sweltering in bed near an open window, I was serenaded by the cellophane crinkling sounds of crickets and locus throbbing in varying rhythms, like ocean waves endlessly ebbing and flowing over sand. The woodland choir would lift their voices to the shadows followed by a sudden overwhelming silence as the chorus paused—interrupted by a sound only they could hear. In the interlude of absolute silence, the mournful lament of the whip-o-will would be heard calling from the dark abyss of the woods while I faded into a deep summer night's sleep.

FOUR BOYS AND A MAN

A LONG A NARROW trail four large boys approached me in a spread formation. The trail was sometimes used as a short cut connecting two parallel streets near our house. It began in a level pasture, plunged down the banks of a stream, crossed the shallow rock-strewed stream of water, ascended abruptly up the banks, and meandered through a dark lonely stand of trees. I was aware that it was too late to turn. It was out of the question that a five-year old could stand up to these larger older bullies and since there was no one around to aid me, I could only continue walking and hope they would allow me to pass them. As I approached, I was comforted to recognize a neighbor, Jack Locke, among the group. I considered turning and running away but I wanted to appear brave and I was certain that Jack was not a bully. As I approached them, I was suddenly reminded of movie scenes where a condemned prisoner walked to his execution. When we finally met, they surrounded me and demanded that I lower my trousers. When I asked why, they replied that they would tell me after I had lowered my pants. I could only stand and stare at them in shock. I almost fainted when one drew a knife and announced that he intended to castrate me. I was, by then, convinced that whatever they intended to do, I was helpless, although a temporary stir of hope arose within me when Jack began an unsuccessful plea to allow me to pass. I assumed that since I could not expect to win a struggle and I could not think of an effective defense, the best strategy was to stall and not cooperate with them. I had no intention of lowering my pants, but indeed, I could not envision a method of escape nor could I hope that something would take place short of a miracle—I was desperate.

One of them said,

"Well, I guess we will have to take his pants off."

My hope for a miracle was near an end when from behind a tree a masculine voice cried out,

"Boys, you touch that kid and I'll cut you with this knife!"

My tormentors froze in mid-motion as an old man, pocketknife in hand, materialized from behind a tree. Slowly approaching, he suddenly shouted,

"Now, get out of here!"

The four boys recoiled as though their faces had been slapped, leaped in unison and disappeared around a bend of the trail, the clatter of their running feet resonating into a melodious diminishing echo as their presence dissipated into the silent forest. My savior, while walking along the trail, was curious and suspicious when he had observed a group of boys blocking the trail before him. He had moved slowly and cautiously behind a tree where he could overhear our conversation. When he was certain that it was time to take action, he had stepped from behind the tree with his knife to threaten my bullies. After their departure, he escorted me to Seale Street and my home.

I will always be grateful for the intervention of my benefactor. No one will ever know what might have occurred that day if he had decided to take another route and the bullies were uninterrupted. It is possible for such a group of boys to stimulate, to challenge each other, and to commit a foolish act that none would commit or even consider alone. When I recall how seldom the trail was used, it seems more than unusual that this man would appear at the exact moment of my need. I choose to believe he was my guardian angel disguised as an old man.

A BABY BROTHER

I RAN AS fast as my five-year-old legs would allow. There was no time to waste for I had a new pony at home to care for. I hurried home to greet this new member of the family. I had dreamed of owning a pony since I could remember, and when my parents sent me to spend the night with their friends, Lee and Mable Jones, I had not questioned why they had sent me away. The next morning, Mable awoke me to say that my mother had telephoned requesting that I return home immediately where a surprise awaited me. For some time I had begged, implored, beseeched my parents to purchase a pony for me and now, certain that I had persuaded them, I could hardly wait to greet this new member of the family. As I happily skipped down the hill from the Jones' house, a man walking in the opposite direction said to me,

"Good morning, young man, you certainly are in a hurry!"

I explained that I was rushing home because I had a new pony waiting for me. He answered,

"I'll bet you are anxious to see that new pony!"

As I bounded rapidly away from him, I began thinking about the word "anxious." It sounded good to me and although I did not remember hearing the word before, it indeed described my feelings that morning. I determined that I would use the word at every opportunity and for many years thereafter, I was "anscous" for this and "anscous" for that.

Upon arriving home, my happiness vanished like dust before a wind as my mother introduced me to my new infant brother! Like most five-year-old children, I had never noticed that my mother was pregnant. Indeed, I did not even know how a pregnant mother appeared,

51

or the meaning of the word. I did not resent my new brother—I was rather captivated by him, but because I had so intensely dreamed of owning a beautiful pony, I had convinced myself that a new pony waited at home for me. As despair is to exhilaration, what darkness is to light, I experienced my first plunge from happiness to dejection while staring at the red faced squirming infant. I think there is nothing so distressing to children as their first encounter with disappointment. Although I would later experience many disconsolate moments in my life, none would ever quite equal the anguish of that five-year-old who had been introduced to reality on a morning long ago—aware for the first time that life is not always what one might wish it to be.

SCHOOL BEGINS

I WAS FIVE years old when school began. My mother faced a dilemma—should I begin school that year or wait until the following year when I would be six? After consulting with the first-grade teacher and several friends, she came to the conclusion that I should begin school at age five. She was aware that I was not quite mature enough to be placed with children older, and in some instances, larger than I was, but she reasoned that I would soon adjust. Unfortunately, the difference in children at that juncture of their development is vast, both in the classroom and in social relations outside the classroom. I was not only unprepared to interact with older children, I had not yet learned to relate to any children. I was only five years old. I lived on an isolated street and there had been no other children nearby to teach me the game of "give and take"; consequently, I had developed into a "loner".

When the first day of school arrived, my mother dressed me in knickers, accompanied me to the schoolroom and handed me over to Mrs. Marshall, my first grade teacher. Until the early forties, golfers and most young boys dressed in "knickers"—short pants that extended to and buckled slightly below the knees. I intensely disliked them because the buckle restricted my legs and was uncomfortable; therefore, at every opportunity, I unfastened and wore the buckle hanging free.

Mrs. Marshall proceeded to issue books, to inform us of the location of the rest rooms, to proclaim the rules of deportment, and to explain what the bell signified at the end of the class. We were allowed a five-minute break between classes when most children ran outside to play. At the sound of the bell my first day at school, I aimlessly wandered outside and began to explore the fascinating exterior of an old building adjacent to my school built in 1859 and known as The Old University of Nacogdoches. There I found massive columns with all sorts of interesting niches and crannies. There were beautiful pigeons nesting above the columns and in the bell tower. Mysterious dark corners beneath an old musty-smelling stairway and a labyrinth of supporting wooden beams criss-crossed the ancient bell tower of the old dilapidated building. It was as though I had been transported in a kaleidoscope of colors and smells to another world—so breathtakingly interesting that time and the classroom of Mrs. Marshall ceased to exist.

"Old University of Nacogdoches and first Band Room, built in 1859"

When the bell sounded, all other pupils returned to their classrooms leaving me alone with my discoveries. The objects and places I explored were so interesting I was convinced that school would be an exciting experience, but my joy was short-lived. A man bearing a long stick suddenly appeared! As he swatted me on the seat of my pants, I instantly became aware that the man's stick was instead, a long ruler used as a paddle. I rapidly lost interest in the delightful items I had only minutes before discovered as Mr. Hall, principal of the Nacogdoches Elementary herded me back to class with his long ruler hovering over my buttocks.

Elementary school then included grades one through seven, followed by high school, grades eight through eleven. Unlike the schools today, there was no junior high or twelfth grade. The elementary principal, the high school principal, and to some extent, the superintendent, were responsible for disciplining pupils. Teachers were responsible for teaching, and whenever a student created disorder in the classroom, the teacher had the authority to either punish or send the student to the office of the principal for punishment. Depending on the severity of an infraction of a rule, the pupil was often paddled or kept after school—sometimes both. My parents had warned me that if I were punished at school, they would punish me again at home. It was not easy to keep secrets in a small town and although teachers regularly informed parents when their child had been a problem, more frequently, parents soon were informed by other means. Teachers enjoyed the utmost respect in the community and most parents wholeheartedly supported their authority to discipline students with a paddle. My parents never doubted the word of a teacher and if I misbehaved, they firmly believed that the bruises on my buttocks were there because I deserved them. In their view, teachers were invariably right, which contrasts greatly with the current practice of blaming teachers for the misbehavior of students while at the same time depriving them of all rights to discipline these students.

. . .

Mr. Hall was an odd-looking fellow. He wore horn-rim glasses ready to slip off the tip of his beak-like nose, his clothes fit so loosely that his coat constantly fluttered in the wind, reminding me of a scarecrow, and he walked leaning forward, knees bent as if headed into a powerful wind. With a ruler in his hand followed by his trembling billowing coattail, he scouted the campus for some ill-starred student late to class. Since most of us had previously felt the sting of his ruler, we would watch with glee whenever he captured another hapless offender. The ruler in his hand was as much a part of him as his glasses and ill-fitting coat. His huge Adams apple mounted above a long curved neck created in our imagination the image of a turkey; nonetheless, he indeed maintained an orderly student body with his ruler. Doubtless, he had long ago learned that the long ruler in his hand inspired respect and lessened the need to use it. Standing in a crowded hallway, waving the ruler as his baton, he reminded one of a symphony conductor directing his orchestra—his children.

SOME DARING ADVENTURES

EACH MORNING I rode with my father to his office, located a short walk from my school and at the end of the school day, I returned home by walking along the Lufkin highway. From Main Street the highway dropped steeply, passed over La Nana Creek to the south of the city, crossed a railroad, and abruptly ascended Fredonia Hill to the summit and home. A swamp would emerge in the low land near our house after a rain, forcing crawfish, snakes and other creatures to the surface for my observation and capture. I would linger observing these fascinating creatures as long as I thought I was safe from the wrath of my mother, but occasionally I would become oblivious to time and suffer the consequences.

At other times, I enjoyed playing games during these return trips from school. Today one of the games could be called "chicken", but I had no name for it then. I began the nameless game by standing at the side of the road waiting to dart before an approaching car. In frustration, the passing driver most often sounded his horn and shook his finger at me as I smiled, satisfied that I had achieved the object of the game. At other times, I played another game of madness at a rail crossing before an audience of delayed automobiles. I would walk to the tracks, wait for the train to stop, fearlessly bend over, walk under it and nonchalantly emerge on the other side. My parents were fortunate that they did not witness these mindless and dangerous diversions. I had no death wish but like most young people, who believe they are immortal, I simply wanted to display my courage before an audience. I am fortunate that today I am able to write about it. However, my mother and grandmother did witness one of my other daring performances.

Fishing was the only activity my grandmother really enjoyed. Lacking social activities or interest, she spent most of her time sitting in the house or on the front porch observing animals or passing traffic. In order to vary her routine, my mother sometimes drove her to various lakes or creeks where she could comfortably sit and fish. She was an excellent fisher-woman with the patience of Job and would quietly sit in one place for hours collecting a string of fish.

One warm sunny day, my mother drove us to a delightful location on the Angelina River where my grandmother could comfortably fish and she could spread a blanket for my baby brother. Being restless and able to remain still for only a short while, I began exploring the area. I soon found an abandoned highway with a metal bridge spanning the river a short distance from my mother, grandmother, and brother. The bridge was framed with a network of metal strips to strengthen and support the bridge. Two metal beams about six inches wide extended along the top of the frame creating an irresistible challenge for me. Like a ladder, the crisscrossed beams on either side of the bridge offered an easy climb to the top, but to walk along one of the two narrow beams required excellent balance and confidence. At the age of six, I never suffered a lack of confidence or doubted that I could easily walk along the uppermost narrow beams, even though they were about forty feet above the water. Mid-way across the top of the bridge, I shouted,

"Mother. Look at me!"

Instantly my mother and grandmother looked up from the banks of the river and saw me forty feet above the water, arms outstretched, slowly walking along the top of the abandoned bridge. Insect and bird sounds were suddenly stilled—momentarily mute from terror, my mother and grandmother began screaming,

"You come down this instant! You get back here immediately!"

Relishing the panic I had created, I smiled as I climbed down from the bridge top. I rarely missed an opportunity to frighten my mother or grandmother—to demonstrate my masculinity, to display my courage—or, by witnessing their terror, was I was only reassuring myself that they loved me?

FREDONIA HILL BAPTIST CHURCH

CHURCH WAS AN important component of my young life. I am filled with nostalgic recollections of church services, Sunday school classes, church socials, Christmas programs, and caroling. Church provided my first job, my first love, my first audience and support for violin solos, but it was also the first institution for which I developed an aversion. Although it had nurtured me as a youth, I could find nothing the church offered me that I needed, not even friends, as I grew older. It was as if I had outgrown a suit of clothes that had once protected and warmed me but in time must be discarded. I became a stranger, no longer able to sustain an interest or relate to any activities of the church; therefore, I gradually began to withdraw until I finally ceased attending around the age of 16. I did not embrace atheism but on the other hand I could not accept the acumen and leadership of those in the congregation less educated than I. During the depression, the congregation was composed of mostly laborers and farmers who had grown up on rural farms around Nacogdoches. They were decent and honorable people with little education. My parents had instilled in me a desire to attend the university and enter a profession that would allow me to enjoy a lifestyle they could never hope to attain; as a consequence, I sought inspiration and companionship with university students rather than with church members.

My father had been instrumental in the establishment of the Fredonia Hill Baptist Church and served for many years as a deacon and Sunday School Superintendent. The church was a short pleasant Sunday morning walk from our house and was the social center for my mother and father. In its infancy it was commissioned a mission, which is a beginning church affiliated with the Southern Baptist national organization but without a full time pastor. Sunday school was held at the mission every Sunday but sermons were held only once a month or as often as visiting clergymen were available. When the mission congregation increased in size and could support a full-time minister, it was then recognized as a Baptist Church. When I was a boy, the mission contained only one large room arranged with green curtains to divide the room into cubicles so that several Sunday classes could meet at the same time. The women members of the mission made the curtains from burlap bags dyed green and converted into curtains. They were attached by rings to intersecting wires around the room and could be moved along the wires, like shower curtains, to form separate enclosures. Upon finishing Sunday school, the curtains were pushed back to the walls creating once again a large one-room sanctuary for church services.

"Fredonia Hill Baptist Church Under Construction 1938"

Christmas programs: pageants, Christmas music and caroling are among my most poignant memories of Fredonia Baptist Church. My father fashioned shepherds' crooks from large insulated electric cables and installed lighting for Christmas decorations and Pageants. He also maintained lights for the mission throughout the year. Various Sunday school classes sponsored Christmas caroling groups that would sing outside the homes of ill and aging members of the congregation. I vividly remember caroling on many cold December nights, but most of all, I remember the pleasant sensation caused by observing the smiles and delight of those we serenaded. My father loved to sing with the Christmas groups and the church choir. Although he could never sing on pitch, he ignored his disability and joined the church choir to joyfully lift up his voice to the rafters of the church each Sunday morning. He was not the only one singing in a different key to the roof beams each Sunday. I listened, and along with the church rafters, I shuddered.

Although I gradually began to lose interest in church activities, as I grew older I continued playing the violin at church services until I graduated from high school. The family continued to attend Fredonia Hill Baptist Church for a short time after I left home for military duty, but disagreeable politics within the church finally persuaded my family to change their membership to the First Baptist Church. It was a difficult decision for my father who had almost single-handedly founded the church and had dedicated countless hours of his time over many years supporting and maintaining it. When my father died, I invited the Pastor of Fredonia Hill Church to conduct his funeral services, for I knew that, despite changing his membership over 40 years before, he continued to retain a love for the Fredonia Hill Baptist Church.

FIRST LOVE

"Author age 7 adores his first love, Letha Mae."

I fell in love with a new member of our Sunday school class when she was introduced. It was the first time that Cupid had discharged an arrow through my heart. As she stood during her introduction, I experienced an overwhelming delight, dizziness, and euphoria—emotions I had never before experienced. I was hopelessly in love at age seven! Throughout the week I waited impatiently for Sunday to arrive so that I might again gaze upon this exquisite spectacle of feminine splendor. Few obstacles were powerful enough to prevent me from attending Sunday school, the only place where I could be near her. I could not bring myself to talk with her; I could only stare at her from afar and fervently hope that she would not speak to me. I am sure that if she had directly approached me, I would have choked, fainted, been unable to reply or I would have run away—perhaps all would have occurred.

Shirley Temple was a movie super-star at that time; a darling to every mother and a model for them to imitate as they dressed their daughters in pretty dresses, starched aprons, and styled their hair in long curled ringlets. My first love was always dressed in such a manner but it created an uncertainty for me—was I in love with Shirley Temple or with her?

I suppose a seven-year-old is not destined to have a long lasting love affair. A short time later, she moved away, leaving me only her memory, a memory of my first love and Shirley Temple. The image remains after 67 years.

MY FIRST JOB

THE MISSION WAS too small and poor to afford a janitor. I suspect that my father who served as a mission deacon hired me for this important job. A church deacon is a member of a committee that makes decisions for the church, somewhat like a member of the board of directors of a business corporation. I will never know if my father requested the board of deacons to employ me or if he simply hired and paid me twenty-five cents a week from his pocket. It was a simple job for an eight-year-old since there were no restrooms to clean. The mission had no running water or plumbing; only two out-houses located behind the mission. My father taught me to sweep the floor, which seemed enormous, move the church benches, sweep underneath, and rearrange them for Sunday services. The floor attracted large amounts of dust and dirt as the congregation walked over the unpaved yard into the building. I was not pleased to spend Saturday morning, my only free day from school and church services, working at the mission but I was content with the salary.

Today, twenty-five cents will purchase a metered parking space for a few minutes, but then my salary would purchase five large bars of candy or five bottles of soda, or admission to a movie. If I saved until I amassed a dollar, I was rich; however, I cannot recall ever saving that enormous amount. My parents provided the discipline I needed by reminding me each Saturday morning that it was time to leave the house and clean the mission. Indeed I was learning to be dependable although I did not understand it at the time. My father had assigned the responsibility of preparing the mission for services each Sunday to me so that the congregation might enjoy a clean neat sanctuary; a duty that others expected me to perform. Despite my complaints, each Saturday morning my parents sent me on my way to the mission until I decided that arguing with them was a waste of time. I found that willingly departing the house was far less difficult; thus, I had taken my first childhood step to learning reliance.

I maintained the mission for two years before it became an accredited church, a new building with running water and rest rooms. A new full time pastor and a janitor at a larger salary were hired leaving me unemployed at age ten. Perhaps the board of deacons believed that I was too young to clean the rest rooms, I will never know, but I am sure of one thing: I was happy, maybe even ecstatic to be liberated from the Saturday morning chore of cleaning the dusty mission. I was free for more important things, like capturing snakes.

REVIVALS

THE PREACHER WAS flamboyantly dressed in cowboy boots, striped pants, vest, and the largest hat I had ever seen. Not only did he stand over six feet in his bare feet, by adding two inches to the heels on his boots and ten inches to the top of his cowboy hat, a seven-foot giant was created. Indeed, this was an impressive man as he entered the tent and strolled down the isle to the accompaniment of piano music. To a ten-year-old, he seemed larger than life.

"How're y'all peckerwoods tonight?" He asked as he ambled to the podium amid the sound of laughter and applause.

Led by the evangelist's assistant, the audience had been singing hymns while eagerly anticipating his arrival. They knew that the traveling preacher would entertain them tonight as he had in the past.

"Where's Jesus?"

A few members of the congregation lamely responded,

"He's here."

"He's where? I can't hear y'all!"

The congregation roared,

"He's here!"

"That's better! He's sitting right next to y'all peckerwoods out there tonight! Look around you!"

And so the Preacher warmed to his sermon. He walked about the stage with a Bible in his left hand while using his right hand to stab the air, underscoring and emphasizing his message. He would often leap down from the stage to be nearer his audience, always guiding and manipulating them. This was no ordinary preacher. He was a brilliant actor with the ability to arouse the emotions of his audience at will. A rivulet of tears cascaded down his cheeks whenever he spoke of his deceased mother, causing clicks to be heard around the tent as women opened their purses to bring out their handkerchiefs. He would lower his voice to almost a whisper as his audience leaned forward to better hear him, then he would immediately energize them by loudly shouting the glory of the Lord! The congregation would react by joyfully crying aloud,

"Amen! Praise the Lord!

There was no dozing or napping in his audience. He held their attention; he mesmerized them, captivated them with his ability to manipulate their feelings over a wide range of emotions. He guided them into the depths of their sadness and directed them back to the heights of their happiness.

Proclaiming the gospel, the evangelist preacher traveled over the south during the warm months, setting up his large circus-like tent in small towns wherever empty grounds could be found. He usually placed his tent on North Street in Nacogdoches where vacant property extended from North Street down into a valley near the railroad station. During the cold winter months, he and other traveling evangelist customarily were invited to hold revivals in various churches to increase membership and renew the faith of current members. At the conclusion of each sermon, with arms extended, he invited sinners to come forward and confess their sins. This summons would usually begin with the congregation softly singing the hymn, "Jesus is calling".

Softly and tenderly Jesus is calling,

Calling for you and for me;
See, on the portals, He's waiting and watching,
Watching for you and for me.

Come home, come home,
You who are weary, come home!
Earnestly, tenderly, Jesus is calling,
Calling, O sinner, come home!

Why should we tarry when Jesus is pleading,
Pleading for you and for me?
Why should we linger and heed not His mercies,
Mercies for you and for me?

Come home, come home,
You who are weary, come home!
Earnestly, tenderly, Jesus is calling,
Calling, O sinner, come home!

The congregation would begin the chorus slowly enunciating the first
line,

"Come home (pause), cooom hooo-ma (slowing to a pause);
you who are weary come-hoooma (another pause)."

As the congregation sang, the preacher sometimes signaled with his
hand for softer music and addressed the congregation in a subdued
passionate voice inviting them to come forward and confess their sins.
With tears staining his face, he would say,

"Ya'll out there who are burdened by a sinful life, who hurt because
you are not satisfied with your life, bring your burden to Jesus. Let
him carry it for you, let him heal your heart. He suffered on the cross
for you so that you may confess your sins and be saved. Come—won't
you come forward? Jesus loves you—Come."

This invitation was the emotional conclusion of the sermon that brought tears to many in the audience. The soft music, the moving words of the hymn, the affectionate voice of the preacher as he blotted his tears with a handkerchief mesmerized his audience. Most attending his sermons were troubled—without money or jobs in the middle of a depression—and with tears, many walked down the isle to be embraced by the minister as he asked each if they would confess their sins and take Jesus as their savior. There was often a long queue in the isles waiting for their turn to confess their sins and be saved.

As a young boy growing up in Nacogdoches during the 1930s, I witnessed many revivals like the one previously described. The people of this era, mostly simple, poor farmers were eager to leave their dreary homes to enjoy an evening greeting old acquaintances and to be entertained by the preacher. There was little home entertainment, few farm homes even had electrical power available for radios; therefore, the traveling evangelist was the best free show in town.

Like many other traditions of our American culture of that time, the traveling evangelist disappeared with the arrival of World War II. War dominated the attention of the public, diverting resources and energies from non-essential activities toward the war effort. During the depression, farmers began to abandon the farm to seek better paying jobs in the city and the government began building power lines to provide electricity to rural inhabitants, affording them accessibility to telephones and radios. There was then less need to leave their homes to seek entertainment. As the war materialized, there was a severe shortage of gasoline, limiting traveling revivals. And finally, education was expanded after the war with the introduction of The GI Bill of Rights providing a college education to returning veterans; consequently, a better-educated generation demanded more sophisticated sermons and entertainment. Thus the era of the traveling revivals faded into oblivion.

LET THE MUSIC BEGIN

MY MOTHER LOVED music. She purchased a piano and began studying music when I first enrolled in school. Her favorite entertainment was listening to violin music on the radio and she often said that to her the sound of the violin was the most beautiful sound in the world. I have poignant memories of her sitting at the piano, slowly, ineptly striking the keyboard in an effort to play church hymns. She found more time to practice after I entered school and eventually developed sufficient skills to substitute for the regular church pianist.

Whenever I grew to the proper age, there was never any doubt that I would study the piano and violin, but the question of when to begin ultimately arose. After a discussion with Miss Penman, who had been selected as my first piano instructor, my mother decided that I was mature enough at age five to begin piano lessons, the same age that I started attending school. In addition to teaching piano, Miss Penman would later become my second-grade teacher.

Within a few months, I found that I intensely disliked piano practice. I had more important things to do; there were cowboys and Indians to be played, trees to be climbed, forests to be explored, trails to be discovered, and dreams to be dreamed. Mother would call for me to suspend my games and practice the piano—my glorious day was ruined! I would apathetically peck at the keyboard for a few minutes, then drift off to dreamland until my mother would enter the room and scold me for wasting time. I whined and complained that I did not want to practice or play the piano and that I wanted to discontinue piano lessons. This repetitious game continued until one day, she surprised me by offering a compromise—she would allow me to discontinue piano lesson if I promised to begin violin lessons. I would have agreed to anything to end the piano lessons.

Author age 8 (note RIO automobile)

She bought me a half-sized violin, and presented me to Mr. Beaucie, the only violin teacher at that time in the Nacogdoches County area. Mister Beaucie was an itinerant teacher, traveling about East Texas teaching violin and other musical instruments. He would arrive at Nacogdoches on a designated day, instruct his students in a rented room used as a studio, and follow a similar schedule the next day in another nearby town. He earned his living from fees paid by parents of his students, and was the predecessor of the Nacogdoches Public School Band Director or Bandmaster. Before The Nacogdoches Public School created the position of Band Director and paid them a salary to teach instrumental music, it was customary for itinerant music teachers to travel from city to city. The musical play, "Seventy-six Trombones" was based on the story of a traveling music teacher. Mr. J.T. Cox was the first Band Director to be hired by the Nacogdoches School District and was my first public school band director.

My mother was wiser the second time around. She accompanied me to each violin lesson so that she could determine my progress and refused to discuss or argue with me when I later expressed a dislike of the violin. Gradually I began to achieve some success with her help and the encouragement of other parents. I did not detest the violin to the extent that I disliked the piano, I only disliked practicing; on the other hand, I rather enjoyed playing and performing at recitals.

I continued to study with Mr. Beaucie until I was about nine-years-old. His fee was one dollar for a thirty-minute lesson, which my mother always kept in her purse ready to pay at the end of my lesson. It is unlikely that Mr. Beaucie collected fees from more than thirty students a week, since his students could only attend his half-hour instruction sessions after school hours and on Saturdays; nevertheless, this small income, even after deducting the expenses of travel and renting rooms, was adequate to maintain a decent living during the depression. I can recall my father earning fifty dollars a week in the decades of the twenties and thirties. It was a time of high unemployment and low prices—a time when five dollars would buy a week's supply of food for a family of four.

While I was in the fourth grade, for reasons unknown to me, my mother discontinued my instructions with Mr. Beaucie and enrolled me as a violin student with Mr. Cox, director of the Nacogdoches Junior and High School bands. Mr. Cox played most wind instruments in addition to the violin, instructed the school band, and taught private lessons after school hours. Perhaps the deciding factor in changing my violin instructor was that my mother no longer found it necessary to drive me to my lessons as she had when I was studying with Mr. Beaucie. Mr. Cox gave me violin instructions in a schoolroom after school hours, but although my lessons required less driving for my mother, the new arrangement proved to create an unexpected problem for me.

While taking violin instructions from Mr. Beaucie, few classmates were aware that I was studying the violin. My mother drove me to a house where Mr. Beaucie instructed students quite a distance from my school. However, my lessons with Mr. Cox made it necessary for me to take the violin to school. Like a magnet, the violin attracted the attention of my classmates as I walked across the campus with it cradled in my arms. I was instantly an object of ridicule by some ruffians who delighted in calling me "sissy", an offensive word for a male youngster in those days that led to many campus fistfights. It was intended as a sneering description of a boy who exhibited feminine behavior or engaged in activities not considered sufficiently masculine. During the decades prior to World War II, ignorant youngsters believed the violin and piano were instruments to be played only by girls; a boy who played either was a "sissy". In rural small towns, bullies with bias dispositions and small intellects ruled most school campuses. Nacogdoches was no exception. The bullies of that time believed that fist fighting was the only acceptable behavior for boys and were constantly on the alert for any behavior that might lead to combat. Connected to the outer world by only a few radios, telephones, and dirt roads, those living on farms and rural areas were for the most part, isolated from the rest of the world. It was 1933. War clouds were beginning to gather in Europe. Hitler declared himself chancellor of Germany, consolidated his power and moved Germany in a direction that six years later would lead to a world war. Every day newspaper headlines and radio spoke about Hitler and his threat of war, yet few in my school classes had ever heard of Hitler. The topic of conversation among adults was the lack of jobs, the price of cotton, and the weather. Few discussed world events. America was gripped in a terrible depression. A few fortunate men worked at low paying jobs, others looked for jobs, and few had completed more than a rudimentary education. In the struggle to survive, there was little time or money for education, reading or listening to classical music. Those who did were subject to ridicule because they were considered different.

To be the object of ridicule by classmates was more than I could bear. As a consequence, I began badgering my mother to let me quit violin and enroll in the school band. For some reason that I will never understand, those same intolerable students that harassed me for playing a violin did not consider playing a musical instrument in the band a feminine activity. With great sorrow, she capitulated and allowed me to begin playing the clarinet in the fifth grade band. Her love of the violin and her dreams of witnessing her son become an accomplished violinist were shattered. She never cared or developed an interest in any bands in which I later participated. It was only after I became an adult that I fully understood her disappointment. Discontinuing violin instruction, however, was not an abrupt end to my violin activities. I continued to occasionally play in church and even resumed taking violin lessons in college after I returned from the war.

THE GREAT DEPRESSION

B ETWEEN THE AGE of five until I was seventeen years old, The Great Depression raged, molding the character and attitudes of my generation. We observed and felt the sting of austerity, hardships, misfortunes, and despair during the decade of the thirties, followed by World War II that brought about more misery and destruction. I grew up in these two decades of instability that molded my life.

On October 24, 1929, the complete collapse of the stock market began, and like an avalanche plunging downhill gathering momentum, it swept away everything before it. Farmers, a large segment of labor, had been in trouble financially for years, but with the collapse of the stock market, compounded with the drought and creation of the Great Plains Dust Bowl, farming became almost non-existent. Banks and businesses failed by the thousands and the salaries of those few fortunate ones still employed shrunk precipitously. Almost everywhere one looked, there was evidence of suffering: people standing in line hoping to receive food being distributed by various agencies, men standing in line to apply for scarce employment, and if they were fortunate enough to have a job, they often worked at undignified tasks. Classmates in school wore second-hand patched clothes, and most tragic of all, there were many stunted, malnourished children. By 1932, U.S. industry had been cut by one-half; twenty-five percent of the labor force or about fifteen million people were unemployed, and for every one unemployed, there were dependents that needed to be fed and cared for. States had barely enough revenue for essential services with little remaining to alleviate the suffering population. There was no such thing as welfare programs or unemployment insurance. Shantytowns began to appear with their unemployed citizens sleeping under newspapers and begging for food. The words "hobo" and "bum" were created to describe those riding the freight trains and hitchhiking along the highways, keeping on the move, hoping to find jobs and food. In only one year, 1931, more than 20,000 people committed suicide. A song entitled, "Brother can you spare a dime?", became the theme song of that period. Those with a few dimes could purchase quite a number of items: shirts cost less than fifty cents, milk cost ten cents a quart, and a loaf of bread cost five cents. President Franklin D. Roosevelt said in his first inaugural address:

"The withered leaves of industrial enterprise lie on every side, farmers find no markets for their produce, the savings of many years in thousands of families are gone. More important, a host of unemployed citizens face the grim problem of existence and an equally great number toil with little return."

Fortuitously, I escaped most of the misery and hardships bestowed on so many of my generation, simply because my father was employed by a company that provided an essential service to many people. The Texas Power and Light Company furnished him a pick-up truck, gasoline and a modest salary from which, with some prudence, we were able to enjoy a meager but comfortable standard of living. We were never denied adequate food or clothing, and my parents had some money left to educate my brother and me, while giving aid to those who were less fortunate. Although my awareness of the hardships caused by the depression was largely a result of observation, I fully understood that we were indeed fortunate to be able to enjoy a modest home, an automobile, and an occasional vacation. That we were mostly separated from the misery of others who were less fortunate, happened quite by accident—a random choice—for my father applied for work with a utility company simply because his older brother was employed by a utility company. When the depression struck, my father had been employed for some time maintaining a source of energy to the city of Nacogdoches.

Almost every day one of the migrant "hobos" would knock on our back door to ask for food. Some were running away from the law, some liked the free life but many more were down on their luck without jobs. My compassionate mother could not deny them a meal. When one of the hobos asked for food, she would prepare a plate of food left over from our meal, and a glass of milk or buttermilk for them to eat in our back yard. When finished, they would return the eating utensils and thank her for the food. Always courteous and humble, it was apparent that they wanted to leave a good impression because they might return and ask for another meal. It was also rumored that they marked the house where they received food so that other hobos would know which house would serve them a meal; although, I could never find such a mark or anything that would serve as an indicator that our house was marked. Hobos continued to flourish until Congress, under the direction of Franklin Roosevelt, passed legislation creating work for the unemployed. Some of the legislation created the Works in Progress Administration (the WPA) that employed men to build roads and government buildings; and the Civilian Conservation Corps (the CCC), that provided a semi-military environment for young unemployed men. The CCC built many roads and national parks that we continue to enjoy today. The Rural Electrification Administration employed workers to build electric lines into rural areas. Most of these projects were approved by Congress in the first two years of Roosevelt's term as President, 1933-1935, and provided jobs to most of those who wanted to work; however, the low salaries did not end The Depression or completely eliminate the sight of hobos until World War II.

A hobo knocked on our back door one day when I was about 10 years old to ask if we would provide him a meal. As he ate, my father asked him if he wanted a job building a barn in exchange for a place to live, meals and some small monthly payment. Because he exhibited an interest, my father conducted him to a small building behind our house that had served as a "chicken brooder house." Dad had built the small one room building, covered the floor with saw-dust, installed a heating device to provide warmth, and had raised baby chickens in it until they were able to survive outside. Because of the filth created by the former inhabitants, I was horrified to consider that anyone would live in the building. The hobo seemed undaunted, and a short time later after accepting my father's offer, began to clean, sweep, scrub, mop, until the interior of the building gleamed and smelled of disinfectant much like a doctor's office. My father then installed a cot, connected an electrical outlet and a water hose for water.

Several months passed as we watched the progress of the barn under construction. Mr. Warner possessed many skills that became more apparent as he fashioned the barn from scrap lumber into a rather pleasant-looking building. We were impressed with his cleanliness, skills, and intelligence, which further fueled speculation within our family about his background and the circumstances that persuaded him to become a hobo. He never volunteered any information about his past and maintained his mystique deep within himself. Any attempts I made to invade his privacy as he worked on the barn were deflected by his silence; however, he was never surly. He briefly answered my questions with an occasional grunt, and once in a great while, with a short sentence. As a bee attracted to honey, our curious guest intrigued me. I was not hesitant to follow him about, barraging him with incessant, unending conversation. He was very patient with me, yet I never gained any knowledge of his background. We knew him only as Mr. Warner, and he politely addressed my mother and father as Mrs. Pettey and Mr. Pettey.

My father invited Mr. Warner to Fredonia Hill Church services. He replied that he would indeed like to attend, but that he owned only one set of work clothes that was not appropriate dress for attending church. The following week, Dad had one of his old suits cleaned and presented it to him. I saw him smile for the first time as he promised my father that he would be pleased to attend church the following Sunday. Although he declined a ride with us in our automobile, saying that he preferred to walk, he kept his promise and appeared at services the following Sunday. At that time, my father was Sunday School Superintendent and routinely made announcements and welcomed visitors before church services began. On that notable Sunday, he welcomed Mr. Warner by announcing that Mr. Warner was attending church for the first time and had recently constructed our barn. Many members of the congregation warmly welcomed him after church services and invited him to attend again. Much to the delight of my father, he appeared to enjoy the fellowship and expressed a desire to attend subsequent services.

A deacon of the church approached Mr. Warner several weeks later and asked him if he would build a house for him. He accepted the offer and the house stands today just as he built it. It was the first of several projects offered him as his reputation spread in the neighborhood. We were proud of his achievements; particularly my father who was delighted with the thought that he had been responsible for saving a "hobo" from a purposeless lifestyle—walking the road to nowhere. Mr. Warner was accepted in the church as an outstanding example of one who had turned his life from that of a drifter to a respected member of the community and almost became an extended member of our family. My brother and I adored him. He was patient, gentle and kind to us as we followed him about his work chattering like parrots. My brother even convinced my parents to allow him to sleep one night in his house.

At the time that my father hired Mr. Warner, he had stated that he would not tolerate drinking alcohol on his property and would ask him to vacate the house if this agreement was violated. Indeed, my dad spoke as a prophet, for one day as he approached my father, Mr. Warner said,

"Hi, Jess."

Dad froze for a moment. Mr. Warner had always addressed my father as "Mr. Pettey"—never as "Jess".

My father asked,

"What did you say?"

"I said 'hi,' Jess."

"Have you been drinking?" Dad responded.

"Just a teensy-weensy bit," Mr. Werner giggled as he held up his thumb and first finger to indicate a small amount.

"I said when you first arrived that I would not tolerate drinking. Do you remember that?"

Without another word, Mr. Warner turned, walked to his house, packed his clothes and departed. My brother and I were heart-broken. His abrupt departure was characteristic of many alcoholic hobos of that time. They remained sober for long periods of time without money to purchase alcohol; however, whenever money became available, many would begin drinking and disappear. My mother and father soon learned to withhold wages owed to itinerant workers until they completed any project assigned to them. Most would simply disappear after being paid, but Mr. Warner remained sober for a long time—longer than most. I never saw him again, although my brother reported that he had returned years later and knocked on our back door. When my brother greeted him, he remarked that he had only stopped by to say hello. He then departed, never to be seen again by any of us. Why did he return? Perhaps he regretted disappointing my father—no one will ever know.

MILKING COWS

M Y FATHER ALWAYS owned at least one cow during my youthful years. The family icebox invariably contained a pitcher or two of fresh milk that provided cool refreshing drinks that we preferred over water. My parents believed that fresh milk was healthier than milk purchased at grocery stores. They were no doubt correct, because milk was not always kept in cold storage then, nor was pasteurized milk always available as it is today. I was assigned the chore of milking a cow or cows, depending on how many he owned at the time, both mornings and evenings. A cow will continually produce milk if she is milked daily, preferably twice a day, but failure to regularly remove her milk will cause her udders to become painfully swollen and she will soon cease to produce milk. It was essential that I milk twice daily if we were to maintain a supply of milk. My father was often called away from his office or home to restore power at various hours of the day; therefore, the responsibility of milking fell upon my shoulders.

Before milking, I would call the cows from the pasture by loudly calling,

"Here Bossy, Bossy!"

Immediately the cows would begin walking toward me, anxious to be fed. When they arrived, I would have their food prepared, an empty bucket available to hold the milk, and a stool on which I would sit as I milked them. Since winter mornings were often cold, I used the cows' bodies as a shield against the biting wind and their udders to warm my hands. After Mr. Warner built the new barn, I found it not only provided protection from the cold wind for me, but also offered a warm place for other creatures and their families as well. Rats enjoyed the warmth of the barn while feeding on stored cow food, and snakes also enjoyed the warmth but fed on the rats. It was a symbiotic relationship we all enjoyed: the rats needed the cow food, the snakes needed the rats as food and we needed the snakes to control the rats. They made themselves at home, and we all tolerated each other.

My father bought an old crippled cow with huge udders, and although her hip was dislocated as a result of an accident, she was the most productive milk cow we ever owned. As much as I disliked milking, I was troubled even more when it was necessary to prod her with a stick to force her to reluctantly walk to the feed trough in obvious pain. As I watched her struggle each morning, I acquired a feeling of compassion for her similar to what one would feel toward a crippled pet.

In order to relieve the boredom of milking, with practice I developed into an expert marksman. Whenever an insect or cat came within range, I would take aim with the cow's teat, squeeze and give the target a blast of milk. Cats, because of their perplexed facial expression and agitation, were my most entertaining and comical targets. Occasionally I even sent an outburst toward my young brother who soon learned to keep his distance from me when I was milking.

How I must have complained when it was necessary for me to abandon my favored activities and perform the disagreeable chores of milking; however, I now feel indebted to my father for teaching me responsibility—the act of postponing instant pleasures to complete necessary and sometimes unpleasant tasks. He seemed to continually find chores for me. In addition to milking and feeding cows, I was assigned other tasks: cleaning the church, cutting weeds around the house, caring for and feeding the chickens, ducks, rabbits, or whatever animal we were housing at the moment. I have no memory of complaining in the presence of my father. It was then a custom for nearly all children to perform chores and I was afraid of him; however, I am sure I whined and complained when he could not hear me. One disadvantage of living in isolation where no neighboring boys could be used as an example was that I could not say to my father, "Why do I have to cut the weeds? Jim doesn't cut weeds"—"Sam doesn't cut weeds. Why do I have to cut weeds?" My father would not have cared whether they cut weeds or not, he expected me to do my chores; therefore, I also understood that any protestations would have fallen on deaf ears.

PREPARING FOR A VOCATION

SNAKES WERE AMONG the many things that fascinated me at age eleven. I began searching books for information that would assist me in identifying and learning about the snake population of East Texas. Books and movies taught me to use a stick with a fork and to pin a snake's head to the ground while capturing it. Whenever I attended a movie about Africa, I was filled with admiration for the hunter, and enthralled with the dream that I also might one day be a hunter of snakes in Africa. Indeed, movies inspired me to select the profession of handling snakes as one of the most appealing, and to resolve that I would begin preparing for this career. There were no lions or other exotic animals to hunt in Nacogdoches, but there was an abundance of snakes in local rivers, ponds, and forest. I had also read about extracting venom from snakes and selling it to laboratories that made an antidote for snakebites. Although I had no knowledge of how to contact these laboratories, I was convinced that an opportunity existed for me to earn money, and an eleven-year-old has little concern or patience for such troublesome items. Later I would turn my attention to such matters, but first, I must first collect the venom.

I procured a wooden box, covered the open top with wire screen, and let it be known at school that I was in the market to buy venomous snakes. In addition to my forked stick, I built a device consisting of a wooden handle with a gadget through which a small rope was passed and formed a loop that could placed around the head of a snake. When the end of the rope was pulled, the noose tightened around the snake's head, rendering it helpless. The snake was released from the noose by holding it firmly behind the head with one hand while carefully removing the rope with the other. As I prepared to extract venom for sale, my mother was quietly having a nervous breakdown.

Eventually a boy heard of my desire to buy snakes and offered me two deadly cotton-mouthed water moccasins he had captured. A cotton-mouthed moccasin is second only to a rattlesnake in its aggressiveness and ability to deliver a dangerous venomous bite. Although the venom is seldom fatal, a cotton-mouthed moccasin is indeed one snake to avoid by all means and handled only by experts. Since I was eleven years old and had never suffered the consequences of snakebite, I possessed the confidence, but not the respect, of an expert snake handler. I was certain that the two snakes represented no danger to me. I had captured and handled non-poisonous snakes; therefore, I reasoned that I was sufficiently experienced to deal with poisonous ones. After completing the sale, I placed the snakes in a wooden box and began preparing for venom extraction by securing a cloth over the mouth of a glass jar. I then captured one of the snakes and forced its mouth open by pressing its mouth against the edge of the jar. The fangs of a snake are hinged to the roof of its mouth and will unfold downward as the jaws open. As the fangs are pressed deeper into the cloth, green liquid venom will drip from them into the jar. Using this method, I was able to extract a small amount of venom from the two snakes.

I had placed several snakes I had previously captured in another covered wooden box and because of my inexperience, I could only identify the non-poisonous ones by meticulously examining each to determine if it contained poisonous fangs. Unlike poisonous snakes, non-poisonous snakes possess smaller teeth rather than two large fangs. While opening the mouth of one of the snakes to observe its teeth, it wiggled free of my grasp and slightly scratched the skin of one of my fingers with its teeth. The small wound created a great deal of anxiety, for I dared not assume that the snake was non-poisonous. I threw the snake into the wooden box, ran quickly to the house and asked my father to cut into the wound with a razor blade. He immediately began to cut where the teeth of the snake had scraped my finger and to suck blood from the wound in an effort to remove the venom. After waiting for some time without pain, we decided that the snake was harmless; however, during the wait, I decided that I had lost interest in the business of selling venom. Within a short time, the snakes were mustered out of service, sold to other innocent hunters and my mother began to recover from her nervous condition. Life returned to normal on Jack Locke Street—until the next crisis.

MY FIRST AIR GUN AND HOUDINI

A TEN-YEAR-old boy with an air gun can be a serious threat to anyone or anything that is unfortunate enough to be near him. Although most air guns are extremely inaccurate at thirty feet or more, the pellets can be dangerous to humans and lethal to birds at close range. During my youth, most parents believed that a cheap air gun presented few hazards, and because they were inexpensive, they were favored as Christmas presents for boys. I am living proof that they were misinformed. I almost decimated the bird population on the south side of Nacogdoches, and poised a danger to my young brother with a low pressure inexpensive Daisy Red Ryder air gun. My favorite pastime was to slowly approach a bird perched on a tree limb until I was sufficiently near for the gun to be accurate, then carefully take aim, and fire. I missed most of the time, but occasionally a bird dropped to the ground.

My four-year-old brother yearned for companionship. As there were no other boys his age in the neighborhood, he entertained himself by regularly following me about and imitating my activities. I was five years older and interested in the activities of older boys, certainly not in entertaining him. I considered him a baby, an annoyance, and a pest. One day, after making several attempts to discourage him from following me wherever I went, I had an idea. It was a cold day. My mother had bundled him into layers of clothing covered with a heavy over coat. I was certain that with these clothes to protect him, a pellet fired from my air gun would not hurt him and might even discourage him from following me about. I therefore made up a rather malicious game to provide me with information so that I could better understand the effectiveness of the air gun at different ranges. Being only four or five years old, I am not sure to what extent he understood my intentions, but because he trusted me, he agreed to my instructions. I instructed him to walk forward until I told him to stop, bend over, and I would then fire a pellet from the air gun aimed at his backside. He could then tell me if the pellets reached him and whether he could feel the pellets.

A faint sound of "Thruumpt" was heard as the first pellet struck his thick clothing from a distance of 30 feet. He laughed with pleasure, as he became aware that he, the younger brother, was an important actor in this game. He shouted that he could barely feel the pellet strike his clothes. I then suggested that he should move several steps nearer me where he could describe the force of the second pellet. Another "thruumpt" sounded as the second pellet struck him, but a bit louder this time. He declared that he felt nothing and that it was fun. He wanted to do it again. Before I fired the third shot, I had incrementally moved him within fifteen feet of me. This was the moment for which I had waited! I motioned him back a few more feet and then fired the third and final time. Energized into alacrity, the small figure leaped like a kangaroo into the air while issuing forth a scream like that of a banshee. It was a colossal shriek that resonated along the ground, echoed throughout the forest, radiating up the hill into the open windows of our house striking the sensitive ears of our mother. He ran toward her—she toward him—and while visions of some terrible accident materialized in her mind, she gathered him into her arms. I knew instantly that I was in trouble, but I could not resist a sadistic smile as I watched my baby brother being comforted by our mother.

As time passed, my brother began to find more interesting activities than following me and allowed me to resume the game of playing cowboy and hunting birds in peace. Until this day, sixty-five years later, I believe that he has never forgiven me for my violation of his trust, and I do not blame him. However, he would enjoy his revenge at a later time.

. . .

I had read about and witnessed in the movies Houdini's extraordinary ability to extricate him from all sorts of restraints. In order to satisfy my curiosity, and perhaps learn the secrets of his tricks, I decided to experiment. I handed my brother a rope and instructed him to tie my arms and legs to a chair. Upon finishing, I then urged him to walk around the chair and me, using the entire length of the rope to bind my body even more securely to the chair. I then announced that I would demonstrate my escape from the shackles he had placed around me. To my surprise, he had fettered me so securely that I could not move, let alone unfasten the rope around me. After trying, unsuccessfully, for some time to loosen the rope, I asked him to untie me. I had failed to notice a sparkle in his eyes as he bound me to the chair or to suspect that he was plotting his revenge for the previous air gun incident. He merely sat in a chair with a smile on his face—enjoying the situation—acting as if he had indeed captured the Devil. I finally became aware of his fervent desire to witness my distress and of his determination not to set me free. For the first time ever, he had gained complete control of his older brother, and he intended to enjoy it as long as possible. I became convinced that I must try some other route to my freedom. I was on the back porch of our home along with my brother who was enjoying his grand entertainment and our mother was cooking in the kitchen two rooms away. I attempted to call her but after several unsuccessful attempts to attract her attention, it became apparent that I must move nearer the kitchen. Although tightly bound with rope, I discovered that I could move my feet a few inches and if I could stand, even with the chair bound to my body, I might be able to slowly move toward the door. Slowly I leaned forward—cautiously placing my feet on the floor and balancing precariously in a stooped position. I began a halting, shuffling, forward movement, gaining a few inches with each slow motion. Like a fly, my brother circled, leaped, and buzzed around me, laughing and obviously deriving much joy from my predicament. After a few shuffling steps, I lost my balance and fell forward into oblivion—I do not like to think that he might have pushed me.

I awoke a few minutes later to the sound of my mother frantically asking me if I was hurt. After she untied me and made certain that I had no broken bones, she then turned to my brother and reprimanded him for not releasing me. His grin reminded me of our past air gun experience, or game, that had caused me to smile, delighted with my demonstration of superiority over him. Now it was his turn to enjoy his revenge—he had at last dominated his older brother for a period of time.

SCHOOL PROBLEMS

EACH YEAR I was promoted to the next grade but I was yet falling further and further behind my class. By the time I had reached the fourth grade I had fallen so far behind that my teachers had began to ignore me, dismissing me as a non-cooperative, lazy student. I was extremely shy, preferring to sit at the back of the class hoping that I would escape attention and the teacher would not call on me. As a result, I convinced myself that I was too dumb to learn the material assigned to me. To compound my feeling of inadequacy, I was moved to the next higher class each year, and as the subjects became more complex, I continued to fall even further behind. It then became apparent to my mother that it had been a mistake to enroll me in the first grade when I was only five years old. Like most mothers, she had believed that I was brighter than other children my age. Teachers, being busy people with a limited amount of time, will often take the path of least resistance and spend more time with the fast eager learners, who require less effort than the silent reluctant ones. Some teachers may dispute this last statement, but I, as a former teacher, experienced firsthand the satisfaction of working with eager bright students, and the frustration of striving to help the less eager and slow ones.

Upon completion of the sixth grade, my mother, in desperation, enrolled me at Stephen F. Austin Demonstration School. The Stephen F. Austin Demonstration School, grades one through twelve, was a teaching laboratory of Stephen F. Austin University where students, majoring in education, gained firsthand experience teaching under the supervision of experienced teachers and college professor administrators. My mother believed that since classes were smaller, and the teaching atmosphere was reportedly better than public school classes, I would be able to recover some of the knowledge I had failed to comprehend in prior classes. By the time she enrolled me in demonstration school, I had completed the sixth grade in public school and was a member of the band. I had enjoyed a genial relationship with other band members, and did not relish the idea of dropping out of the public school band to attend a small experimental school without a band; consequently, the change of schools did little to improve my schoolwork as my mother had hoped. I returned to public school the following year, none the better for the experience.

By the time I returned to Nacogdoches High School, the band director, Mr. Cox, had discontinued rehearsing the band in the gymnasium, and had moved into a band room in the Old University of Nacogdoches building. The University had been chartered in 1845 by the Republic of Texas but not built until 1859. The building was used during the Civil War as a Confederate Hospital, and after the war, headquarters for the occupying Union Army. When the University finally closed it's doors in 1900, the Trustees transferred the land and building to the Nacogdoches Independent School District where it served the school district as a classroom for chemistry and band until it was finally closed in 1960. It was then turned over to the Historical Commission and is now a museum.

When I attended band, the old building was in such disrepair that it was a hazard to band students. Today, I can still smell the musty, moldy odor that radiated from the ancient wooden floors. The band room was on the second floor at the top of a curved creaking wooden staircase without banisters. It was a miracle that the stairs did not collapse or that no one fell from them. Even so, I doubt that the school would have been held responsible, for at that time we lived in an age where litigation was almost unknown. During the depression most people were unable to afford a lawyer, and it was customary to exercise old-fashioned common sense. We simply walked next to the wall in single file as we descended or ascended the open staircase.

. . .

It was common knowledge in school that Melvin, an usher at the Austin Theater, would allow youths to enter the movie theater without tickets. Someone informed me that if I would walk past the ticket window, stand at the rear of the theater surveying the audience as if searching for someone, and then take a seat, Melvin would ignore me. I seldom had money to purchase a theater ticket, yet through the courtesy of Melvin at the Austin Theater, I was able to see movies that featured famous movie stars of the "Golden Age": Mickey Rooney, Judy Garland, Rita Hayworth, Betty Davis, Clark Gable, Randolph Scott, Tyrone Powers and so many others who influenced the character of America prior to World War II. The public regarded movie stars as upright, moral role models and emulated them at every opportunity. It was not until after the war that personal scandals involving famous persons began to be reported in the news media. During those years almost every citizen of the USA recognized names of movie stars and enjoyed discussing their favorite stars and movies. I believe most movies of that era inspired healthy emotions and inspiration. Most were romantic, sentimental, cheerful, musical with romantic lyrics, and ended with happy moral conclusions. One usually left the theater feeling inspired and more cheerful than when one entered. The decades prior to World War II was indeed the innocent era in America, when movie studios controlled almost every aspect of a movie star's life and movie scenes were carefully censored to protect the public from witnessing anything that could be considered immoral behavior.

I will always remember Melvin, the usher, for his contribution to unknown numbers of young people, who, like me, enjoyed an escape from boredom. The movies kept us occupied and provided a more wholesome entertainment than we might otherwise have found. One might think of Melvin as the patron saint of the idle youth of Nacogdoches.

MESMERIZED BY JAZZ

THE CENTENNIAL YEAR of Texas was celebrated in 1936 at the State Fair in Dallas. Because my father wanted to attend this historical event, he made plans to drive to Dallas and visit a cousin. The fair was a wonderful collage of colored lights, food, calypso music, carrousels, Ferris wheels, and historical exhibits. After wandering around the fair grounds and becoming separated from my family, I found an orchestra playing popular jazz music in one of the exposition tents. For the first time in my life, rather than seeing big bands in the movies or hearing them on the radio, I was able to experience the thrill of seeing and hearing one in person. As in a dream, I found myself mesmerized standing as near as possible to the stage near the end of the saxophone section. My parents soon found me, but I was unwilling to surrender my place to anyone, not even to rejoin my family. They agreed to leave me if I promised to remain in the tent until they returned. The saxophone soloist, Fuzzy Combs, was so near that, had I wished, I could have touched him. I remember his name after sixty-one years, although I cannot remember the name of the orchestra leader. As I stood transfixed, watching every move and hearing every sound he made, I became aware that he was producing an effortless saxophone vibrato. His bottom lip moved in such a way that it produced a pulsating musical sound, much like the violinist produces by tilting his fingers forward and backwards on a violin string. It was a thrilling experience for me to discover how vibrato is created with a saxophone from a professional musician! I could hardly wait to return home and practice it.

As a result of this trip to Dallas, I became interested in the famous jazz bands and artists of that time: Benny Goodman, Artie Shaw, Duke Ellington, Woody Herman, Louis Armstrong, and many others. I rarely gave thought to my studies, sometimes missing classes to listen and study records of those great bands. I enjoyed discussing jazz solos from these records with four friends who were also members of the school band. We memorized the player's name, discussed whether the soloist played to our satisfaction or not, and attempted to imitate their solos with our instruments. In time, we were able to identify most jazz soloists by their tone and style. In time we expanded our knowledge of famous jazz bands by memorizing the names of the entire band members and the instruments they played.

I devoted countless hours listening to Benny Goodman's "Sing, Sing, Sing", recorded in New York in a 1936 Carnegie Hall concert, Bunny Berrigan's vocal and trumpet recorded solo, "I Can't Get Started Without You", clarinet solos of Artie Shaw on his record of, "Begin the Beguine", and my favorite solo of all, a saxophone solo, "Body and Soul", recorded by Coleman Hawkins in 1939. In my opinion, these are and will be forever four of the greatest big-band era jazz classics of all times.

It is noteworthy that we were the only five students in Nacogdoches High School that had any interest in playing jazz at that time, although jazz flourished throughout the nation. That we were among the best musicians in the marching band may partially explain why we were alone in our quest for jazz, but I believe it was because there was a lack of local role models. Unlike cities such as New Orleans, there was an absence of jazz groups and jazz stars in Nacogdoches to attract students to jazz. There was little or no support from parents, teachers, and very little from other students as we searched for a means to learn jazz. Records and radio jazz programs were the only available resources for our study and emulation. We did, however, support each other.

. . .

During the decades of the 20s, 30s and early 40s there was such a demand for big bands that many jobs were created for musicians despite the depression. The nation experienced a dance-craze. Perhaps it was a way to forget the suffering and deprivation caused by the depression, but whatever the reason, there has never been before or since, such public interest in dancing, dance music and jazz. The need for dance bands to satisfy this demand was so great that it was necessary for dance bands to maintain an exhausting schedule of travel over much of America. As vaudeville entertainers had traveled over the country living out of their suite-cases in the 1920s, so too dance band musicians found it necessary to live out of their suite-cases during the 20s and 30s while playing "one-niters" in small cities around the nation. Even small rural towns in East Texas could attract famous jazz bands because audiences were willing to pay dearly for the opportunity to dance and listen to a well-known band. The small city of Jacksonville, then with a population of 2000, was able to attract Joe Venuti and his Orchestra, a well-known music personality of movie and radio fame during the 1930s, to play for a public dance.

A famous band playing in a nearby town was irresistible to me. Even though I was too young to have access to any transportation or money, there was always hitchhiking, an accepted safe method of travel in those days. Jacksonville was only a short distance from Nacogdoches and with a friend to keep me company, we began our journey to Jacksonville with the certainty that we would be soon be offered a ride and be able to hear this great band. Indeed, if necessary I might have walked. Crime was then almost non-existent and drivers felt a need to share a ride with others less fortunate. Money was scarce and two fourteen-year-old boys represented little threat to a driver. In addition to the problem of transportation, our pockets did not contain enough money to pay entrance fees to the dance, but at age fourteen; one optimistically makes plans without considering obstacles or solutions. Miracles seem to, and do appear incessantly at that age. It is only after growing older that we begin to doubt that there will always be a miracle, and we are usually correct.

We had only a short wait before a driver stopped and offered us a ride to Jacksonville. We arrived at the high school gymnasium, where the dance was to be held just minutes before the band began playing, but without tickets, we were unable to enter the front entrance. Undaunted and optimistic, we began to search for other places of entry. We almost immediately found an open unlocked back door used by the musicians to move their equipment from the bus to the bandstand and walked inside. As though we belonged, we stationed ourselves behind the band—near enough to read the musicians' music over their shoulders. It must have been obvious to the musicians that we were students, but I am sure that it must have also been disturbing to have two youngsters peering over their shoulders during the entire evening.

During the evening my attention and curiosity became focused on one of the saxophone players who drank numerous glasses of water held in his trembling hands. I was so intrigued by his enormous intake of water, that I was compelled to ask one of the band members why he seemed unable to quench his thirst. He informed me that the saxophone player was recovering from a binge of drinking alcohol over a long period of time. Since no one in my family abused or even drank alcohol, I had never before witnessed such a scene. Somehow, I became a Water Bearer during the evening and assumed the task of refilling and placing the musician's water glass within his reach. It was an exhilarating experience for me to be near professional musicians, but to be able to grant one of them a favor was beyond all expectations. I don't remember much about the music that night but I vividly remember the saxophone player, his shaking hands, his thirst, and a feeling of importance as I continually placed a full water glass within his reach.

We waited beside the road for a ride home but there was little traffic at such a late hour. Hours ago the band had finished packing their equipment and boarding their bus as we stood on a lonely deserted road waiting for a return ride to Nacogdoches. It was nearly three o'clock in the morning before a car stopped and offered us a ride to Douglas, Texas, a small town along the route to Nacogdoches. We waited at Douglas, standing on another deserted road until daylight before someone offered us a ride into Nacogdoches. To my surprise, my parents appeared calm and unconcerned that I had not returned home the previous evening; however, now I am sure they worried more than was apparent.

I was a spectator of several other famous bands during the decade of the 1930s and 1940s. I hitchhiked to a nightclub near Longview, Texas, about 60 miles from Nacogdoches, where many famous bands, including Jimmy Lunsford and Tommy Dorsey performed at various times. The nightclub was a large barn-like building containing a huge wooden dance floor with a bar and a bandstand. There were few decorations; only a large, unpretentious plain dance floor crowded with people who came from all over East Texas. The Tommy Dorsey Band appeared with a group of singers called The Modenaires featuring a twenty-one year old skinny singer named Frank Sinatra.

Despite my love of music, the many years I devoted to playing in various bands, and the pleasure I derived from these activities, I now believe that I made a fortunate decision when I chose to not enter the music profession as a full-time musician. Although I had performed as an amateur or semi-professional musician while attending school, my interest in aviation in 1942 prompted me to enlist in the Army Air Force rather than in a military band. Most professional musicians of my generation received excellent training while serving in military bands and continued to play professionally after leaving the military. On the other hand, I acquired the responsibilities of caring for a family before separating from military service and became convinced that traveling with bands contributed little to marital bliss. If I had been single at that time, I have no doubt that I would have joined a band as a full-time musician rather than return to school to earn a music degree and teach music; however, I have no regrets. With a family to support, I chose to become a band director and later an insurance executive with a large company offering generous medical and retirement benefits. I was content to only play in bands as a diversion. Over the years I have witnessed often the tragic plight of professional musician friends who found it necessary to continue working long after retirement age. Like many artists, they had willfully sacrificed their earnings in their early years for their passionate love of music, only to grow old without sufficient retirement income and medical care.

LATENT LOVE AND SUNDAY

AFTERNOONS

IT WAS 1937, and The Depression continued. Hitler raged incessantly about the need for more living space for Germany, although it would be two more years before he invaded Poland and plunged Europe into World War II. Occasionally I glanced at the headlines of newspapers or listened to a radio station broadcasting his speeches, but like most youth of that time, I believed the United States was isolated and that Hitler poised no danger to America. War was something that a boy of thirteen would not worry about, for I had greater concerns—I was convinced that I was unattractive, awkward, and dumb. I disliked school and discipline. I understand now that I was merely full of overactive hormones that interfered with my ability to concentrate on tasks assigned to me in school. In order to compensate for and to escape from these problems, I took pleasure in playing the saxophone in the high school band and playing the violin during church services. By the time I entered high school, I had discontinued private violin lessons with both Mr. Beaucie and Mr. Cox, but continued to play duets at church with Marjorie Woods, daughter of Reverend Woods, our pastor of Fredonia Hill Baptist Church.

Reverend Woods was the first full time minister hired after the Fredonia Hill Mission became a church. He had four sons, age sixteen, nineteen, twenty-one and twenty-five and a daughter my age. I believed Marjorie to be the smartest and most lovely member of the family, but I was also thoroughly fascinated by her brothers. Their ages extended over a span of about nine years, lending humor and interesting diversity to their interchanges of conversation. They also served as four surrogate fathers to Marjorie. Although the brothers always made me feel welcome and comfortable in their presence, the fact was never far from my mind that if they suspected I had taken any liberties with their little sister, I might be accountable to them.

The older brothers lived and worked in Houston, but almost every weekend they would drive to Nacogdoches to be with their family. Even though my mother often prepared my favorite chicken, accompanied with peas, greens with sweet potatoes, and a grand pie for dessert for our Sunday lunch, I could barely finish it. I was eager to walk to the Woods' home before they finished their Sunday meal and abandoned the dinner table. They invariably invited me to join them at the table, where I enjoyed the banter and clever repartee between members of this large family. Their laughter and good-natured teasing was very different from what I experienced at home. When alone, my mother and father did not converse often during a meal nor was my brother and I invited to participate in their rare conversations. My parents believed in the trite platitude that children should be seen and not heard.

Upon conclusion of the Sunday meal, the sons of the Woods family would invite me to join them in a backyard game of touch football, followed by a Sunday afternoon radio broadcast of a symphony orchestra. It became a Sunday custom for other neighborhood youths to join us and form two touch football teams. We would fling long passes, feint, run, and catch the football until we tired and it was time for the regular Sunday afternoon radio broadcast of classical music. As we listened to the music, we enthusiastically waved our arms about to the rhythm of the music as if we were conducting the orchestra. At various times, the family would gather at the mother's piano to sing. When it was time to take leave of this wonderful family, it was indeed a somber moment for me.

I fondly remember those Sunday afternoons filled with football, music, and most of all, joyous laughter. The lovely Woods family clearly demonstrated to me that wealth contributes little to the joyful celebration of life; that a family of meager status, yet rich with love can freely enjoy boundless simple pleasures that are so often overlooked by the affluent. I now understand what an enriching experience it was for me to share those Sunday afternoons with this family.

Marjorie studied piano and violin at the same time I received violin lessons. In addition to our attending many of the same classes in school, accompanying the church choir with our violin music, rehearsing and playing duets for special church services, our mothers were friends. During their frequent visits and the other activities, we were continually brought together. It was predestined that I sooner or later would discover that she was a girl, even though it required some time. This discovery added pleasure to the activities that we shared, but a thirteen-year-old is grievously inhibited from inexperience, timidity and a lack of imagination. Marjorie did not play an instrument in the band; consequently, my interest in the school band, jazz and other activities led me to gradually lose interest in our church music activities. We were eventually placed in different classes at school and my youthful latent love never quite blossomed. Our interests developed along different paths.

A DRY COUNTY

NACOGDOCHES COUNTY WAS a dry county until after the Second World War. Occasionally liquor interests would seek a referendum attempting to legalize the sale of liquor but on every occasion churches managed to combine strong campaigns to defeat their efforts. Several weeks before the voting date, church pastors would begin a series of sermons condemning the use of alcohol while organized groups canvassed various neighborhoods, handing out literature highlighting the evils of alcohol and soliciting opposition to the legal sale of alcohol. Advertisements were also purchased in the local newspaper beseeching citizens to vote against legalizing the sale of liquor. The electorate of Nacogdoches was not persuaded to vote for the sale of alcohol until after World War II when citizens from other parts of the country began moving into the city and returning World War II veterans brought home a more tolerant attitude toward the consumption of liquor. Liquor supporters also helped convince voters that they were losing tax revenues by not allowing the sale of liquor. My youth occurred at a time when it was illegal to sell liquor in Nacogdoches County.

Despite laws dating back to the 1920s prohibiting the sale of alcohol, enterprising persons living in Nacogdoches County had incessantly devised methods to outwit the law in order to sell or obtain liquor. "Bootleggers" or "Moon Shiners" have existed over much of the United States ever since prohibition laws were first passed but it has always been a high risk and dangerous profession. A safer method was conceived in Nacogdoches during the Depression by having a law passed that made the sale of alcohol legal if it was prescribed by a licensed physician and used for medicinal purposes. As I waited each Saturday afternoon for the Movie Theater to open, I was continually aware of a queue of men waiting to enter a drug store located next to the movie house. An elderly retired doctor sat at a small desk located near the entrance writing prescriptions. He would ask each person that approached his desk,

"What is your problem?"

The answer was always the same,

"I have a sore throat and a cold."

As he wrote the prescription and handed it to the patient to present to a pharmacist, the doctor would respond,

"Take a tablespoon every three hours as needed."

The pharmacist would ask the patient which liquor he preferred. The patient then walked out of the drug store with a bottle of liquor legally sold in a county that legally banned the sale of alcohol.

After the elderly doctor died, the drug store discontinued the sale of liquor making it necessary for those who wished to legally purchase liquor to drive about 50 miles to the nearest "wet" county where liquor could be purchased legally. Since the surrounding dry counties inhabitants constituted a large market for the sale of liquor, a number of liquor stores and dance halls, called "Honky Tonks," had evolved along the boundary of the wet county. This portion of the highway was called "The County Line." It was littered with countless empty beer cans, twinkling like stars after dark as they reflected the headlights of automobiles traveling along the highway. The number of glittering stars, or beer cans, increased along the road as one neared the "county line." The liquor merchants had a monetary interest in preventing nearby counties from voting to legalize the sale of alcohol and it was rumored that they contributed substantial sums of money to those organizations opposing the sale of liquor in Nacogdoches and adjoining counties. Banning the sale of alcohol made it necessary for those desiring liquor to drive almost a hundred miles round-trip; often returning after the driver had consumed alcohol. This, of course, contributed to a number of auto accidents, injuries and deaths. A dangerous curve on a highway leading from Nacogdoches toward the "county-line" was aptly named, "dead man's curve". When the curve was straightened and the sale of liquor was legalized, the number of automobile accidents, deaths, and injuries decreased.

There were a number of "bootleggers" in the county where liquor could be purchased illegally at any time. They usually operated by hiding bottles of liquor outside and around their house after dark. Customers would drive to their house, wait in their car until the "bootlegger" approached, place their order, and then wait in their car for the "bootlegger" to retrieve the hidden liquor and deliver it to them. Occasionally law enforcement officers would raid and arrest a "bootlegger" but usually the he would be in business again within a few days.

Jesse E. Pettey Jr. age 15

TOUGH LOVE

"BEND OVER", HE said as he raised his paddle preparing to bestow five whacks to the seat of my pants.

Mr. C.K. Chamberlain, principal of Nacogdoches High School, was administering a penalty of one stroke of a paddle for each class I had missed the previous day. Rather than attending classes, I had spent the entire day at a Boy Scout cabin located on the banks of a nearby lake basking in the sun and enjoying the company of a friend who was also cutting classes. When questioned by Mr. Chamberlain about missing classes, I falsely replied that my mother had given me permission to remain at home with family visitors. When he requested my written permission, I replied that I had forgotten to bring it. Being very unwise at age 14, my friend and I had failed to consult each other in order to fabricate a good alibi; consequently, my friend had given Mr. Chamberlain a silly excuse that contradicted my alibi. Mr. Chamberlain, cocked his head, looked at me, and said,

"You are insulting my intelligence. That will be five strokes with the paddle, and you'll stay after school in my office for the next three days."

I hated staying after school more than I feared the paddle. We even boasted to each other about the number of blows or "licks" that we could tolerate from his special paddle. Most male teachers of that time designed their paddles to strike fear in the hearts of their students, and Mr. Chamberlain, as principal and chief discipline enforcer, indeed was no exception. It was expected that he would possess and brandish the most fearsome paddle of all. His paddle was about two feet long and eight inches wide with holes carved in frightening shapes. Common wisdom was that the holes made blisters on the delinquent's buttocks duplicating the precise pattern and shapes of the holes in the paddle. Mr. Chamberlain reinforced this rumor by repeatedly boasting that none of his victims could sit for many hours after their punishment. This information fueled our imagination about the effects of his paddle. Although he was severe, we knew that he was fair and I, like most other students, liked and respected him. Our respect was well founded because his self-discipline, integrity, hard work, and the years he spent working on his graduate studies ultimately earned him a professorship at Stephen F. Austin University. A school was later named in his honor.

"Standing L to R—Author, Father
Sitting—Mother, Brother, H. Gordon"

MY SHORT ATHLETIC CAREER

COACH YELLED AS a ball carrier ran toward me at full speed, "Keep your head down—Hit 'em headon!"

I did not want to tackle him head-on. I knew that a collision, "The Big Bang" was about to take place, and I did not want it to occur in my face; instead, I ran toward him at an angle, closed my eyes and turned my head at the last moment—completely missing him. The coach was furious:

"Didn't I tell you to tackle 'em headon? Let's do it again!"

The ball carrier was again running at me with all the speed he could generate. I ran toward him—head lowered—a charging bull at full speed. There was a huge explosion—red lights flashed, horns blared, and bells rang! As I lay stunned on the revolving ground, the coach walked toward me and said,

"Thata' way son! That was a good clean tackle. Now everybody line up for some more!"

I had difficulty associating "clean tackle" with red lights and ringing bells. A friend who played football had convinced me that football was fun; however, he had omitted the part about flashing red lights. I could find nothing enjoyable about tackling another player running at full speed, even though the coach had flattered me by praising my ability to run quickly. He announced repeatedly that I would be his next "scat back", a small but quick ball carrier in the back field with the agility to evade tackles. It was an honor for me as a freshman to make the team and I was flattered that he would allow me to run with the ball; however, my band director informed me that I must choose either the band or the football team. It was a rather easy decision for me because I loved music much more than running full speed into another football player. I had never experienced red lights and clanging bells while playing a saxophone.

When I informed the coach that I had chosen band over football, I felt a cold contempt radiating from him as chilled vapor rises from a frozen lake. It so overwhelmed me that I could feel myself shrinking into nonentity—insignificance—a pariah—I had lost the privilege to be in his eminent presence. But this was only the beginning. From that moment on, he seized every opportunity to embarrass me in the presence of other boys. Although I avoided him whenever possible, our small school building afforded few places that I could escape him indefinitely. On those occasions when we did meet, he would say to the boys around him,

"See that boy? He is a coward. He quit football! He doesn't have the guts to play football. He wants to play a horn in the band like a girl."

In his eyes, I had committed the unforgivable—the greatest of all sins—I had quit his football team. His contempt for me was deliberately designed to send a message to any boy who might consider quitting his team, "quit and you can expect the same treatment from me." He aroused in me such anger that I constantly fantasized about how I might extract my revenge from him, but he was a large man. There was little that a small boy could do but wait—wait until he tired of the game, which he did ultimately and with the passing of time, my hatred for him subsided. The coach's actions sent an unmistakable message to me, and undoubtedly to other students within hearing range, that rather than acting with grace, a man should seek revenge and behave as a bully whenever he objects to a decision made by another. Many years would pass before I could again enjoy a football game or feel respect for a coach.

THE GREAT EXPEDITION

I AM SURE that by now the reader has perceived that, like most young men, but perhaps more than most, I craved adventure. I could not comprehend how my friends could resist my invitation to join me in some thrilling escapade. One such friend, Frank, not only accepted one of my invitation but also enthusiastically shared one of my dreams.

Frank and I had spent many nights near Douglas, Texas, on the banks of the Angelina River, fishing and hanging out with friends, but we had traveled only a short distance from our camps. I often pondered over what lay beyond. As time passed I became obsessed with the unknown river territory between Douglas and a river bridge between Nacogdoches and Lufkin. I was certain that these miles contained unexplored jungles, exotic birds, dangerous wild animals, and abundant fish. I wanted to be one of the few who had ventured into these wild areas along the river and enlisted Frank to share this expedition with me. We estimated the number of days it would require, the amount of food we would need, the essential equipment we should take, and how we might acquire these items, but it soon became apparent that we were without one important item—a boat! This predicament presented a most difficult problem for us since we did not have money to purchase a rowboat and a motor was beyond question.

We began frequenting stores that sold boats, asking the owners if they had, or knew of any discarded boats. One storeowner informed us that he had an old wooden boat in need of repair, and if we would be so kind as to remove it from his storage lot, he would give it to us. With the help of my father, we joyfully moved it to the river and began unskillfully restoring and caulking the rotting wood. With the certainty of youthful optimism, we were certain that we could make the old boat watertight again. After much labor and many tests, we decided that we had restored the boat sufficiently for the forthcoming trip; thus we began loading it with the items we had acquired for the estimated three-day trip. On the day of departure before daybreak, we eagerly sailed from our overnight camp to embark on our great expedition.

During the first day of our voyage, we began to comprehend that our restoration of the boat had not been quite adequate, for we observed water covering the bottom of the boat; nonetheless, we managed to row until late afternoon while bailing water from the boat with a tin can. In our enthusiasm for the journey we considered a leaking boat only a small problem. We refused to allow it to dampen our spirits as we began to cheerfully make camp and prepare our evening meal.

We had selected a thick growth of timber as a location for our camp, but because of our lack of experience, we were unaware that trees create dark shadows. Dark shadows together with the dampness of the river provide a dark, cool, wet breeding grounds for mosquitoes—not a few, but many mosquitoes. Immediately after beaching the boat and long before darkness, we were attacked by troops of huge swamp-river mosquitoes. Our only defense against them was to build a large fire and pray the smoke would drive them away. To our dismay, the fire merely attracted more of them. They enveloped our exposed faces, bit our hands, stung our legs, pricked our arms and attacked the remainder of our body through our clothes. Despite the heat, we attempted to protect ourselves by sitting near the fire covered with a blanket while unsuccessfully endeavoring to sleep. The dampness of the river bred mosquitoes, the darkness protected mosquitoes, our fire attracted mosquitoes, and our blood nourished colossal swarms of mosquitoes. We sweated under the blankets, inhaled smoke from the fire, frantically swatted mosquitoes away from our face, and endured their whining chorus as they serenaded us around our ears throughout the night. Only those who have witnessed and suffered East Texas Swamp-River Mosquitoes can truly appreciate our torment as we camped on the banks of the river that first night of our great expedition. Although, I have been challenged by some who contend that their mosquitoes are larger than East Texas Swamp-River Mosquitoes but they will never convince me. For a fact, there are few fiercer or meaner vermin existing on earth today than those buzzing critters living on the banks of the Angelina River near Nacogdoches, Texas, and I have scars to prove it.

During the night, a roar followed by a loud cough from the bushes suddenly startled us. Although dreadfully frightened, I had enough composure to reach for the .22 rifle we had brought with us. I had heard that sound before in zoos. A quick unanimous decision was reached that one of us would remove a burning bough from our fire and hold it while the other held the rifle. We had read that all animals fear fire and it seemed better protection than the light .22 rifle. As we waited, we heard a few more grunts and noises, then complete silence. We continued to wait, alert with the burning limb and rifle for a long time before we were sure the source of our fear had left the area. Because of our intense concentration and fear that the suspected lion might return, we paid little attention to the mosquitoes during the remaining few hours of darkness.

There were lion-like creatures usually called Mountain Lions that roamed isolated forests in East Texas at that time. As a child, I can remember hunters exhibiting cougars, bobcats and lynx killed or captured in the forests near Nacogdoches. While participating on hunting expeditions since that time, I have heard similar sounds to those heard by Frank and me that night. I am yet convinced that it was some sort of a lion-like creature.

Blessed morning finally arrived. Whenever I feel despondent, I endeavor to recall that terrible night and the following sunrise. At first light, birds began singing a fervent adoration to the rising sun while leaves pirouetted, curtsied and murmured secrets to courteous breezes, swaying clean sunlight between tree branches. During the placid silence of dawn, a lonely leaf silently drifted to earth interrupted only by a distant woodpecker knocking on a tree door. In those untroubled moments, I was aware of the ubiquitousness of a superior entity and knew that all was well. In retrospect, the previous night had been a nightmare—a horror that had finally ended with the dawn—nevertheless, precisely as the sunlight had cleansed the terror of the night, it also revealed another reality — a beached leaking boat.

Following a breakfast of peanut butter and grape jelly, we began to load the boat in preparation for our second day of a great adventure. Soon after launching, we found that not only did the water leaking into in the boat slow our progress, the leak was rapidly becoming worse. It was apparent that one of us must continually bale water from the boat while the other wielded the oars. With this arrangement, we managed to cruise until noon, eat and rest a bit, then continue rowing until mid-afternoon when we decided to beach the boat and prepare a camp for the second night. As the sun began to sink into the velvet shadows of the forest, clouds of hungry mosquitoes descended on us once again. Our face and hands were covered with red lumps caused by previous mosquito bites but that did not deter the determination of our new whining guests to begin another feeding frenzy. On the other hand, we were grateful that we did not again hear the frightful cough of a lion.

Following another long sleepless night of inhaling smoke from our campfire and sweating under blankets as we attempted to evade our buzzing tormentors, morning finally arrived. The mosquitoes departed to wherever they go and the peaceful sounds of the forest returned. Although our spirits lifted as the sun rose, restoring our enthusiastic determination to complete the journey, we were indeed sore and tired from lack of sleep.

We had not traveled far the third morning, when we recognized that our method of bailing water from the boat was less effective with the passing of each hour. Our speed was seriously reduced as the boat filled with water, soaking our clothes and provisions; forcing us to beach the sinking boat about noon of the third day. Our bedding was soaked, we had very little food, we were less than halfway to our destination, and we were exhausted from lack of sleep during the previous two nights. Our immature imagination had led us to expect an adventure much like the movies had portrayed of African hunters, with natives rowing their solid boats filled with provisions, sailing the Congo. Instead, our boat sank, we were without provisions, exhausted from two sleepless nights fighting mosquitoes, and our great expedition had turned into a nightmare.

Dejected, we sat on the banks of the river quietly considering the looming reality of a very long walk ahead. To add to our misery, we had not heard or seen anyone to help us during the entire trip, it was impossible to walk along the riverbank because of underbrush, and we did not know the location of inland roads that would lead us home. We were two youngsters isolated in a wilderness. We indeed, needed a miracle.

For several hours we sat on the river bank discussing various but unproductive solutions when suddenly we froze—somewhere in the distance there was a sound different from that made by insects or birds of the forest. It was but a whisper; a sound so faint it could be the wind stirring the leaves, but it was different. It was this small difference that had captured our attention. We tilted our heads; leaned toward the sound while remaining utterly motionless in a desperate attempt to determine from which direction the almost silent reverberation came. As it increased slightly above a rustle, we began to detect a sound like that of a far away insect propelled by the shifting winds. It flowed forth from the forest, alternately augmenting and subsiding as it ricocheted over the water along the twists and bends of the river. As a bee slowly buzzing toward us, it gradually grew louder. I began to recognize the sound of a boat motor, but the bends of the river concealed the sight of a boat for yet a long time. Our spirits lifted as we began to think that we were not alone and that help may soon be approaching.

After what seemed an eternity, a small object appeared from far away, maneuvering around a bend in the river. As it drew nearer, I observed that it was a large boat containing four men dressed in some sort of uniform with a fifth person sitting in the middle wearing civilian clothes. Approaching even nearer, I could determine that the uniforms were those of firemen, and the civilian sitting in the center of the boat was none other than my father! I was astounded—how did he know that we were in trouble? My father was indeed my hero at that moment.

As we loaded our soggy possessions into their boat, Dad explained that he had been tormented with the thought that the old leaking boat would sink, leaving us marooned along the river or even worse, drowned. After two sleepless nights, he had requested some of his firemen friends to accompany him and search the river for us. As a longtime member of the volunteer fire department, he was well acquainted with both firemen and policemen. His timing could not have been better because we were not anxious to spend another night alone with mosquitoes and lions. Although, I cannot remember if I ever thanked my father for rescuing us, he was indeed my guardian angel as we concluded our great river adventure. I had witnessed yet another miracle.

Soon after we were rescued, Frank and his family moved from Nacogdoches and within a few more years, I volunteered to enter the Air Force. Although I met his younger brother shortly after the war, I never met Frank again. He was a fellow band member, a buddy, and a good friend—indeed, he must have been a friend to share with me the hardships and dangers of our great expedition.

TWO RUNAWAYS

WE STOOD AT the side of a highway with our thumbs extended hitchhiking. Many automobiles rushed past before a huge truck pulled over onto the side of the road and stopped. The driver patiently waited as we scrambled up into an enormous cab, and said,

"Hiya, boys. Where ya'l goin'?"

He was a large man dressed in overalls. His weather-beaten face was like that of a boxer who had endured too many punches, his arms were those of a weight-lifter grown soft, and his huge belly came to rest between his legs underneath the steering wheel. As we stared at him in amazement, I was mute; I could only think about how I might distance myself from this awe-inspiring giant. His size and intimidating appearance was so frightening that it aroused in me an urge to turn and run away.

At length I said, "We're goin' out west."

He responded, "Where ya'l goin in the west?"

"Just anywhere in the west," I answered.

It all began many months before. For some reason unknown to me, my mother was troubled when I began dating a young girl who lived nearby. Too young to own an automobile, I had walked to Mary's house a few times to visit her. Her parents had been present and I had departed at an early hour; therefore, I did not understand my mother's concern, nor could she explain it to me. I was fifteen—almost grown I believed—and our conduct had been beyond reproach. For almost a year I had visited Mary at her home but one day my mother ordered me to stop seeing her. That was the day I resolved to leave home. I believed her decision was unfair and I perceived her command as interfering with my life; consequently, in anger and a desire to make her regret her decision, I began to think long and hard about how I would leave home. I lacked the confidence to go alone; I needed a companion. Because Billy was a fellow band member and a Boy Scout, he was the quintessential companion for me. After some persuasion, Billy agreed to accompany me on my western adventure, even though he was not angry with his parents. The High School Band was scheduled to attend a band contest in Tyler, Texas, one day before a Boy Scout Jamboree began in the same city. A Boy Scout Jamboree is an annual gathering of scouts from Boy Scout Troops all over the state and where games and contests are held. I had convinced myself that the Jamboree would provide the best opportunity for me to run away from home because it was to be held in Tyler, half the distance to Dallas, my gateway to the west. My parents had given me permission to attend the jamboree and therefore, would not be aware of my departure until I was far from home.

Before daylight the first morning of the jamboree, we arose, spread two wool blankets on the floor, placed our folded clothes in the center, pulled the four corners of the blanket together, and tied them into a knot. I then placed one arm through the blanket under the knot, lifted the bundle to my shoulders and carried it as if it were a backpack. We quietly sneaked away from our Boy Scout tent before the wake-up bugle call and walked to the side of the Dallas highway, where we began hitch hiking.

Our truck driver continued,

"Well, I can take ya'l as far as Dallas. What ya'l goin' to do when you get out west?"

I responded, "We're gonna git a job."

My friend Billy said, "We like horses and we thought we'd like ta get a job on a ranch."

"I see," He acknowledged.

There was a long pause while he seemed to think about two young teenaged boys with a bundled blanket, each carrying a musical instrument, hitchhiking, and seeking a job on a ranch.

"Where ya'l come from?"

"We're from Nacogdoches." I responded.

"Do your Momma and Poppa know where ya'l at?"

There was a long silence—he stoically waited.

Finally I said, "no, sir."

After another long pause he asked, "Ya'l boys have any money?"

"We have a quarter!" Billy volunteered.

"I'ma fixin to stop up here at a truck stop an I'm a gonna buy ya'l boys some dinner," He said.

We were intensely hungry. We had not eaten since the evening before. Because of our early departure from the scout camp, we had missed breakfast. It was not a difficult decision to accept his offer for a meal.

After lunch, the sound of the truck engine and a full stomach made me content, drowsy, and silent as I drifted into a reverie. I thought about home, my mother, our running away, our kind gentle giant-like truck driver, our destination, how far away home seemed, and tried my best to remember why I was running from home. At length I felt compelled to continue our explanation of our trip to the west. For some time our driver had driven in silence and had not asked questions.

"We're goin' out west to work," I repeated.

He turned his head toward us, taking in everything at a moment's glance, turned back toward the highway and said after a long pause,

"Ya'l mighty young to be goin out west."

There was even a longer period of silence as Billy and I struggled for a proper response. Unable to think of one, we waited for him to resume the conversation.

"Ya'l boys wouldn't be runnin away from home would ya?"

After a long pause, I answered sheepishly, "yes, sir."

There was another long pause as I contemplated his uncanny ability to ferret out the truth with only a few short questions. It never occurred to me that our driver might think it unusual for two young boys to be hitchhiking, with a bundle of clothes, and musical instruments in their hands.

"Do ya'l boys know what tomorrow is?"

Remembering that it was Saturday, I proudly answered: "I guess it's Sunday."

"Well, that's right. Do ya'l know what else it is?"

"No, sir."

"It's Mother's Day!" he responded in a booming voice. He paused for a while and said,

"How ya'l think your mamas gonna feel tomorrow when they wake up and you boys ain't home?"

After another long interval, he asked, "Where ya'l boys gonna sleep tonight?"

It had not occurred to us that we had no place to stay. A Texas northern had blown in that afternoon bringing a cold north wind, and dropping the temperature about 30 degrees within a few hours.

"I'm fixin to stop upheer at a garage. I gotta friend that owns this-heer garage and maybe he'll let ya'l stay there tonight. It's kinda cold to be sleeping outside."

We arrived in Dallas without additional conversation while I quietly meditated about Mother's Day and home. The truck driver parked beside his friend's garage, and went inside while we remained in the cab. After a few minutes, he returned to announce that his friend had agreed to allow us to sleep in his garage.

He then said,

"Well, boys I gotta leave ya'l here. If I was ya'l, I'd turn around tomorrow mornin and head back where yal come from. Your mamas will be mighty proud to see ya'l. Good luck."

With that bit of advice, he thrust a 25-cent coin in each of our hands and drove away. Hunger began to gnaw at our stomachs soon after our friend had departed. From a hamburger shop located across the street, we purchased a hamburger for fifteen cents and a coke for five cents. Although it was not sufficient to satisfy our hunger, we had a place to sleep and money from our driver/angel to buy food the next day. We returned to the garage as the owner was preparing to depart for the night. He locked all the doors and warned us that if we opened any door, it would close and lock automatically. The garage was unheated, and we each possessed only one woolen blanket to ward off the increasing chill. As the night progressed, we could only shiver and hope that morning would soon arrive. It seemed an eternity before the sun rose. We began gathering our belongings without speaking, both understanding that we needed to return home.

As I reminisce over this adventure, I am reminded how vulnerable we were and how many pernicious events might have confronted us without our truck driver's assistance. Two fifteen year old boys with only twenty-five cents between them, without shelter and lacking mature judgment would have been easy prey for an evil predator. I have been blessed many times over the course of my lifetime when someone appeared at the moment that I needed assistance. I believe our gentle, giant, truck driver was a guardian angel, and we were two very lucky boys.

After a short wait by the side of the highway, we were offered a ride directly to Nacogdoches. Fortunately, there was little conversation by the driver of the Nacogdoches-bound automobile, for it afforded me time to fashion responses to questions that I anticipated my parents would ask. I was certain that they would be angry and I expected to be punished.

Upon arriving at my home and meekly entering the front room, I could see into the bathroom where my father was shaving. Through the mirror he observed us entering the front room but he continued shaving without speaking. He was obviously waiting for me to speak first. As the pressure from the silence began to build, I cautiously said in my most carefree, casual voice,

"Hi, Dad!"

"Well, did you boys have a good time?" he asked as he looked at us through the mirror and continued to shave.

"No sir, we were cold and hungry."

He continued shaving without commenting. My mother heard our voices and entered the room to ask if we were hungry. It was afternoon and we had only a small hamburger for breakfast—we were starving! As she prepared food for us, I knew that she was disturbed, and to further ease the tension, I said,

"Happy Mother's Day!"

Although her only response was a slight, "Thank you," I could see a shadow of a smile on her lips and a sparkle in her eyes. After we finished lunch, my father drove Billy to his home where he lived with his parents and a large number of older siblings on a farm several miles from town. Because I felt some responsibility for influencing him to leave home with me, I was determined to be at his side when he faced his family. I hoped to make them understand that he did not want to run away, that I had persuaded him to join me.

The brothers were gathered in the front yard when we arrived. I thought to myself, "He sure is in trouble!" The entire family had assembled at the house. The brothers approached as my father stopped the car and one older brother, apparently the leader of the group, said to Billy,

"Meet me behind the house."

The brothers then walked toward the back of the house to wait for Billy. We entered the house where Billy's mother and father were seated. I said in a meek voice,

"It wasn't Billy's fault. I talked him into it."

"That's even worse," remarked one of the brothers.

I determined at that moment that I was not helping Billy, and that perhaps I should remain silent.

After a few minutes Billy and his other brothers came into the house. It was evident that he had been crying. He approached his parents, embraced them and expressed his regret for causing them to worry about him. My father arose from his chair and began walking toward the front door, for he knew that it was time for us to leave the family to their Mother's Day reunion.

Neither my father nor my mother ever brought up the subject of my leaving home again and I quietly continued to date Mary. The experience of leaving home taught me how indeed fortunate I was to have two understanding parents rather than a house full of older brothers to discipline me. Poor Billy.

ANOTHER MIRACLE

AT THE BEGINNING of my tenth grade, my guardian angel produced another miracle by placing me in a class instructed by a history teacher who became one of the three pivotal influences of my life. In previous years I had been satisfied to just "get by" in school, but in my tenth year Miss Dora Grant kindled in me a desire to achieve what I believed was unattainable for me. Her challenges and encouragement motivated me to study and to strive for grades I had never thought possible; consequently, my self-confidence improved in direct ratio to my improved grades. Somehow she caused me to suspect that she liked me, an experience that I had never before enjoyed. It was the first time that I had ever believed a teacher respected me just for what I was or could be. Perhaps her great insight had accurately lead her to believe that I lacked confidence; that I had convinced myself that I was inadequate; that I had given up. Slowly she began to convince me that she had singled me out of the class for special attention and that I was a special person.

During class, she often approached me from behind my desk, placed her hands on my shoulders, leaned over one shoulder, her face inches from mine, and asked if I had completed yesterday's assignment. She was so physically near that I found myself unable to tell her a falsehood. After several clumsy attempts to make excuses, I found that it was much easier to complete the assignment than to explain to her why it was not completed. She made me feel so special that I wanted to please her. Soon I found myself completing assignments with great care; I yearned to bask in her praises. My grade of C began to replace a previous F, a grade of B replaced a grade of C, and for the first time, my name appeared on the honor roll. Being on an honor roll was far beyond anything I had ever believed that I could accomplish or cared to accomplish; rather it had occurred because of her teaching skills, her intuitiveness, and the commitment of a caring teacher.

I can not remember much of the subject matter she taught me, but she was indeed my most important teacher. She helped me discover confidence, to understand that through hard work I could accomplish goals, and with achieving goals, I could succeed in almost anything I desired. I shall be forever grateful to her for self-confidence; a belief in myself that she instilled in me, which I believe is the greatest gift any teacher can contribute to a student.

Music and military service were the other significant determinants of my life. Successfully playing a musical instrument made me aware of my abilities and contributed to my self-confidence. My successful military experiences raised the bar of expectations beyond and above that which I had previously believed were my limits. By the time I was discharged from the military, I had accomplished so many difficult objectives set by those in command, and had survived so many terrifying situations in combat, that I was convinced that, indeed there were no future obstacles that I could not overcome. I feel extremely fortunate that I was exposed to these positive experiences; however, Miss Dora Grant was the first and most important of all.

OLD CORA

Cora was our housemaid. In addition to her duties of cleaning the house, she cooked meals for the family and was treated as a family member. She was ebony black, skinny, unattractive, and deceptively dumb. At that time, most blacks pretended to be dumb simply because white people expected them to be dumb. It was much easier and safer for them to carry out this charade, to always appear to be searching for a solution to a problem, for there was nothing more uncomfortable for some white people than being in the presence of an intelligent black. On the other hand, apparently feeble-witted blacks aroused compassion among many whites. Most whites wanted to think of blacks as simple, agreeable, lovable children, whereas a smart, intelligent black was perceived as a threat. Only a generation before Cora, blacks had been held in slavery and some yet lived who could remember those years. They had passed on to her generation the ability to appear submissive and humble. I believe that Cora, like most other blacks of her time, was more comfortable acting dumb in the presence of white people.

Cora lived in her home located in a section of Nacogdoches, called "Nigger Town", where only black people lived. Whites used the word, "nigger", often without maliciousness because it had been used as far back as present memory exists; however, we are now aware of how much they disliked the word. Black people were polite and protective of white persons in their neighborhoods but few whites would venture into the area after dark simply because there were few incentives for them to be there. Many white businessmen and salesmen found it necessary to conduct business with blacks during the day and black workers ventured into the white section of town during the day to work, but it was not safe for them to be there after dark. Some black people were allowed to enter restaurants or hotels for work but never to eat or remain over night. Signs were posted over rest rooms and drinking fountains announcing, "For the use of white people only", and other signs were printed, "For Colored Only". All buses or trains regularly posted, "Colored must sit in back of the bus". When I was a youth, the word "Negro" and "Colored" were interchangeably used on these signs, but the words were so extremely unpopular with blacks, they were replaced with the words "colored" or "black" after World War II. The black community possessed their own churches, schools, movies, and so we lived peacefully within our own communities. It was not until the later 1950s, however, that all "colored" signs began to disappear and Congress passed laws abolishing segregation.

There were some in Nacogdoches who had been taught to hate blacks; however, within my circle of acquaintances, blacks were only objects of ridicule—not hate. They were stereotyped and segregated simply because it was a 200 year old custom. Whites accepted segregation as a matter of fact and those few who attempted to change the practice were extremely unpopular; even sometimes endangered by extremists. On the other hand, there were many truly compassionate people like my mother who often aided blacks in need of help. I can remember accompanying her to visit Cora in her home when she was ill and when she delivered Christmas food to other poor black families.

I never questioned anyone about how Cora acquired her house—whether she was a widow or not—I only knew that she lived alone. She could not read, write, or state her age. We could only guess that she was in her 60s when she died.

My brother enjoys telling the story about Cora's coconut pie recipe. The event took place after I had left home to serve in the Air Corps, and I have no reason to doubt the creditability of his story. He claims that after our mother had taught Cora to bake an acceptable coconut pie, she made one for a Thanksgiving meal. It was a beautiful pie covered with browned, foamy meringue, so enticing that our family could hardly wait to taste it. After the pie was served, my brother took the first bite and began to spit it out while complaining about the terrible taste. Later my mother discovered that, because she could not read, she had mistaken soap flakes for dried coconut shreds.

I remember Cora with more fondness, as I grow older. I recall how we considered her a simple buffoon; how she amused us by the manner in which she wore her colorful bandanna around her head; how her mouth glittered with gold teeth; how she attempted to cover her glittering teeth with her hand; and how she addressed me as "Mr. Junior". Although she is now only a distant memory, I will always remember her with affection. She was utterly incapable of telling a falsehood or stealing an item that did not belong to her. She was born of a generation that accepted hard work as a way of life—a time when honesty was its own reward and honoring a promise was presumed. She was from an era unlike any since.

EARNING MONEY

MR. POPP WAS a German immigrant who had lived in Nacogdoches for many years. Despite the fact that he was an excellent repairman and his skills were in demand, he had encountered resentment because of his German background during the First World War. When I was about 13, he opened an appliance repair shop near my father's office prompting my father to suggest that I visit him to inquire if he needed help. I suspect that he had already suggested to Mr. Popp that I was available to assist him after school and on weekends. My father never admitted that he had set up a job for me. He always let me believe I had found the job with my own efforts. I began a new career when Mr. Popp offered to train and pay me one dollar each Saturday to sharpen lawnmowers for his customers. The salary was better than the 25 cents paid me for cleaning the church, my previous job.

Mr. Popp was a tall, skinny man with a long nose. He consistently wore a large brimmed black hat, a khaki shirt and khaki trousers supported with black suspenders. Whenever I see a photograph of the scarecrow straw man character from "The Wizard of Oz" movie, Mr. Popp immediately appears in my mind. I did not learn anything about lawnmowers that would benefit me in later life. The old fashioned reel-type mowers gave way to power mowers but my fascination with things foreign, inspired by Mr. Popp, remained throughout my life. He was different and more fascinating than anyone else in Nacogdoches was at that time. Although I found it difficult to understand his German-flavored English, he held me spellbound whenever he spoke. He was the first person I had ever met from a foreign country. Perhaps he kindled in me the first glow of interest in foreign people and different cultures or maybe I was simply fascinated with anyone or anything different from what I had been accustomed to in Nacogdoches; whatever the reason, this fascination with things foreign has motivated me throughout my life to travel, to live in a foreign countries and even to chose a foreign bride for my wife.

A brief time after I began working for him, Mr. Popp closed his shop, moved from Nacogdoches, and was never heard from again. My second career suddenly came to an end.

. . .

Without the help of my father, I soon found another part-time job unpacking and stacking food on the shelves of the largest grocery store in Nacogdoches. It was owned and operated by Novel Bright, a pleasant man who provided part-time jobs for numerous high school and college students. He was a generous employer with a pleasant, relaxed personality that contributed to an affable environment for both employees and customers. He always positioned himself at one of the cash registers so that he could greet the public and supervise the business. He allowed student employees to work whenever they wished. We simply reported to him when we were ready for work on school holidays and Saturdays. If we failed to report for work, he never questioned why. He would log the time that we began and pay us at the end of the day.

The twenty cent an hour wages I earned at the grocery store allowed me to earn two dollars each Saturday—more than double what I had earned working for Mr. Popp. I enjoyed the company of the employees; assisting customers and working for Mr. Bright was a pleasure. He never displayed anger or displeasure, but instead wore a continuous smile and was courteous with both employees and customers. It was also this job that helped me begin to feel that I was no longer a child.

It was this job that taught me to recognize the smell of garlic. My mother had never used garlic with her cooking and I was informed that it was worn around the neck as a cure for colds or other ailments in past times. East Texans rarely seasoned their food with it, yet it was an East Texan who visited the store every Saturday morning that first introduced me to the odor of garlic. He not only smelled strange to me, his appearance was also amusing: he was extremely fat, red faced, always wore loose hanging overalls and waddled like a duck as he walked. I was aware immediately that he had entered the premises because of a terrible stench that radiated from his clothes, his skin, his breath, and wafted down each isle of the store like a fog, shrouding everything in its path. The odor of raw garlic is not repulsive to me, but when the aroma is discharged through the skin or breath of a person, it can be unbearable. I think he must have eaten enormous quantities of garlic with his breakfast, for I have never before, or since, encountered such a strong fragrance; however, I also must admit that my ability to smell was much more acute then.

. . .

During the summer vacation of my sophomore year of high school, my father arranged a full-time job for me as a "grunt" with a construction crew building power lines for the Texas Power and Light Company. A "grunt" is one without skills but contributes muscles for hard labor and often groans or grunts from exertion. It was such a desirable full-time job, and jobs were so very scarce during the depression, that my father applied for me immediately upon learning that the job was available. Until I graduated from high school, I worked eight hours a day, six days a week during summer school vacation with the same construction crew earning twenty five cents an hour. The work was hot, dirty, laborious and exhausting, but I was able to save a small amount of money for the first time.

The construction crew erected new electrical power lines in rural areas by setting wooden poles into the ground and connecting them with electrical wires. We would dig a hole about six feet deep, unload a 30 foot creosote treated pole from a truck, lower one end into the hole, lift the other end until it was vertical, and refill the hole around the pole. Several years would pass before machinery was used to do this sort of labor, but then we did it with our hands and back muscles. I soon learned to cover my skin as much as possible when exposed to creosote, which was a black coating used to preserve the poles. Direct contact with the creosote blistered the skin. Only a few days working near the poles caused the skin of my face to turn a flaming red.

After the poles were set upright, electric copper wires were lifted by ropes to be secured by linemen waiting at the top of the poles. My job was to stand at the foot of a pole and send tools up to the waiting lineman by a rope and pulley. Since I was only fifteen years old and the lone youngster working among a crew of adults, I was constantly teased. In order to entertain themselves, they delighted in telling me stories so that they might observe my reactions. Being young, inexperienced and naive, I would sometimes believe them. Their favorite joke was to tell a story about snipe hunting. A snipe was, by their description, a bird that could not fly and hid in bushes. In order to capture them, an innocent youth was designated to hold an open sack while the group presumable herded the snipe into it. Of course, the perpetrators, rather than herd the snipe, would conceal and amuse themselves by observing the victim waiting for the snipe to appear. He remained in place holding the bag until he realized he had been duped. Perhaps that is how the old cliché, "left holding the bag," originated. I was fortunate to have heard the tale before and refused to participate in their snipe hunting game; however, they were able to outwit me in some of their other schemes. Another favorite joke was to send a new unsuspecting fellow worker to fetch a pair of "stents" from the foreman. When asked for a pair of stents, the foreman would send him to another worker quite a distance away that purportedly was using the stents. When the stents was requested from that worker, he would in turn be notified that another worker was using the stents until the novice became aware that he was the butt of a joke.

. . .

Near the end of my junior year in high school, my high school band director, Mr. J.T. Cox invited me to become a member of The Stephen F. Austin College Marching Band and later to play in a college dance band, "The Austonians". A high school student playing with college students in the Stephen F. Austin College band and orchestra was an experience I had never expected, but to be paid for performing with a band while yet in high school was beyond all expectations. The Austonions appeared at movie theaters, college dances, high schools, and various dance halls over East Texas. While most of our performances were devoted to promoting and advertising the university, we were paid for playing dances on weekends.

I had been working at various jobs earning pocket money since I was very young: cleaning a church, sharpening lawnmowers, stocking groceries, and building power lines. These jobs taught me how to work with people, but more importantly, they taught me to be dependable. It was not necessary that my father teach me responsibility and punctuality—he needed only to help me find employment and my employers taught me to be dependable. The usual penalty for irresponsibility was to be fired or laid off, the worse thing that could happen to most workers during the depression. In a small city where everyone was acquainted with each other, reputations were revered and fiercely protected. If one's reputation became tainted with a history of irresponsibility, the entire population of Nacogdoches was aware of it, jobs suddenly became scarce and the family name was tarnished. For this lesson learned early, I am grateful to my father.

. . .

While I continued to date Mary through my senior year in high school, we were inseparable friends with two other couples that had been dating for some time. We shared activities, and even attended our Senior Day in Galveston together, but Mary and I had few other interests that we could share. She was younger than I was and one class behind me in school. It was inevitable that I would lose enthusiasm for our relationship. I wanted to be involved with older and more fascinating college students. I was busy playing in the university band, and all my other interests focused on college activities. Upon my graduation from high school, we discontinued dating and I enrolled in fall classes at the university. My mother could have spared herself much anxiety had she been able to foresee our eventual separation; but then, I would have missed the experience of leaving home.

A GRUNT IN A SHIPYARD

AFTER GRADUATING FROM high school, I responded to a rumor that the shipyard in Houston needed more employees to help build ships. Although a year would pass before the U.S. would declare war on Germany, England was already in a debilitating war with Germany and desperately needed additional war supplies. America was feverishly building more ships to transport those needed amounts of food and war machinery to England and her allies. I found the shipyard, indeed, stirring with activity and hiring workers at above average wages as fast as they could be processed. Although inexperienced, I was hired to work full time at a pay rate of one and one half-dollars per hour with additional earnings for working more than forty hours per week. In 1941, sixty dollars a week for forty hours was considered exceptional earnings but I also earned an additional thirty dollars each week by working longer hours and Saturdays. I found myself, at age seventeen, with a job paying higher wages than my father earned. He could, like many other men living in Nacogdoches, quit his job to work for better pay in the Houston shipyards, but he had so many years invested in his retirement plan that he could not afford to terminate his employment with Texas Power and Light Company. Although I found the pay generous, I was aware that it was a temporary wartime job and that soon I would be called into military service. The previous year Congress had passed the first ever peacetime draft that would summon me for military service the next year at age seventeen.

I was assigned to a crew of six that installed a large magnetic cable in the ships. The cable was designed to interfere with the magnetic field of a floating mine, repelling rather than attracting it to the metal hull of a ship. Our job was to cut the cable into sections and pull it through designed openings in bulkhead partitions around the ship. The cable was about the size of an adult's thigh. Because of the weight, it was cut it into smaller lengths so that we could pull it through the openings and splice it together to form a continuous cable around the ship.

A few days after I began working, our foreman said to us,

"Boys, we can't finish this cable until the welding crew gets out of our way. They are behind schedule. I'm sure you don't want to be laid off, so just disappear so no one can catch you loafing. I'll find you when they are finished. Pettey, you go with Ed; he'll show you how we disappear."

The crew headed for their hiding places while Ed introduced me to a dark unfinished area of the ship. I rapidly acquired the skill of "disappearing" whenever a delay occurred and I discovered that it occurred often. A ship under construction offers many convenient, deep, dark recesses between unfinished bulkheads where one may remain out of sight, unnoticed, and not be missed for days. Construction workers, numbering in the hundreds, were organized into small crews and worked on various projects on different parts of the ship. They worked under a very complicated, coordinated schedule that must be accurately followed so that one crew would complete a project and move to their next project. Another crew, working on a different project, would take their place. The second crew must finish their project on time and move on in order that the third crew could take their place. With so many employees and schedules to coordinate, inevitable chaos developed from time to time. When our scheduled work project was delayed, we had two choices: inform the ship foreman and wait, without pay, until we could resume work, or disappear from sight, with pay, until the obstacle was removed. I never knew anyone who chose the former, and if we had elected to do so, there would have been such an overwhelming number of workers dismissed, only to be rehired, I question that it would have been cost-effective. Few cared about cost under war conditions. Inefficient management was the norm when America was building war machinery as rapidly as possible with unlimited taxpayer's money. To paraphrase a famous quotation regularly used at that time,

"Damn the cost, full speed ahead."

At the end of the summer of 1941, I relinquished my job at the shipyard to return home and enroll at Stephen F. Austin University. I had saved sufficient money to pay my college tuition and buy a tenor saxophone to replace an alto saxophone my parents had given me several years before. The summer of '41 was a significant time in my life. It was the first time I had lived away from home, the first time I was able to pay all expenses from my earnings, and the experience ended forever my reliance on my parents. I thought I was an adult, but I needed several more years to prove it.

CLOUDS OF WAR

WHILE I WAS enjoying that thrilling period of growing up, another eventful period of world history was taking place. Germany had invaded Poland plunging Europe into war and England was fighting for its very existence. While these events were inexorably drawing the U. S. into war, I rarely devoted any thought to the dangers that threatened my generation. I was aware that England had entered the war and that Hitler was persecuting and conducting a program of liquidation for certain ethnic groups, but I felt somewhat detached from all of the horrible incidents we heard and read about—there was an ocean separating us from the war.

I graduated from high school in the spring of 1941, unaware that we would be at war by the end of the year. My summer job at the shipyard ended. I eagerly anticipated attending fall classes at SFA University and participating in school activities. I impatiently waited for the moment to arrive when I could register at the university as a freshman and join friends I had made while playing in the band as a high school student. I would at last become a college student. When the time finally arrived, I was further elated with an invitation to join the Sawyers fraternity and become a "pledge". A pledge is a temporary member of a fraternity organization that is placed on probation during his freshman year. During this trial period, the pledge is continually hazed while the older members evaluate his reactions. If accepted, he was elevated to full membership his second year and as an upper classman, he could then haze freshmen on probation.

Hazing usually took the form of indignities invented by older members: beaten with a paddle, being released blindfolded from an automobile at night on an isolated road and other clever humiliations too numerous to list. I was resolute in my determination to be accepted as a member of the fraternity by demonstrating a good attitude and toughness under adversity.

"Initiation night" was held each year to initiate pledges. It was ostensibly to impress on the pledges their obligations to the fraternity and to allow senior members to become better acquainted with them. Some wag remarked that initiation night was held only to satisfy the sadistic tendencies of upper classmen. Like initiations in many adult brotherhoods, we were blindfolded and led from one location to another where the senior members read us instructions. At one station I was instructed to signal my loyalty by eating worms. Being blindfolded, I was unable see a raw oyster tied to a thread held over my mouth. As it was slowly lowered, I could taste something moist and slimy. The power of suggestion convinced me that it was indeed a juicy worm. With a command to swallow it, the worm was repeatedly dropped into my mouth and retrieved from my throat just as I began to swallow. This was repeated many times until I vomited and the tormentors tired of the game. I was then placed in an automobile blindfolded, driven a circuitous route to a deserted road, and set free many miles from the city. Walking until daylight, I eventually found a familiar road and walked to a highway where I was able to flag down a car and return home.

I continued to live at home with my parents and was one of the few students who did not live in a dormitory. In spite of the indignities inflicted on me as a pledge and a freshman, I had fun—or was I having fun?

In order to be identified as freshmen, we were instructed by upper classmen to wear "beanie" caps. These baseball-like caps also served to cover many strange and comical haircuts that were imposed on freshmen by various school organizations. If, during FRESHMAN WEEK and often throughout the year, a freshman was discovered without his beanie cap, he was usually hazed with a paddle by an upper classman.

A girl friend and I sat in a campus drug store enjoying a dish of ice cream. Unexpectedly, an upper classman who was know as a bully approached our booth and loudly announced to my date,

"I'm going to beat his butt for not wearing his freshman cap."

I calmly replied that I had dressed to be with a girlfriend and did not deem it appropriate to wear my cap. Unimpressed, he ordered me outside and announced that he would administer his paddle so that I would remember to wear my freshman cap in the future. I calmly countered with a counter-offer to meet him outside the drug store at a specific hour—after I had escorted my date home—and trade alternate blows with the paddle until one of us surrendered, unable to bear further pain. Because the entire drug store crowd overheard our conversation, he was unable to refuse my offer without seeming a bully or a coward, although he was indeed both.

When I returned to the drug store later, a crowd had assembled outside, eager to witness a struggle of endurance between a freshman and an upper classman—the epic story of David and Goliath! We agreed that we would flip a coin, and the winner would deliver the first blow to the other. We would then alternate strokes of the paddle until one declared a halt to the contest.

"ONE!" chanted the crowd as I received the first stinging blow.

It indeed hurt because he attempted to make it as painful as possible for me. I straightened and prepared to deliver a strike as severe as I could. We continued to deal blows to each other.

"FIVE!" the crowd yelled as they counted each strike of the paddle.

I felt the blow somewhat less as numbness began to slightly replace the pain.

"FIFTEEN!" The crowd yelled as they became more excited.

The pain had become a stinging burn with each whack of the paddle, but I was determined to endure any pain my opponent could deliver. But oh, how it hurt! Could he withstand more pain than I could? Would I pass out before winning? He began to pause longer between strikes as though he wanted a respite from the pain before the next one struck. I began to sense victory, although my buttocks felt like they had been ground through a meat grinder.

"TWENTY!" The crowd counted as I clinched my teeth and awaited the next blow.

"TWENTY-FIVE!" shouted the crowd. He threw down the paddle and said,

"ENOUGH!"

I was confident that he would never bother me again. I had disarmed him; he could never again bully any other defenseless freshman for fear that someone might remind him of that night when he had said, "enough!" I was a campus hero for a short time, but while enjoying my fifteen minutes of fame, I was unable to sit.

. . .

Students were enlisting in the armed service by increasing numbers as my first semester drew to a close, and the war drew nearer. I tried to delude myself into believing the U.S. would remain neutral or that I would be overlooked by the military, but young men in uniform were to be seen everywhere. I was constantly reminded that my time for service was rapidly approaching. I had registered with the draft board in 1941, a requirement for all age seventeen and over. Now I was approaching my eighteen birthday at which time I would be old enough to be accepted in the military service; however, I continued to make an effort to ignore the inevitable. Japan finally burst my bubble of hope.

WORLD WAR II ARRIVES

IT WAS AROUND one o'clock on a peaceful Sunday afternoon December 7, 1941. I sat at a desk in my bedroom writing a theme for my freshman English class while a small radio broadcast a background of soft music. Only a few minutes before, my family had finished our Sunday meal and I had withdrawn to my bedroom to compose the theme. The assignment, due the next day, was to write a description of a memorable event I had experienced during my past life. The assignment was never completed—without warning, a radio announcer interrupted the music broadcast and with a trembling voice said,

"We interrupt this program to bring you the latest news; Japan has, within the last hour, bombed Pearl Harbor in Hawaii! I repeat; Japan has just bombed Pearl Harbor! There have been many causalities. We do not know at the moment how many, but we will keep you informed. Congress is calling for an emergency meeting tomorrow morning!"

The hairs on my arms stood on end. My entire body tingled as I dropped my writing pen and turned up the volume of the radio. Leaning forward, I put my ear near the radio as if I must be close to the source of the announcements in order to assure myself that I had correctly heard—to understand what was happening to my country. I sat mesmerized, in shock for a few minutes. I bounded from my desk and ran into my parent's bedroom where my father was listening to the news as I entered. We were staring vacantly at the floor, trying to understand the terrible news broadcast when my mother entered to ask what was taking place. As we continued listening to the radio, my parents must have considered the possibility that I might be called to war and the anguish that was certain to follow. I was thinking about turning eighteen the following month and the inevitability of being called to serve my country. At that same moment, the entire nation was being informed of the tragic attack that cost over two thousand young American lives—over two thousand hopes and dreams eternally squashed. As we attempted to comprehend the rising number of causalities—more that eleven hundred on one ship—a hatred for Japan, like bitter caustic bile, arose in my throat. It would be many years before I would be able to look at a Japanese photograph or person without feeling this hatred coursing through my body. Several years would pass before this hatred would, like all emotions, dissipate into a state of objectivity. It was not until 50 years later while visiting Japan and being hosted in the home of a beautiful Japanese family that the neutrality turned into a sincere admiration and affection for the Japanese people. However, for the next four years of war, we would be incessantly reminded of that dreadful "Day of Infamy." Posters were everywhere announcing, "Remember Pearl Harbor!"

Dr. Birdwell, president of Stephen F. Austin University, called a general assembly of the entire student body the next morning to listen to a speech by President Franklin Roosevelt:

"YESTERDAY, DECEMBER 7, 1941, A DATE WHICH WILL LIVE IN INFAMY, THE UNITED STATES OF AMERICA WAS SUDDENLY AND DELIBERATELY ATTACKED. . . . I ASK THAT THE CONGRESS DECLARE. . . .

I was only seventeen years old at the time I attended this assembly to hear President Roosevelt's famous speech, but I am certain that I was an adult when the meeting adjourned. Our lives had been unalterably changed in only a few hours, and even more tragic, many had been shortened. Congress declared war on Japan that same day, December 8, 1941. Germany and Italy declared war on the United States December 11, 1941. It was no longer possible to mute the sounds of war for it was unmistakably loud and indisputably clear as it reverberating throughout the world.

. . .

Before enrolling in my second year of college in September of 1942, a friend and I discussed the pros and cons of voluntarily enlisting in the service rather than waiting to be drafted. We concluded that by volunteering, one could select the branch of military in which one wished to serve. Many draftees were placed involuntarily in the infantry, where soldiers slept in the mud during the night and walked in mud by day. If one must engage in a war, we thought the Air Force offered a much more clean, tidy and civilized way to fight. The most compelling evidence that we could present to each other was that airmen slept in warm beds. We began immediately to make plans to enlist in the Army Air Force, then known as the Army Air Corps.

One evening, as my father and I listened to the radio, and my mother prepared dinner in the kitchen, I asked him if we could all talk together. He called my mother into the room and I announced my decision to enlist in the Army Air Corps. I explained further, that if I were accepted, there was no need for me to enroll in school for the fall semester. It was a terrible moment for them as they courageously came face to face with the reality that their son was going away to war and might never return. At that time parents all over the world were being confronted with the same frightful awareness. I pray that none of us will ever again undergo such an experience!

Within a few days, my friend and I hitchhiked to Houston and the Air Corps recruiting office where we were greeted with the usual military courtesy,

"Stand in line over here and wait until your name is called."

We asked if we might take the tests needed to qualify for flight training, and before we realized what was happening, we were poked, probed, instructed, blindfolded, asked what colors we saw, and given the famous "short arm inspection". To the reader who has never undergone a military "short arm inspection", words are inadequate to describe the experience, although, I will attempt to describe it in the next section. I was informed the next day that I had qualified for pilot training, and I immediately chose to enlist by signing the necessary papers. My friend was not so fortunate. He was rejected. After taking the military oath, I was ordered, as a new member of the armed forces, to return home and wait for further instructions by mail. At that moment, I lost all interest in school and although I had decided to enroll in the fall semester of Stephen F. Austin State College, it was unlikely that I would finish the semester before being called into service. I attended classes and enjoyed the social life of college, but I was convinced studying would be a waste of time, and indeed, the semester was never completed. I anxiously awaited my first orders from the U.S. Army Air Corps—just one more letter before I would become an aviation cadet.

PART II

WORLD WAR II

"Your blood and my blood is naught but the sap
that feeds the tree of heaven"

Kahlil Gibran

THE LIFE OF A CADET

BASIC TRAINING

THE LETTER I had anxiously awaited finally arrived. It was a letter from the government congratulating me for being selected as a pilot trainee in the Army Air Corps and ordering me to report for Basic Training on my nineteenth birthday, January 29th, 1943, at Shepherd Field, Wichita Falls, Texas. Although I was not to report for active duty until January 29th, the letter stated that I would become a member of the armed forces effective November 30, 1942. I was 18 years old at that time.

I would soon learn that I was about to receive the same rigid military discipline and training that existed at the top military academies of that time. The Air Corps cadet-training program was organized somewhat like the Army and Navy academies, and despite the urgency of providing a constant supply of trained pilots for the war, it attempted to produce the best-disciplined officers in the U.S. military. I fear this ambitious goal was not always met, for military pilots generally believed that they were quite different from the regular army because of their flying skills. We were also enchanted with popular Hollywood movies that portrayed pilots as undisciplined but brave and magnificent heroes. During flight training, however, I found discipline to be absolute and strict; it controlled every aspect of my life. I was to discover that discipline would teach me to extend myself far more than I ever thought possible and to make rapid decisions in stressful situations. Military discipline would prove to be most difficult and unpleasant but when I could look back on my life with more objectivity, I resolved that military training was the best thing that had ever happened to me. It occurred at a time of my life when I was struggling to achieve my identity—a time when I direly needed it.

Basic training was the first phase of military training and introduction to military discipline for Aviation Cadets. It was a three-month intensive course of physical training, orientation, and most of all, discipline. After finishing basic training, I would encounter 12 more months of arduous flight training; but further training and discipline would continue long after graduation and until such time that I would leave the service. The letter instructed me to travel by train from Houston to Wichita Falls, Texas, where I would report to Shepherd Field for basic training.

Upon boarding the train, I found that most of the passengers were young men like myself reporting to Wichita Falls for basic training. After basic training, some would fail the requirements of pilot training and be sent to other destinations for different training. The successful ones in my class would graduate in March 1944, from cadet flight training and become pilot officers of the class of 44C. As we played cards, talked, or slept during the long train ride to Shepherd Field, none of us exhibited any apprehension about our destiny. Like most optimistic youths, I never envisioned encountering an unfortunate event. I soon learned however, that such events do happen but it never caused me to abandon my firm belief that adversities would never plague me. I could only comprehend that I would be training for a war from which many would not return, and although this awareness drifted just beneath my consciousness, I was certain that I would not be one of them; furthermore, I dared not think about it.

As we slowly approached Shepherd Field, I stood in the area between railroad cars staring out the window in rapt concentration. I had previously known a very limited life in Nacogdoches. I was always surrounded with familiar faces and my parents had always been there to protect me. Now I was about to be subjected to a life that was completely different from any I had known or imagine. On this cold early morning of January 29th, 1943, I could see soldiers dressed in military uniforms shouting at groups of motley disheveled recruits in civilian dress. "Oh boy! Happy Birthday!" I said to myself, as I suddenly became conscious of the reality that in my entire lifetime, I had never missed a birthday celebration. I had been accustomed to people singing birthday greetings to me but now I was facing the prospect of having someone shouting commands at me.

A military drill instructor develops an ability to paralyze a trainee with fear by screaming in his face. As we stepped from the train, our welcoming drill instructors, dressed in starched neat uniforms, were waiting and prepared to instantly demonstrate their skills. A recruit soon learns that there is little hope of satisfying a military instructor short of perfection; but he had better try. Immediately they began shouting at us to line up and answer roll call. One of the instructors began shouting for us to "line up at arms length!", indicating that we were all to raise our left arm to touch the shoulder of the soldier on our left side. After several minutes of chaos and with the help of several instructors, we had formed three lines of recruits an arms length apart. Another instructor shouted that we were to respond to our names being called by yelling in our strongest voice, "Here, sir!" If the volume of the response did not please the instructor, he bellowed in the face of the recruit, "I couldn't hear you, soldier!" The soldier then shouted louder, "Here sir", until the instructor was satisfied. The sound of, "I can't hear you soldier!" and "Here Sir!" resounded across the countryside repeatedly that morning. The instructors wanted assurance that we fully understood how to respond to roll call. This was my introduction to a long series of lessons in military discipline.

It was early in the morning when we arrived at Shepherd Field and none of us had eaten since boarding the train the previous day. It seems that the army understands that soldiers function best on a full stomach, for we were soon informed that we were to experience our first army meal. As we were marched toward the mess hall, we were greeted to the refrain of, "you'll be sorry", sung by passing uniformed soldiers. Experienced servicemen seemed to delight in tormenting newly arrived civilian recruits by yelling at every opportunity, "You'll be sorry" until their civilian clothes are replaced by a military uniform.

Breakfast is considered an important meal for servicemen and that day the mess hall offered coffee, juice, and gravy thickened with canned tuna served on toast. I quickly learned that soldiers called tuna gravy on toast, "s—on a shingle." I did not like the taste, although I was famished and ate it, but after hearing the name, I abhorred it. To this day it conjures up an image of what the title described. It was one of my two most disliked army dishes; the other army dish was lamb. East Texas is not sheep country, and as a consequence, I had never tasted or become accustomed to the strange odor of lamb. I could smell it long before entering a mess hall and invariably the odor caused me to lose my appetite. The wartime army also served dehydrated potatoes and eggs tasting like sawdust but I could stomach them when sufficiently hungry.

We were marched to the supply depot after breakfast and issued our first army clothing: long woolen underwear, socks, combat boots, fatigues, military caps, woolen green shirts, pants, a jacket, and a steel combat helmet. We were then marched or, more correctly, herded to our barracks where we were instructed to discard our civilian clothes and change into our new military uniforms. What a sight we were in our new GI-issue clothes! The quartermasters had totally disregarded size when issuing our clothes; instead, we were issued what was available. Like the character "Dopey" in Snow White And The Seven Dwarfs, our sleeves and pants were too long or too short and most of us could not get our feet into the boots. Few items fitted! We paraded around the barracks ridiculing each other and laughing until our sides hurt at the sight of such a ludicrously dressed army. Our barracks sergeant ordered us to trade clothes with one another until we could find a proper size and to exchange the remaining ill-fitted items at the supply depot. I discovered that the supply depot often could not exchange items for another size because they were not available. Many other recruits and I were forced to wear ill-fitting army clothes until they could be replaced by purchasing them from a government supermarket called the Post Exchange or PX. I will always suspect that the tailors who made those military uniforms had a strange sense of humor.

The next morning we began our training in earnest. Our days were long: bugle call at 5 AM for roll call outside the barracks, calisthenics from 5:30 to 6:30, breakfast from 6:30 to 7:30, roll call again outside the barracks at 8:00, march in formation to the drill field to practice military drills until 10:00, break until 10:15, continue drilling until 12 noon, then lunch until 1 PM. Most afternoons were spent jogging in formation and running through obstacle courses consisting of walls to be scaled, ditches to leap over, and ropes to climb. Certain times were set aside for gunnery practice at a firing range and learning to disassemble/assemble firearms. We were taught to accurately aim and fire a rifle and a .45 caliber pistol at moving targets. The many hours I had spent with my little air gun shooting at birds back home contributed to my earning a "good marksman" medal in a short time. If we drew Kitchen Police (KP) or guard duty, we would wash dishes or stand guard until the wee hours of the morning. There was little or no time for recreation and I was so exhausted each evening, I only wanted to sleep.

We continued this schedule for the next three months with interruptions only for weekly barracks inspection. I dreaded hearing the barracks sergeant announce,

"Barracks inspection tomorrow morning at 8 AM,"

I soon learned that inspecting officers could be very picky and disagreeable. They seemed to delight in perversely issuing demerits for the tiniest perceived infractions of rules. We would stand at rigid attention at the foot of our beds until the inspection was completed. An inspector would move among us, choosing to inspect whatever might draw his attention and selecting individuals at random for abuse.

Standing almost nose to nose, he would often demand the name and serial number of a victim. The name and serial number of the trainee must be shouted without hesitation while the victim's eyes stared straight ahead, fixed on an object—perhaps an object on the face of the inspector. Some inspectors enjoyed making comical or sarcastic remarks but any trainee who smiled or moved his eyes received a berating and demerits. I found it difficult to refrain from smiling or even laughing at some comical remarks when the inspector was facing away from me but it certainly was not difficult to wipe the smile from my face when he turned to glare at me. Inspecting officers usually wore white gloves. The gloves displayed dirt whenever they were wiped over various parts of the room. The favorite targets of most inspectors were areas around windowsills, because they often found dust. All living in the barracks were issued demerits when this occurred. Sometimes a coin was dropped on our beds to see if the blankets had been pulled tight. If the coin did not bounce, the cadet was given demerits. Certain number of demerits would result in KP (kitchen duty), lost free time or marching around the drill field with a full pack during the evening. Somehow I managed to escape these penalties because I was lucky not to incur the wrath of an inspecting officer. We soon learned to minimize our chances of attracting their attention; a slight eye movement or a smile could bring an inspector shouting into our face. However, many poor souls around me were not so fortunate. Some seemed to be demerit magnets and attracted the attention of inspectors on a regular basis. After dark the drill field resembled a horror movie, as silhouettes of shadowy zombies with full backpacks could be seen wandered aimlessly around the field. They marched as if seeking a return passage to the world of the living.

If the humiliation of the barracks inspection was not enough, we were subjected to periodic venereal disease inspections. In the middle of the night a voice would shout the brutal order,

"Ok, everybody fall outside. Short-arm inspection in fifteen minutes! The uniform of the day is a raincoat only!"

They say that military complaining or griping is a sign of good morale. If so, it could be said that we possessed excellent esprit-de-corps and high morale at two o'clock in the morning as we formed outside our barracks, sleepy, shivering from the cold winter morning, and covered with only a raincoat. Our barracks sergeant called out our names as we answered, "here sir!" When he was confident that all were present and accounted for, we were then marched to the medical clinic to form a single file while we waited for a medical doctor to individually examine us. The doctor was seeking signs of venereal disease, which, we were told, was more obvious at night. From the line, we stepped forward one at a time and stood before him with our raincoat open so that he could examine us.

If these "short arm" inspections were not humiliating enough, as an added measure we were subjected to venereal disease movies once a week. The movies were designed to make us aware of the terrible consequences of venereal diseases and how such diseases are spread. Often we were subjected to repulsive views of various body-parts infected with a venereal disease, which caused me to dream of wearing rubber gloves while in the company of a female. This was, I suppose precisely the objective of these training movies but at our young age it would require more than a movie to deter our determination to seek female companionship.

My busy training schedule provided me little time to pay more than a momentary glance at the news of the war during early 1943. Since the United States had entered the war in December of 1941, the U.S. and Allied Forces had been fighting losing battles in the Pacific. In Europe, the Germans had invaded and were occupying Denmark, Norway, France, and conducting massive air raids on England. By the end of 1942, the time I entered military training, the tide had slowly turned in favor of the Allies with the invasion of North Africa under the command of General Dwight Eisenhower. Then in early 1943, the Allies and the U.S. invaded Sicily establishing a foothold from which Italy was later invaded. The seat of the Italian government in Rome had fled to northern Italy. Meanwhile, around the clock the U.S. bombed by day while the English bombed occupied Europe by night causing massive destruction. As these events unfolded, I concentrated only on pleasing my training instructors and adjusting to military life. I seldom thought of the future as anything more than the next training session. Furthermore, graduation was too far in the future to give it much thought.

Eventually, our motley assortment of individuals began to resemble a cohesive group as we learned to work together to make sure that everyone complied with the rules. Each trainee made sure that not only his own personal area, but also the areas of those around him were clean. Only one small over-looked area, when detected, could result in a more thorough inspection and punishment of all. This attitude spilled over into non-inspection events as well and each began to watch out for his comrades.

As the weather grew warmer, we began to notice a rather pungent odor permeating the barracks. "Whew, someone stinks," a trainee shouted from his bed. "Somebody died," said another as everyone in the barracks began to check their own feet while preparing for LIGHTS OUT and TAPS bugle call. A few more days of searching passed before the perpetrator was finally discovered. He was a young man from a rural settlement in Arkansas who disliked water and rarely bathed. A few mates who bunked near him met and decided that he should take a shower in order to cleanse away the unbearable fragrance of his feet. That same evening before LIGHTS OUT, they surrounded him, pulled him to the shower room, forced him under a showerhead and turned on the water. He was warned that if he did not shower each day with soap, they would drag him into the shower again. The problem was solved.

After three months of rigorous discipline and physical training, we were ready for our next assignment at Texas A & M University in Bryan, Texas, where we would be enrolled as college students. Prior to the war, the Air Corps had selected only college graduates for training as flying officers but during the war, because of an increased demand for pilots, this requirement had been eliminated. Most of us who had been accepted as a flight cadet in the Air Corps were former college students but because the age requirement had been lowered, few of us were old enough to have graduated; consequently, those in command believed that we needed further education to make up for this deficiency. As we left basic training, we were separated into three groups: those who would be trained as navigators, those who would be bombardiers and those who would be pilots.

"Flight Cadet Jess Pettey"

TEXAS A & M

W E ARRIVED AT Bryan, Texas on March 1, 1943. From the train station, we were transported by trucks to an old dormitory on A & M campus that surely must have been home to the first freshman class ever to enroll at A & M. Goodwin Hall was a stately old building, wearily supporting a tumultuous assortment of gables, turrets, and spires like a medieval cathedral. Also like an ancient cathedral, the building was slowly and inevitably crumbling as it succumbed to the ravages of time; in fact, the building was standing empty as it had been deemed unsuitable for habitation and condemned for destruction. Possibly because soldiers were expendable, the utilization of the building as our dormitory offered the university a surreptitious way to enjoy government income with little or no expenses. The thought occurred to me that perhaps there had been some fervent lobbying in Army Headquarters by the university to persuade the Army to rent the old building. Indeed, my fear was that the building would collapse while I was quartered there.

Soon after our introduction to our ancient quarters, we were marched to an office where we were enrolled in classes. A & M University had not suffered a drain of students due to the draft as had other colleges. Most of the students at A & M were enrolled in ROTC (Reserve Officer Training Corps) and upon graduation would be called to service as commissioned officers; therefore, they were granted the privilege of remaining at the university in officer's training until they graduated. We were assigned classes and shared the same classroom as these civilian students.

I had recently been accepted for flight training, and as I sat in classes at Texas A & M, I struggled to understand why I was enrolled in an algebra class. I will always suspect that because of the great number of young men being trained for flying duty, there was a shortage of facilities and instructors. We were therefore enrolled in classrooms to delay our turn for flight training. I was impatient to begin flying instructions and annoyed with the announcement that we were being returned to the classroom; as a result, I daydreamed through classes. My speculation was confirmed when we were informed, after only three months of uncompleted studies that we would be assigned to pre-flight training in San Antonio, Texas. I must add that all of us were greatly relieved that we managed to escape Goodwin Hall before it collapsed on us.

PRE—FLIGHT TRAINING

A TIRED ANXIOUS but happy group arrived at San Antonio Training Command Center June 5, 1943. After three months of what we believed to be wasted time in classrooms at Texas A & M, we were delighted to be stationed at an airfield and see airplanes. I was anxious and eager to begin pre-flight training; the first stage in pilot training where our training for the first time included the words "flight" and "airplane." Eight months before, I did not know what to expect when I was accepted for flight training, but I was certain that it would be about flying airplanes. For the past six months, I had not heard the word "airplane" spoken during our training.

While we were being assigned to various squadrons and classes, the war continued to rage in Europe and Asia. Although I had little time to keep up with the news, occasionally I read about the Allies invading North Africa and landing on the shores of Sicily. At the end of each movie we viewed newsreels about General Chennault's P-40 Flying Tigers in China and General Doolittle's B-25s in the Pacific that had bombed Japan after taking off from Navy carriers in the Pacific. We heard on the radio that our bombers continued to pound Europe by day and that English bombers were hitting the Continent by night. Hollywood saturated movie theaters with scenes of daring, handsome pilots with their sloppy rumpled caps, bravely flying their missions through enemy fire and returning home to revel in the admiration of the public. All of this ballyhoo only served to increase my ambition to emulate these flying icons. I could only wait and dream of the day when I could pilot my own airplane and shape my cap in a fashion similar to those worn by movie heroes. Military pilots of that time frequently removed the grommet from a new officer cap before twisting, sitting, and sleeping on it until the cap became misshapen and appeared to be much used. It was called a "50-mission cap" and was a badge of distinction for veteran flyers.

Although we would not be piloting an airplane for another three months, we were assigned classes where we studied airplane engines, propellers, controls, how these controls work, what makes an airplane fly, and aircraft identification. There was also much arduous physical training. When I was informed of the physical minimum requirements that I must exceed in order to graduate as a pilot, I was overwhelmed. I had expected some vigorous physical requirements but never had I anticipated such strenuous prerequisites nor been aware that combat aviation required athletes at the controls. Could I perform 100 sit-ups and 50 chin-ups hanging from a bar, run five miles within an hour with a full backpack, and at the same time learn the intricacies of navigation, radio, communications, and other complex flying skills in order to graduate from cadet flying school? I certainly was not confident, but despite my doubts, I decided that the best course of action was to remain in the program until such time that I would be "washed out" or eliminated. Since most that failed to graduate as pilots were accepted for Navigator or Bombardier training, I decided that I had little to lose.

We were issued new summer uniforms consisting of khaki shirts, khaki trousers, and khaki caps. When the weather became cooler, we were issued winter uniforms of olive drab wool shirts, trousers, jackets, and caps. We were also issued metal insignias shaped like an airplane propeller with wings that were to be worn on the front of our caps and on each shirt collar. The brass propellers signified that we were Aviation Cadets in training to be flying officers. Although we were not saluted as officers, we were referred to as "sir", a most impressive title to young girls within hearing range. In fact, most girls thought that I was an officer—a mistake that I usually failed to correct.

Due to its size, San Antonio offered more diversity in entertainment and opportunities to meet girls than any place we had been stationed. For the past six months I had mostly been restricted to military bases and busy with training. Now that we were aviation cadets we were allowed to spend our weekends off base and permitted access to a huge social-center on base. The social center sponsored a dance band composed of Aviation Cadets that rehearsed each week under the direction of a Special Forces Sergeant and played for weekend dances. When a notice was posted requesting volunteer band members, I immediately responded and was assigned the solo tenor saxophone chair. I played for a dance at the recreation center every Friday evening until I graduated from pre-flight training and was sent to primary flight training.

The Gunther Hotel, where the beer flowed freely and the local girls were plentiful, was the weekend "hangout" for the San Antonio military. It was a quintessential battleground for the attention of young females, for there were numerous soldiers from four air bases for every local girl who chose to grace the tables at the sidewalk cafe of the Hotel. Because of the number of servicemen, the girls could exercise their selective talents, which encouraged the servicemen to new heights of aggressiveness. They competed in every conceivable method for notice and approval. I was nineteen years old, shy, and lacked confidence. The poise and ingenuity demonstrated by some servicemen while approaching and meeting girls was for me a source of amazement and admiration. My feeling of inadequacy was further enhanced by listening to the many stories of conquest told by my classmates and watching Hollywood movie heroes confidently approach the opposite sex. At that time most young single men possessed their own unique method of introduction or approach, which they called "a line". I was young, inexperienced, and had never developed "a line"; therefore, I did not know how to approach and meet a young lady who was a stranger. It had not been necessary for me to learn such a technique while growing up in small town Nacogdoches because I was already acquainted with most of the girls through church or school activities. More than likely we had played together as children, but as a cadet in a strange city, I became aware that I must develop new methods if I was to succeed in finding a girl friend. Occasionally at a dance, I would force myself to approach a table of young ladies and ask one to dance with me, but it overwhelmed me to approach a table occupied by girls at a sidewalk cafe. I intensely disliked this method of meeting girls for fear that I would be, and often was, rejected. Usually I could not think of anything interesting to say to them even while dancing, nor was I a good dancer. I believed myself to be a boring dance partner and I was somewhat surprised when a girl did agreed to dance with me. Soon I began to develop a "line", a series of questions and statements used to ease the tension as we danced together but I never developed an approach to use for approaching a sidewalk cafe table of young ladies. It never occurred to me that many young girls, because of their lack of confidence, suffered from the same anxieties that tormented me. I might have found some comfort in that knowledge.

Pre-flight training passed in a blur of images—an amalgamation of jogging through hills and hot valleys during physical training, participating in a dance band, a drill instructor shouting at us to gather and make piles of rocks while amusing himself by yelling that he only wanted to see "asses and elbows", bending over rock-strewed terrain picking up rocks in an impossible task of cleaning the ground, and knowing all the time that all this was only to keep us busy. Fifty-four years later, I yet have mental images of San Antonio, of drill parades, cadets fainting and falling like autumn leaves while standing at rigid attention in the hot Texas sun, and walking along the River Walk and the Breckenridge Zoo.

Members of the Pettey family have appeared in every major war beginning with William Pettey, a 16-year-old soldier of the Revolution. My grandfather, William Holloway Pettey, volunteered to become a member of the Texas 4th Calvary during the Civil War. My father, Jesse E. Pettey Sr., served as a soldier of the Army during World War One and I, Jesse E. Pettey Jr., served as a bomber pilot in the 15th Air Force during World War II. Although I possess no other photographs of the earlier Petteys in service, I have one photo of my father, age 19, wearing a First World War uniform taken at San Antonio Breckenridge

Park in 1918. It was an extraordinary set of circumstances that placed me in San Antonio in 1943 as a pilot trainee, also age 19, twenty-five years and a generation after my father. I can only speculate that he, like his son, attempted to meet girls at the Gunther Hotel, but also like his son, found little worthy of remembrances or discussions later in life. He never talked about his experiences in San Antonio, but perhaps I failed to ask him the right questions.

"Author and Restored PT-19"

PRIMARY FLIGHT TRAINING

"A PT-19, WHAT is that?" Someone asked as we eagerly looked at photographs showing several rows of PT-19s parked in front of a control tower waiting to fulfill our dreams of flying into the wild blue yonder (words from the official Air Corps song). I had completed pre-flight training August 30, 1943 and the next day, September 1, 1943, was sent to the Primary Training Center located in Uvalde, Texas, about 80 miles west of San Antonio. Garner Air Field Primary Training Center then, and still does consist of a few buildings, a small air field with gravel taxi strips and two runways. It was a small training air base located in a tiny town in a desert populated with horned toads, jackrabbits, and a few single high school girls. Most girls either married or left town upon graduation. Uvalde was also the home of former vice-president John Nance Garner and the training base, Garner Airfield, was named in his honor. Since he seemed to own most of the land in Uvalde, I wondered if he might have also owned the airfield. We had eagerly waited the moment that we would step into an airplane, receive instructions, and learn to fly. That time had finally arrived.

After finding our barracks and unpacking our equipment, we were introduced to our flying instructors. I was momentarily taken aback as we approached the men who would teach us to fly airplanes. I had assumed that our instructors would be military pilots; instead I saw a group of civilian men wearing smart double-breasted military khaki uniforms and caps with strange insignias. They also appeared to be much older than military pilots. I later learned that many of them, because of age or health did not qualify for military duty, but because of their valuable skills gained over years flying as "barnstorming" pilots or as pilot instructors, the government hired them to train military student pilots. "Barnstorming" was a term then used to describe early aviators who made their living traveling over the country exhibiting stunt flying and offering the public short airplane rides for a fee. They were a group of "tough old birds," as we affectionately called them and knew more about flying than most young military officers who supervised them. I was assigned to a C Flight and introduced to Mr. L. D. Prewitt from Bastrop, Texas, who would be our flight instructor. Mr. Prewitt was a small man with traces of gray in his hair, dark brown eyes and a wrinkled weathered face that apparently had been exposed to many years of wind and sunshine in an open airplane cockpit. I assumed that he was about 50 years old but a 19-year-old youngster is a poor judge of age for those over age 25. I never asked or inquired about his age but when I view his photograph today, he appears to have been in his early 40s. Lieutenant Knight, a military pilot, was introduced as our "check pilot" and later proved to be a formidable presence in the cockpit. The principal duty of a "check pilot" was to schedule and conduct test flights with students in order to determine their rate of progress. Cadets dreaded their presence in the instructor's seat because they were assigned the unpleasant duty of "washing out" or eliminating those who could not attain a minimum standard of progress. If a cadet failed a flight check, the "check pilot" handed what was called a "pink slip" to the cadet at the end of the check flight. A list of maneuvers the cadet was expected to adequately perform was printed on the pink colored form with space for the "check pilot" to make comments about why the student pilot did not perform to his satisfaction. Since the word "adequate" is subjective, a "check pilot" was allowed complete freedom and discretion in his judgment of a student's performance; as a consequence, he soon earned a reputation for being either tolerant or very strict. Lieutenant Knight seemed to enjoy a reputation for being very strict and was feared by the trainees. If a student received three "pink slips" during any phase of his training, he was removed from the pilot training program and transferred to other duty. I was fortunate to have survived all my "check pilots", including Lieutenant Knight, but many others were not so fortunate.

Following the speeches of welcome and introduction to our instructors, Mr. Prewitt accompanied me and three other cadets that made up Flight C to the flight line to introduce us to a PT-19. I stared in awe at the machine that was to be our first training airplane. It appeared to me to be a large airplane although the PT-19, in reality, was a small simple airplane with two open cockpits, one forward and one aft, a single low wing, a non-retractable landing gear and a wooden propeller. Mr. Prewitt demonstrated how to start the engine. He inserted a crank in the cowling behind the propeller and turned it by hand, much the same as drivers once started automobile engines. After demonstrating proper use of the hand crank, Mr. Prewitt explained that when the engine started, the student must quickly climb into the front cockpit, buckle his safety belt, buckle his parachute, connect the chin straps of his flying helmet, don a pair of goggles, and connect a tube called a gosport to his ear phones. The instructor spoke to his student through a device attached to the end of a tube running from the instructor to the earphones of the student in the forward cockpit. It was a simple tube that carried the voice of the instructor to the student, assuming that the student had remembered to connect the tube to his earphones in the first place. The student pilot could not reply or talk to the instructor in a PT-19; he could only nod his head if he understood the instructor's comments or point to his ears when he did not understand. Of course at that time my hearing was very good and I could clearly understand instructions over the noise of the engine. As a result, I gave little thought to the extremely loud engine noises I endured while flying airplanes until I began to lose my hearing later in life.

Mr. Prewitt gave us our flight schedule for each day of the coming week. We flew each morning with Mr. Prewitt and attended classes in the afternoon where we studied basic navigation, the PT-19 engine, Morse code, and enemy aircraft recognition. We were assigned flash cards with pictures of enemy aircraft to memorize. In order to graduate from pilot training we must learn to recognize allied and enemy aircraft in a 1/50th of a second display from a flash projector. A split second in reaction time in recognizing the difference between friendly or enemy aircraft could mean the difference between life and death for pilots under combat conditions. I had few problems in learning to identify aircraft but Morse code presented great difficulties for me. Military pilots were taught to send and receive Morse code as a safety measure in the event of an emergency, but for some reason I was never able to recognize an entire word instantaneously. I passed, however, on the basis of my being able to translate each letter into a word.

. . .

I was standing on the wing of the PT-19 as Mr. Prewitt sat in the cockpit preparing for my inaugural training flight. He said,

"You watch me as I set the controls and turn off all switches so that you can insert the crank. After I shout that all switches are on, you begin turning the crank to fire the engine. After the engine fires, you put away the crank, get into the student cockpit, connect your earphones and buckle up. Be very careful of the spinning propeller. When you are all buckled up, I will begin instructions then."

I watched him check the controls, the fuel gauge and making sure that the ignition switch was in the "off" position until I was in position and ready with the crank. He instructed me to shout "switch on!", indicating that I was clear of the propeller and ready to turn the crank. He then shouted out loudly so I could hear, "switch on!" I began turning the crank to start the engine. I had heard many frightful stories about spinning propellers decapitating individuals who became careless. Mr. Prewitt constantly reminded us that it is wise to be aware and cautious when near a spinning propeller.

As I cranked the engine for the first time, I was shaking from nervousness. I had anticipated this flight for so long that I had dreamed about it in my sleep; I dreamed how I would feel soaring between clouds and about the scenery around me—now the moment had arrived and I was shaking like a frightened schoolboy. Somehow I managed to start the engine and step into the cockpit. Mr. Prewitt immediately began to taxi toward the end of the runway as I buckled my equipment.

Since a pilot cannot see the taxi strip ahead over the engine of a PT-19, it is necessary to continually make short turns in order to see the taxi strip from either side of the engine as it turns. After a zigzagging taxi ride, we arrived at our take-off position where Mr. Prewitt paused to check the instruments on the instrument panel.

The small craft shuddered, vibrated, and appeared to be out of control as Mr. Prewitt confidently guided it down the runway at full throttle. The PT-19 seemed too fragile to withstand such intense buffeting but suddenly the vibration and noise ceased as we lifted from the runway. Buildings beneath us appeared to shrink into the landscape as we gained altitude, climbing toward billowing fleecy clouds constrained by an azure sky. Words are inadequate to express the elation I knew at that instant. There is a moment during every flight, after one is free of the ground, where no earthly limitations exist to impede one's speed or direction, and with clouds only a reach away, that one truly feels omnipotent. At that mystical moment, one is entirely free of worldly concerns. One can soar like an eagle, glide like a gull high above the islands of clouds that obscure the sun from earth-bound prisoners below. I had entered a world I could not have imagined as a boy growing up in East Texas.

My reverie was brusquely interrupted by Mr. Prewitt's voice explaining each movement of the controls through the gosport and instructing me to follow his movements with my hands on the controls. After gaining a few hundred feet, he reduced the power and continued to climb through the clouds. As I watched the fluffy clouds roll by I thought, "this is what I want to do; this is what I was meant for."

Upon reaching five thousand feet, Mr. Prewitt demonstrated and explained the maneuvers that I would be expected to learn. He began by describing a stall, explaining how a pilot raises the nose of the aircraft until the aircraft loses its forward speed and begins to fall, diving and spinning out of control. The PT-19 was too slow to perform rolls and snap rolls, but it did spin very well. Mr. Prewitt lowered the nose until he gained some speed and then raised the nose as far as possible by pulling the control stick back as far as it would go. When the craft stalled, he kicked one of the rudder pedals with his foot and at the same time shoved the stick forward. This maneuver caused the aircraft to rotate violently as it fell off to one side and began to spin earthward. I was not anticipating this, and the extreme movement lifted me from my seat as he pushed the stick forward. I was restrained only by my seat belt which, fortunately, I had buckled before take off. Desperately I grasped anything I could hold onto while my stomach churned with each spin. After spinning downward several thousand feet, Mr. Prewitt regained control by kicking the rudder pedal in the opposite direction of the spin and pulling the stick back into his stomach. I would learn this maneuver later, Mr. Prewitt explained. Meanwhile, I attempted to find my stomach, which had been discarded far above me where the spin commenced. Indeed, a roller coaster ride back home on earth seemed almost tranquil after that spin. Mr. Prewitt calmly explained that this maneuver was one of many used by fighter planes to escape enemy fighters.

One of my classmates, unfortunately, forgot to buckle his seat belt while preparing for a training flight. During the flight, the instructor demonstrated a spin unaware that his student had failed to fasten his seat belt. When he suddenly lowered the nose of the airplane to begin the spin, the student floated upward away from his open cockpit seat. Subsequently, the cadet opened his parachute and landed near a farmhouse. He gathered his parachute and walked to the house to ask the wife if he might telephone his commanding officer. The wife volunteered to drive him to the air base several miles away. Several weeks later, while flying alone, he experienced engine failure and found it necessary to land in a field near the same farmhouse. When the door was opened in response to his knock, the same startled housewife shouted, "No! not you again!"

Mr. Prewitt allowed me to control the aircraft for short periods of time during our subsequent flights, although he made the takeoffs and landings. Our first few flights were devoted almost entirely to performing a stall and a stall recovery, with a few other maneuvers thrown in to keep the flights interesting. Mr. Prewitt repeatedly demonstrated how to recover from a stall, explaining that stall recovery was important because it could save my life someday. Fatal stalls are more likely to occur during takeoff or landing, when the airplane is flying slower than at other times. With practice, however, the pilot may recognize stalls only moments before they occur and be able to recover. Before I was allowed to make take-offs and landings, I had to demonstrate to my instructor's satisfaction that I had mastered this maneuver. Soon Mr. Prewitt allowed me to control the aircraft during take-off and landing with his hands slightly touching the controls. As I gained more proficiency in flying, he would take his hands off the controls and inform me that I was entirely in control of the airplane.

During my training, Mr. Prewitt demonstrated a figure-eight maneuver explaining that this procedure was part of my training designed to improve coordination between my hand on the stick and my feet on the rudders. He selected a road for a reference and taught me to align the aircraft directly over the road. He lowered the nose to gain speed, pulled the nose up and banked the aircraft to the right away from the road to gain altitude. I discovered that we had turned away from the road as if following the bottom of a $ sign. Mr. Prewitt instructed me to pretend and visualize the vertical slash in the $ sign as the road. He then executed a 180-degree turn back toward the road, heading in the opposite direction, while losing altitude. It was like flying the middle part of an S in a $ sign. Another 180 degree turn while gaining altitude caused us to head toward the opposite side of the road and was like flying the top part of a $ sign. When another 180-degree turn was completed, it was as if we had closed the S and completed the top of an 8. Another 180-degree turn and we had closed bottom of a completed 8. Mr. Prewitt observed my smoothness and coordination as I repeated this procedure until he was satisfied that my coordinated movements would become a habit. He suggested that I practice the figure eight every day. Nature allows no tolerance for disproportionate or uncoordinated flight control movements while in the air. Uncoordinated movements can and often do result in fatal accidents when there is insufficient altitude or time to correct the error. Such accidents are labeled "pilot error."

In the course of these flights, Mr. Prewitt taught me to use the instruments on the instrument panel: the artificial horizon, needle and ball, air-speed indicator and altimeter that supply important information to the pilot. They inform him of the position of his aircraft in the air and are still used by pilots.

Mr. Prewitt soon allowed me to take off, climb, bank, stall and land the PT-19. When he wanted to demonstrate something new or felt a need to correct me, he resumed control of the airplane but he always returned control to me. As I grew more adept and confident, even these interruptions became less frequent.

. . .

As I taxied toward the hardstand parking area, Mr. Prewitt said,

"Stop the airplane. You take it up alone this time,"

He climbed out of the cockpit and leaped to the ground. Shouting above the noise of the engine, he said,

"Take it up, circle the field, land and taxi back to me. I'll be right here."

I was stunned! It seemed to me that I had only been flying the airplane a short time and I certainly believed that I was not ready to "solo." I was not sure that I could fly it alone without crashing back to earth.

Competent instructors know the student better than the student knows himself. They instinctively sense when a student has become an adept pilot. They have a measure of his confidence, his emotional stability, and somehow they identify the moment when a student should, in order to gain more self-confidence, fly alone. Mr. Prewitt knew my time had arrived although I did not recognize it. He was a civilian, yet his instructions were commands and since he was the superior officer in charge of my training, I must obey. Of course, my answer to his instructions was,

"YES SIR!"

I turned the airplane and began to taxi toward the end of the runway. I desperately wanted the end of the runway to move further away so that I might continue to taxi forever, but I was also aware that the moment was close when I must push the throttle full forward and fly the aircraft into the air alone. The knuckles of my hand were white from squeezing the control stick as perspiration trickled down both cheeks. Suddenly I was sitting at the end of the runway going through a pre-flight checklist:

> Throttle forward to 2800 revolutions per minute.
> Left magneto switch on. Did the revolutions slow? If not,
> Right magneto on.
> Check flight controls.

A pre-flight check was to ensure that the engine, powered at full speed during takeoff, had little chance of losing power and all controls were working properly. As I taxied forward and turned into the runway I was no longer afraid. I now must focus my concentration on flying the aircraft and there was no time to think about failure. Without a radio, I waited in the center of the runway for the tower to flash a green light signifying that I was clear to take-off. I pushed the throttle forward to the maximum RPM and the aircraft began to roll down the runway.

I was alone! I could not depend of Mr. Prewitt to take over. I turned my full attention to the airplane and felt the tail slightly lift and the rudder become more sensitive to my control as the air resistance increased on the controls. The PT-19 continued to accelerate. I sensed that I had gained enough speed to lift the airplane into the air by gently pulling the control stick back toward me. The aircraft responded by effortlessly leaving the runway and drifting upward into the sky. There was no time to enjoy the exhilaration of my first solo takeoff, I needed to concentrated on making a 45 degree turn to the right in order to leave the flight path and fly away from the traffic pattern. I had experienced no difficulties thus far in my first solo flight; however, I was well aware that landing the airplane was the most dangerous part of any flight and that I must immediately return to the ground where Mr. Prewitt was watching and waiting for me.

I had gained an altitude of six or seven hundred feet when I began letting down, losing altitude, in order to enter the landing pattern. At 500 feet, flying downwind and parallel to the runway, I concentrated on the end of the runway on my left side. A few moments after I had passed the end of the runway, I began a left 90-degree turn onto what is called the "base leg". When the runway was almost parallel with my left wing, I began another 90 degree left turn onto what is called the "final approach". The two 90 degree turns had aligned and headed me directly toward the runway. I pulled back the throttle to lower my speed and lowered the flaps to further slow and cause the airplane to begin a slow gliding descent to the ground near the end of the runway. A gradual descent is necessary to place the airplane near but past the end of the runway an instant before the wheels touch the ground. A moment before I touched the runway, I began easing back the throttle and pulling the stick back hoping to execute a smooth stall before the wheels touched the runway. Pilots say, "a perfect landing is simply a controlled crash". If the stall is coordinated properly with the airplane's descent, the plane will glide a short distance with the wheels just inches above the runway until its slower speed causes it to stall and lightly drop onto the runway. The pilot is said to have "greased it in," whenever he executes a near-perfect landing with hardly a bump. I thought I was making a good landing. Every move had been properly executed but I had leveled and stalled my airplane too high above the runway, dropped, slammed onto the runway and ballooned again into the air. When a light airplane stalls too high above and drops onto the runway, it will frequently bounce back into the air. I had two choices: quickly restore full power to the engine and gain altitude for another landing or give the engine a short burst of power and attempt to stall again much further down the runway. More often the student balloons back into the air two or three times before managing a hard landing that will allow him to remain on the runway. Observing a fledgling pilot bouncing like a balloon down a runway was a comical sight to behold; however there was a serious risk that he would either run out of runway before bringing the plane to a halt or damage the landing gear of the aircraft. Judging the height from which I had dropped and the difficulty of coordinating the bursts of power needed with each bounce of the craft, I made an instant decision to gain altitude and fly again into the landing pattern for another attempt to land. The second attempt was much better. My coordination of the descent, speed and stall resulted in a smooth landing. The craft did not balloon again into the air and I was able to slowly apply the brakes to slow its forward motion. I was certain that I had failed my solo flight but Mr. Prewitt had instructed me to taxi back to where he waited at the flight line and although I was disinclined to face him, I was compelled to follow his orders and face my destiny.

As I taxied to where Mr. Prewitt waited, I visualized him criticizing my terrible landing, notifying me that I had failed my solo flight and informing me that I needed additional instruction before I could solo again. I imaged him wearing a stern face, with his arms folded on his chest like an executioner awaiting his next victim, but as I taxied nearer to him, I could see only a smiling face.

"Well, that wasn't too bad considering that the ground was too low or was it your airplane was too high?" He said with a big grin. "I know you are a little nervous but I want you to take it up again and try to be a little easier on your landing gear this time. OK?"

My elation knew no bounds as I taxied again to the end of the runway and prepared for my second solo takeoff. He had forgiven me for the poor landing, had not lost faith in me, and even made a joke so that I could save face. I thought, "what a man!" as my anxiety dissipated. He had given me a second opportunity to prove to him, and more importantly to myself, that I had the ability to fly an airplane. I was resolved to do my best, and for the first time since I had been accepted for pilot training, I was certain that I possessed the ability to successfully complete the training requirements of a military pilot.

The second solo takeoff and landing was almost perfect—no bounce, no drop, no jerky inept movements; instead, I executed a smooth coordinated approach to the landing field until the moment my wheels gently touched the runway. I knew that it was a good landing but as I taxied toward Mr. Prewitt, I was further assured when I saw the big grin still on his face.

There was, and I assume still is, a strong camaraderie and amity among pilots. This comradeship developed from a commonly shared phenomenon that only fellow pilots can identify; an emotional exultation, a euphoria, an elation unlike any other ecstasy ever felt prior to man's discovery that he could fly. Once man found that he could soar into the air leaving all earth bound institutions and creatures behind, pilots were then bound into a fraternity that shared the thrill of transcending the laws of nature. We could fly away from the limitations of our planet, free from man-made structures; we could soar like the wind. And like the wind, we were a part of nature, yet by defying gravity, we defied nature. We instinctively understood, without arrogance or conceit, that we alone shared this magical moment. We also understood that however great the effort, we could never describe that feeling to another. I had just experienced that phenomenon and from that moment on, another member of the esoteric brotherhood of pilots was born.

Three months of Primary Training School passed quickly while we endeavored to learn flight maneuvers, navigational problems, airplane engines, aircraft recognition, and improve our physical conditioning. We were sent out alone daily to practice flying procedures, we endured the heat that inevitably accompanies physical conditioning, we survived barrack inspections, we fought sleepiness from fatigue during classes, we withstood the stress of check flights, and worst of all, we said farewell to classmates who had received their third and final pink slip. We also had fun during our few free hours, but most of all, we learned to fly.

BASIC FLIGHT TRAINING

O N NOVEMBER 5TH, 1943, my cadet class, 44-C, reported to Waco Basic Training Command located at Waco #1 Airfield in Waco, Texas. There were two flight training airfields in Waco: Waco #1, a basic training field, and Blackland Airfield, an advanced multi-engine pilot training school. I had successfully completed Pre-flight and Primary flight training and was now eager to begin Basic training, the third phase of our training. We had been informed that those with marginal flying abilities would be eliminated in this third and deciding component of our training. On the other hand, it was almost certain that those who survived basic training would graduate, for few cadets were washed-out during the fourth and final stage of our training, called advanced training.

During our first group meeting, Lt. D. E. Ulrich called my name to join a group of four other cadets. He introduced himself, informed us that he would be our instructor, and instructed us to follow him to a BT-13, our new training airplane. I stared in awe as I approached this huge machine standing 12 feet above the tarmac with a 42 feet wing span. It appeared to be a monster, and indeed Lt. Ulrich informed us that it was nicknamed "The Vultee Vibrator," because of the loud engine noises and vibrations it produced. He opened the canopy so that we could stand on the wing and view the cockpit as he explained the function of each apparatus that controlled the airplane. For the first time, he explained, we would be instructed in the use of a two-way radio, a variable pitch propeller, and other complicated radio equipment installed in the aircraft. He climbed into the cockpit seat demonstrating the controls, various toggle switches, buttons and how to operate the canopy so that we could bail out in an emergency.

Lt. Ulrich was from New Jersey and like most easterners, spoke rapidly, pouring forth a flood of articulation like water cascading over a waterfall. He was short in stature—only a few inches over five feet—and appeared to be haughty or cocky from the habit of constantly looking upward. His small body was a quintessential fighter pilot physique, but instead, he had been selected to train cadets. Because I had been accustomed to slower southern speech, his rapid speech and cockiness intimidated me until I became better acquainted with him. In time, I found him to be a very supportive and caring instructor who was liked by all his students. Twenty-three years later, while waiting for a train in New York City, I instantly recognized him among a crowd of passengers also waiting for a train. When I approached and asked him if he had been an instructor in Waco, Texas, his face instantly lit up as he said,

"You are Jess Pettey, I remember you."

He was also able to recall the names of the other four cadets in my class, which was an amazing feat of memory. We were only one of many flights that had been assigned to him over the years that he instructed—but I am getting ahead of my story.

I made my maiden flight in the "Vibrator" with Lt. Ulrich the second day of my assignment to basic training. I was soon to discover that the BT-13 was a much more complicated aircraft than the PT-19 we had flown at Garner Field. It was heavier, had more horsepower and was more dangerous because of the weight and power. For the first time, I was introduced to filing a flight plan with the operations office prior to takeoff. The flight plan was a standard form on which the pilot recorded the name of the pilot, passengers, estimated time of takeoff, destination, time of arrival at destination and estimated time of return to the airfield. The operations office was to be notified by radio of any changes that altered the flight plan and would order a search soon after the estimated time of arrival had passed and the pilot had not arrived. At the time of filing, the pilot was also given weather information.

Painted on the side of our airplane were the numbers 642. During our taxi to the end of the runway, Lt. Ulrich radioed the tower to ask for permission to prepare for takeoff.

"Tower, this is 642, over."

"642, this is tower, over."

"Tower, 642 requesting permission to taxi to runway, over."

The controller in the tower answered,

"Roger, you are cleared use taxi strip B to runway two-ninety."

We had been given permission to taxi on taxi strip B, identified on a map of the airport, to runway 290, and the controller had recorded aircraft number 642 en route to runway number 290 for takeoff. By not saying, "over" at the end of his transmission, he had informed us that he expected no reply. As we taxied toward the runway, Lt. Ulrich switched the radio to intercom so that he could talk with me and not be overheard in the tower or by other pilots in the vicinity. He invited me to taxi so that I could become comfortable being in command of the aircraft. Because of its size and the height of the engine of a BT-13, the pilot had a very limited view of the taxi strip. As a consequence, it was necessary for him to turn the aircraft in wide turns to either side in order to observe the taxi strip directly in front of him. The movement was called "fishtailing".

When we arrived at the end of the runway, Lt. Ulrich instructed me to read aloud a checklist that was attached to the instrument panel. I read aloud,

"Propeller pitch set in low position."

Since the engine was more powerful than our previous airplane the checklist was longer and contained a procedure for checking the propeller. This was my first introduction to a variable-pitched propeller. Pitch was the angle of the propeller edge to the aircraft. During takeoff, it should always be in a low pitch position that allowed it to take a larger bite of the air and produce more power. For cruising, it was changed to a high pitch position, lessening the drag or friction and consuming less fuel. As I read each item from the checklist, Lt. Ulrich responded by saying "check," signifying that the item was in a correct position for take off. After completing the checklist, he switched the radio from intercom back to the radio and said,

"Tower, 642 ready for take off, over."

"642, you are cleared for takeoff on runway 290. Wind is from the northwest at 15 miles per hour and visibility is 10 miles, over."

"642, roger and out."

This last transmission was to inform the tower that we had received and understood his message. There would be no further communication unless either the tower or the pilot found it necessary to resume conversation. It is imperative that air silence be maintained whenever possible so that other pilots may use the same radio frequency to receive instructions from air controllers.

Lt. Ulrich slid the canopy shut, turned the airplane from the taxi strip into the runway and eased the throttle full forward as we gained speed. I had never heard such a loud engine reverberation; it deafened the pilot and the entire countryside with its shuddering, quivering vibration. I could then understand how the BT-13 had earned its appropriate and deserving nickname, "The Vultee Vibrator".

After climbing a few hundred feet, the lieutenant moved the throttle from the full forward position to about 3/4 position and instructed me to take the controls. When I had climbed to seven or eight thousand feet altitude, he said over the intercom,

"I am about to demonstrate some aerobatics you will be required to learn and show you the limits of this airplane: first, the 'snap-roll.'

The earth suddenly moved a complete circle of 360 degrees around me. At the completion of the circle, the earth remained in place as it was before, causing me to think that perhaps I had only imagined the earth's movement. I had felt nothing; the earth had simply revolved in a surrealistic motion around me. I was to learn later that whenever a snap roll is rapid and well coordinated, one retains the sensation of gravity attaching him to the airplane. It is easy for one to believe that the aircraft remained stationary while the earth merely rotated around him. The lieutenant explained that he had quickly depressed the right rudder to initiate a roll to the right, then pushed the stick forward as the aircraft rolled upside down, released the rudder at the end of the roll, returned the stick to its normal position and depressed the left rudder to counter and stop the rolling motion to the right. This maneuver was accomplished in one coordinated movement. He instructed me to feel the controls as he executed another snap roll. At the conclusion of the roll, he raised his hands into the air indicating that I was in control of the airplane and said,

"Now it's your turn. If you get into trouble, I'll be here to get you out."

I nervously kicked the right rudder and immediately dived toward the earth executing a beautiful half loop before I leveled the airplane. Instantly I realized that I had not pushed the stick forward when the craft was in an upside-down position to maintain the nose in a level position; consequently, the nose dropped, causing us to plunge toward the earth.

After Lt. Ulrich had a hearty laugh, he demonstrated another snap roll and instructed me to implement another roll. This time I remembered to push the stick forward. The roll was completed in a somewhat rough and untidy manner resulting in a loss of only a few hundred feet altitude. Lt. Ulrich said,

"To maintain an upside down position, you merely stop the roll half way through, push the stick forward because everything then is in reverse. To point the nose down when in an upright position, you push the stick forward but if you are upside down, to point the nose down you must pull the stick back toward you, in the opposite direction."

At that instant the earth suddenly was above me—I was hanging upside down in my safety belt, the blood rushing to my head. The force of gravity had changed from my seat to my head and the sole restriction that prevented my body from falling earthward was my safety belt. The lieutenant had suddenly kicked the left rudder and pushed the stick forward in order to maintain our altitude. We were flying level, but upside down. After a few moments, he depressed the left rudder again, pulled the stick from its forward position and the airplane completed a 360-degree roll. The earth returned to its normal position underneath me and gravity once again forced me down onto my seat.

Our weeks were filled with flying, learning aerobatics, instrument flying, aircraft identification, Morse code and navigation. We were also introduced to formation flying, night flying and navigation for the first time. We flew short cross-country assignments, located checkpoints on the ground, identified them on the map and plotted our heading to the next checkpoint. Night flying consisted mostly of night takeoffs and landings but we were introduced to night formation flying. I found it comfortable landing at night by using the angle of the runway lights to judge the height of the aircraft. Indeed, I seem to have made smoother landings than those made in the daylight, but night formation flying always caused me to be apprehensive and tense. Often one can only distinguish another aircraft by its wing tip lights: green on the right or starboard side and red on the left or port side. The tiny lights inform a pilot which direction the approaching plane is flying but it is difficult to judge the distance of the craft until it is quite near. It then becomes a large ominous shadow. It was disconcerting for me to be unaware of an approaching airplane and then suddenly discover its presence. Formation flying was more pleasant in the daytime when I could see. We flew close together with only a few inches separating our wings and we could hand-signal the other pilots—even see their facial expressions. We flew only in groups of three airplanes, but later in combat, we would fly in groups of six or seven bombers. For defense, a combat bomber would fly on either side of a leader, another group of three would fly behind and slightly lower to avoid the prop-wash, or turbulent air created by the first three bombers. A seventh aircraft would fly behind the second group but still lower to avoid prop-wash. The seventh aircraft flew in much turbulence caused by the other six aircraft and was extremely tiring for the pilot. Close formation flying was a matter of life or death for bombers in combat for it provided defensive firepower from several aircraft flying close together. Enemy fighter pilots relished the discovery of a single bomber damaged and unable to keep up with the formation. Like a pack of wolves, they would attack the helpless victim; consequently, we were trained to fly in formation for our future safety.

THE HEMPSTEAD KID

"627 TO TOWER, over."

"This is tower, 627, over."

"Sir, I am almost out of gas and need to find a field to land before dark."

It was almost dark; I was low on gas and lost. Common sense dictated that I find an open field to land for the night or prepare to abandon the airplane and parachute to safety.

"627 where are you? Over." replied the tower in Waco.

"Tower, this is 627. I don't know but will radio you my location when I land, over."

"Roger 627, good luck and keep in contact."

That morning I was given my first solo cross-country assignment and had taken off from the base full of confidence and excited. This flight was to be a test of my navigation skills, utilizing all the knowledge and skills that I had recently been taught. Before takeoff, I had been given the direction and velocity of winds so that I might calculate the compass directions I must fly in order to reach each checkpoint along the way to my destination. Checkpoints are places, usually cities, along a flight path that can be identified on the map and allows the navigator to continually determine his location. The map was attached to my knee so that my hands were free to fly the plane. I had previously determined the compass directions that I must fly. My compass assured me that I was on the correct heading, the weather was clear, visibility was unlimited: I could not imagine that I was about to experience one of the most dangerous events in my flying career.

The first leg of the flight was exactly as I had envisioned it to be. I had departed on time, arrived over the first checkpoint at the correct time, and recognized each town along the way. I turned east in order to fly the compass direction I had calculated in order to arrive at the second checkpoint. After the turn, everything began to go wrong. I could no longer locate visible cities, highways and railroads beneath me on my map. I was certain that I was flying in the correct direction and believed that I would soon observe something that I could locate on the map. I continued to fly a heading that should have led me to my second checkpoint, but my estimated time of arrival passed and still my checkpoint was not in sight. I even flew lower in order to read the name of a town painted on a large water tank but I could not locate the city on my map. This further increased my confusion and anxiety. I began to worry until I remembered that the Brazos River ran north and south from Waco. Since I was north of Waco and had not crossed the river I reasoned that I could abandon my second checkpoint, continue to fly east until I intercepted the river, and then simply follow it south to Waco. When I observed the river on the horizon, I began to relax. I could now turn right and follow The Brazos River south, secure in the knowledge that soon I would see the city of Waco and return to my air base. I certainly did not intend to tell anyone that I had missed my second checkpoint. I estimated that it would take me about an hour to reach my airfield at Waco.

An hour passed without sighting Waco, nor could I identify any other landmarks from my map. Although I was puzzled, I was sure that I was flying in the correct direction. I had abandoned the use of my compass long ago and was merely following the river on my right side. Another hour passed and I had not yet arrived at Waco. I began then to face the reality that the sun was setting, my fuel was low and I was lost. Something had gone terribly wrong.

As I pondered over my dilemma, three things became apparent. First, I must take actions to protect my life. Flying an airplane after dark, lost, and with insufficient fuel was not only foolish but also very dangerous. Second, I must make an attempt to save the expensive airplane. Certainly, if I continued to fly until the gas was depleted, I would be forced to bail out leaving the airplane to crash in the dark. Third, I must make an attempt to save other lives. If I bailed out of the aircraft, I would be unable to prevent it from possibly crashing into a populated area. I must, therefore, begin to look for an open field to land the airplane before dark. We had been trained almost from the first day of flight instruction to follow a procedure for an emergency landing. One of my instructors had said,

"There are three things a pilot needs to know to stay alive. How to fly off the ground into the air, how to bring it down again, and last, how to land if your engine is dead. Everything else that you do in the air unimportant."

We had devoted countless hours to making emergency landing approaches to open fields. We were trained to quickly select a field and circle it in order to search for obstacles that would damage the plane. If the engine had failed and lacked power, the selected site must be viewed only during the approach because the pilot was limited to only one final approach. If we were fortunate to be flying at a high altitude when the engine failed, we were taught to circle the field to make certain that the field was clear of obstacles. It was an unfortunate event if the engine failed while flying at a low altitude. We could only then hope to reach an open field and pray there were no obstacles on it—there was no second look. While conducting training flights, instructors would frequently pull back the throttle and order the student to execute an emergency landing procedure. The student was graded by how well he followed the emergency procedure, his judgment in selecting a field and his approach to the field. While we were selecting a place to land, we were without power and losing altitude. An instructor would judge whether the student would have landed safely or failed to reach the selected field. An instant before touching down, the instructor would restore power and instruct the student to regain altitude. This experience can be very unsettling for the student if he happens to be flying over rugged terrain. Flight instructors emphasized the reality that a pilot is helpless to choose the moment when he will lose power but he can and must make wise decisions based on good judgment and skills.

There were many open fields below me and I fortunately possessed full engine power. I enjoyed a luxury not afforded most emergency landings. A simple course of action lay before me: select a field, fly down to inspect it, test an approach, assure that the field was sufficiently long for the airplane to roll to a stop before crashing into a fence at the end of the field, and finally, land. At the time I was executing the first approach, I noticed a small hill on my right that ran parallel to my selected field. The first approach was almost perfect as I dropped over a fence and floated a foot or so over the ground inspecting and deciding where I intended to land. At the end of the contemplated landing space, I pulled up and turned right in the direction of the previously noted hill. As I banked I noticed someone rushing down the hill into the open field but I was concentrating on flying the airplane and had little time to observe the movement below me. While making the second and third inspecting approach, turning each time into the foothill, I could see someone or something running down the hill into the open pasture each time I turned into the hill. I decided that I would touch ground and land on my fourth approach since the field seemed adequately long and the ground seemed to be firm. The landing was smooth and the airplane rolled almost to the fence at the end of the field and safely stopped. I was thrilled to be safe on the ground and to know that the airplane was undamaged.

"Lawsey, Mister, I thought you wus one of Mister Tojo's men!" A breathless, perspiring black woman shouted in amused agitation as she and several curious farmers approached.

I then understood that she was the one I had observed running from the small hill into the open field as I flew over it. From the crest of the small hill on my right she had observed me making several approaches to the field below her. As I turned toward the hill where she stood, it appeared to her that I was deliberately heading toward her. The dreadful noise made by the BT-13 Vibrator contributed to her terror as she imagined a Japanese airplane about to open fire at her. She then ran down the hill onto the open field where I made the second approach directly at her again. Now, certain that I intended her harm, she ran up the hill only to observe me again heading toward her as I made another turn into the hill. In panic she ran down the hill into the open field again as I made another approach toward her. By now she was frantic as she struggled breathlessly back up the hill the second time where she could observe my airplane finally roll to a halt. The rigorous noise of the B-13 had attracted the attention of the entire countryside and a group of 15 or 20 persons, mostly black farm workers, gathered at the end of the field. As she observed them approach me, she felt sufficiently safe to advance in order to inspect that extraordinary being sent my Mr. Tojo to harm her. Her curiosity was no greater than mine, for I desperately wanted to know where I had landed.

I climbed back into the cockpit.

"Tower this is 627, do you read me?"

"Roger, this is tower, I read you loud and clear, 627, where are you, Mister? This evening an alert was called after you lost radio contact. Over."

"Tower, this is 627 I have landed in a farmer's field near Hempstead. Everything is OK, no injury to me or damage to the airplane. I was almost out of gas and it was getting dark, over."

"Roger 627, we will send help tomorrow morning. Mister, tonight you stay with the airplane. Is that understood? Over."

I replied, "Tower, this is 627, I understand. I will stay with the airplane tonight, over."

"627, this is Tower. No further instructions. I will call you tomorrow morning, out."

As I climbed back out of the plane, one of the black farmers who had gathered around the airplane asked me if I was hungry. When I answered that I was, he invited me to accompany him to his house, located a short distance from the aircraft. Although, I had been ordered to remain with the airplane, I could think of nothing in the order that specified the distance I was allowed to be away from it. I reasoned that if I could observe the aircraft, I was guarding it; moreover, I was hungry. I walked with the farmer to his shack-house, a crudely built house devoid of paint or other amenities. I had been inside homes of some black families while accompanying my mother as she delivered Christmas food to them, but I had never shared a meal with a black family. He invited me inside his house where his large family waited and served me a huge plate of excellent southern food: black-eyed peas, turnip greens, buttermilk and corn bread. The children were mesmerized, staring at me in astonishment as I ate. I am sure it was a sight they would remember for years: a white flier from the sky, dressed in flying coveralls covered with pockets, and a helmet with earphones and goggles covering his head. I thanked the family for their kindness as I prepared to depart, explaining that I had been ordered to remain with the airplane. It was dark as I walked back to my aircraft; with nothing more to do, I prepared for a long uncomfortable night in the cockpit.

I was suddenly jolted awake as the radio began hissing and crackling.

"627 this is tower, over."

As I reached for the microphone, I was momentarily dazed from the instant awakening.

"Tower, this is 627, over."

"There are two lieutenant instructors on their way to pick you up. One will fly your aircraft back to the airfield. State your position in relation to Hempstead, over."

I replied, "Roger tower, according to local farmers, I am about five miles southwest of town, and since I was following the Brazos River when I landed, I must be near the river. Over."

"Roger, I will pass this on to the lieutenants. Be on the lookout for them in about an hour, over and out."

I climbed down from the airplane for a stretch while I watched someone approaching me from a distance. As he came nearer I could see that it was the same black man who had provided dinner the previous evening. He carried a covered plate in his hands filled with bacon, fried eggs, biscuits and potatoes and wore a big smile on his face. What a welcome sight on a cold December morning after a miserable night sitting in a cramped cockpit of an airplane! I have never tasted anything better. I was deeply touched by the kindness of this poor black family. They wore patched clothing, and more than likely, possessed little surplus food to share, yet they were concerned that I, an absolute stranger from the sky, might be hungry. They embodied the true spirit of Christmas. Experiences like this have strengthened my belief that the poor are many times, more generous and willing to share their meager possessions than are the rich.

I could hear the Vibrator long before I could see it—throbbing, buzzing, and vibrating like a chain saw. No doubt the noise jolted awake all creatures that happened to be below. A few moments later I could see the source of the noise; a blue BT-13 loomed ever larger as it circled overhead. I again heard the radio crackle,

"627, this is 340, do you read me"?

"340, I read you loud and clear sir, over." I answered.

"627, are their any obstacles like rocks or ditches we should be aware of?"

"This is 627 sir, the field is clear and level. Over."

"Roger and out."

It was apparent to me that the airplane was approaching much too high for an attempt to land, but I remained silent, for a student cadet never tells an officer instructor how he should land his aircraft. As the aircraft floated over a fence at the edge of the field, the pilot became aware of his height and elected to restore full power to make another approach. I was greatly relieved because I had made a safe landing. I would have been embarrassed to witness a poor landing of an officer instructor. His second approach was much lower and successful; however, despite frantic use of brakes, he was barely able to stop his landing roll before colliding into a fence at the opposite end of the field.

"Mister, why did you select this field when there were so many better ones?" The pilot instructor demanded as he descended from the cockpit.

I thought to myself, but dared not say aloud, "why was I, an inexperienced student, able to safely land in this short field without a problem?" The lieutenant was in fact embarrassed that the other lieutenant and I had witnessed his poor landing.

With the use of a gas can delivered by the instructors, we transferred some gasoline from their airplane into my airplane and prepared to depart. One instructor started the engine of my airplane while the other instructor and I prepared to fly together in the other BT-13. He said,

"I want you to put on the instrument goggles and fly on instruments to Waco airfield. You will only use your magnetic compass. I want to show you that you can rely on your instruments. If you had believed your compass yesterday, you would have not been lost. Now, calculate and tell me the compass heading you will follow to Waco, and our ETA."

I worked with a map attached to my knee and a protractor, a semicircle instrument used to measure angles on a map. After completing my flight plan, I replied to his question,

"Sir, our heading is 355 degrees, and our ETA is 50 minutes or 11:20."

"OK, let's go" the lieutenant said as he began to start the engine.

A few minutes after take-off, the Lieutenant placed a red plastic cover over the inside windshield. The cover was transparent and allowed the instructor to see through the windshield to watch for other aircraft, but when my goggles were in place, I could see only the incandescent instruments on the instrument panel. Like nighttime, I was unable to see through the completely black windshield. He instructed me to take over the controls and set our heading at 355 degrees. He was silent for the next hour as I flew our compass heading to Waco.

"OK, mister, let's take away the cover. You may remove the goggles. It is 11:20."

I could not believe the scene below me. The time was 11:20 and we were directly over the runway of the Waco airfield. I had accurately plotted our compass heading and my ETA, estimated time of arrival, was precise to the minute.

"Mister, do you believe now that you can believe your instruments"? He asked as we circled the field.

Although it was a frightful experience, I had learned a valuable lesson, and the memory remained with me throughout my flying career; however I cannot yet understand how I flew along the Brazos River without passing over Waco. The only plausible answer is that I mistakenly flew along a tributary of the river believing it to be the main river.

Upon landing, I was ordered to report to the commanding officer. After he commanded me to stand at ease, he asked me to explain why I had lost my directions during my return flight to Waco. He sat with a stern countenance listening to my explanation of the previous day's events, but at the conclusion of my reply, he smiled and said,

"Well Cadet Pettey, you have certainly had an interesting cross-country flight, but I hope that you learned something. What did you learn?

I replied, "Sir, I learned to trust my compass and not to depend on visual references."

He replied with a grin, "You are dismissed."

I was so elated and relieved, I ran the entire distance to my quarters. I had been certain that I would be washed out of the program, instead, the commanding officer saw fit to use the experience as a training lesson. However, I was soon to discover that it was more difficult to persuade my classmates to overlook the incident. During my remaining basic-training period I was referred to as "Wrong-Way Corrigan", an allusion to a pilot who, some say, had mistakenly flown to Ireland a few years before. Many believed that it was intentional.

The final lampoonery was revealed in our class book, "The Bee-Tee". Under my photograph appeared the caption,

"Jesse E. Pettey, Nacogdoches, Texas—"The Hempstead Kid."

. . .

While training to be an Air Corps Pilot, the war with Germany and Japan continued to rage on another planet, or so it seemed. I was totally engrossed in my studies and flight instruction from morning until the late hours of the night. While I struggled to master the BT-13, the Allies invaded Sicily, Italy surrendered, and Germany occupied Rome. I seldom thought about the war or about being engaged in air combat within a short time. Fighting for survival in the midst of a horrendous war was beyond my comprehension.

HURRIED LOVE

WACO WAS A larger city than Uvalde, where I had been previously stationed and it offered much more entertainment. Unfortunately, my leisure time was limited to Sundays only. The USO, an organization devoted to providing entertainment for military personnel, held a dance every Sunday afternoon in a building located in the center of Waco. Young single ladies volunteered to act as hostesses, serving food and making themselves available for conversation or dancing with lonely servicemen. The rules were strict and enforced by older volunteer chaperons: no use of alcohol on the premises and the girls were never to leave with a serviceman. I had never cared for USO-sponsored dances because I considered the rules too severe and I had never cared for dancing. I judged myself a poor dancer and never a "ladies man." Indeed, I could barely dance across the floor. My reservoir of small talk was also severely restricted; nevertheless, one Sunday I resolved to attend.

Blood rushed to my head as we twirled, glided and circled, blocking all else from my vision but her lovely face. I had completely forgotten that I could not dance well. She was the center, the essence of my giddy circles. Never before had I met anyone so beautiful or been so intoxicated from the presence of such an angelic face.

I had observed her serving punch to soldiers during my first visit to the USO. Staring at her from afar, I held a long conversation with myself bolstering my resolve to invite her to dance with me. Upon her acceptance, I was so dazzled and overwhelmed that I was compelled to request every dance with her until the USO closed. This was the beginning of a profound romance that continued for the next six months. We were together whenever I could find a free moment from my military training. She discontinued her work at the USO in order to have more time with me. Since I was dependent on taxi transportation to and from the air base, most of our time together was spent visiting and playing cards in her living room. After greeting me upon my arrival, her parents would graciously retire into the kitchen to allow us total privacy. Alone, we soon became bored with card games and embraced, which I found much more interesting. If they needed to return to the living room, they sent a signal to us before entering by scraping their chairs as they arose and banging doors as they entered the living room. These noises allowed us time to disengage and resume our card game before they entered. After a time, I became confident that our alertness assured her parents that we were merely playing a game of cards, but I am quite sure that they understood more than I thought. Soon after graduating from cadet training, I purchased an automobile, which liberated us from the confinement of her living room. With the use of the car we were then able to spend most of our time going to movies, dances, or leisurely driving around the countryside.

During the war gasoline was severely rationed and could only be purchased with gasoline coupons allotted to each owner of an automobile. As a result of their scarcity, coupons appeared on the "black market" and were sold or traded like currency; however, there seemed to always be an abundant supply of gasoline coupons on military bases. I managed to obtain a sufficient supply for my needs.

. . .

On November 28th, 1943, Roosevelt, Churchill and Stalin met in Teheran to plan the invasion of France. Christmas was rapidly approaching. I was homesick, as were most of my fellow cadets, and anxious to spend Christmas with my family. I had not been home since entering service, almost a year earlier, and had a great deal of empathy for other cadets who lived so distant from our air base that it was impossible for them to return home during our short Christmas leave. As a result, I invited Cadet David Swartz to spend Christmas with me in Nacogdoches. David was a young Jewish fellow cadet from New

York who, like most of us, had never before been away from home during the holidays. He readily accepted, but was uncomfortable with my plan to hitchhike because he had never hitchhiked before. I was able to reassure him when I explained that I had traveled many times using this method and that most drivers considered it a patriotic duty to share a ride with servicemen. Almost all drivers shared their automobiles with military hitchhikers along the road, and frequently hitchhiking was the most rapid method of travel for a soldier.

A car slowed to a halt after passing us on a street in Houston, Texas. We had hailed a ride earlier from Waco to Houston. The driver had recommended that we try hitchhiking from where he had stopped to let us out of the car. As the door opened for us to enter the waiting car, we became aware that this driver was a young lone female. Somewhat startled, we settled in the front seat, as she had indicated, wondering how we should behave or what would follow. Throughout the war years, it was not unusual for single females to offer a ride to a soldier. It was usually a patriotic act and presented little risk for them during the war. Almost all had a husband, brother, father or close relative serving in the military, and some had even lost a member of their family. In those days of patriotism, it was a rare event when a driver was attacked or robbed by a hitchhiker. She immediately asked us our destination and when we said we were headed for Nacogdoches, she replied that, although she could not drive us to Nacogdoches, she would drive us to the city-limits of Houston; there we would have a better opportunity to hail a ride into Nacogdoches. Our conversation was casual, with normal questions and answers until she reached the city-limits where she stopped to let us out of the car. We thanked her and said good-by. In spite of our initial fears, she had acted properly and most likely, she was a lady who felt pride in her contribution to the war effort.

Only a few minutes passed before we were offered another ride into Nacogdoches. My parents lived near the highway that we would use to enter the city; therefore, I asked the driver to let us out of his automobile near our house. I had only informed my parents that I would arrive in time for Christmas, but I was uncertain about the day or the time. I wanted to surprise them.

It was a joyful Christmas reunion for my family and me, but for David, it must have appeared unreal. He had never before celebrated Christmas in a gentile home or visited a family in a small East Texas town. Decorating a Christmas Tree, participating in a Christmas dinner, attending a Baptist Church service and observing the ritual of opening packages on Christmas morning was far removed from his customary Hanukkah celebrations. I am also sure that by listening to his description and history of Hanukkah, my family and I enjoyed a better understanding of our different religions.

Newspapers and radios announced that our ally Russia had advanced into Poland. It was good news for the allies, but little was reported about the Russian army halting on a river embankment before crossing into Warsaw. There they patiently waited to observe Polish underground soldiers place children in underground sewers, smuggling them outside the city away from the vengeance of the advancing Germans. Even though the Polish Underground Resistance Army was fighting Germans, Russia made no effort to aid them. Instead they waited for the Germans to finish their slaughter of the underground, then entered the city to battle the already weary and weakened Germans. The Russians were not alone as they ignored the Poles' plea for help. The U. S. and her allies also silently stood by as the Poles valiantly and desperately battled until the end. It is a sad chapter in our history.

Upon returning from Christmas vacation I immediately began preparing for flight tests that would determined whether I would be accepted for advanced training. Lieutenant Ulrich intensified my training. We practiced rolls, snap rolls, loops, spins, cross-country flights, flying formation, night flying, emergency landings and instrument flying, everything I might encounter during flight tests.

With a grin on my face, I raced to the barracks holding a white piece of paper in one hand, unable to contain my excitement. I wanted to shout to the world, "I passed the flight test!", but upon entering the barracks, I immediately sensed that not all the cadets present were as elated as I was. Several sat on their bed with bowed heads—some even crying. They had received a third pink slip, the most dreaded piece of paper in the Air Force Cadet Program. A few had failed the flight test, and although they had not received their third pink slip, they would be delayed until they were able to pass the test or be "washed-out". Humiliated before their fellow cadets, those who had "washed-out" packed their bags in readiness to transfer to wherever the Air Force needed them. Sadly, they would never become Air Force pilots.

ADVANCED TRAINING

ARLY INTO BASIC flight training, we were given the opportunity to indicate our preference for single or multi-engine advanced training. I had chosen to be trained in multi-engine airplanes and expected to be transferred to an airfield that offered multi-engine training. Those selecting single-engine training would be sent to an advanced school that offered single-engine training. After final graduation, those trained in a single engine would be sent to another training school that trained combat fighter pilots; those graduating from multi-engine advance training would be sent to flight schools, either to train as a bomber or transport pilot. There were some exceptions to this training proceeding but they were rare. Flying a large powerful airplane appealed to me although the Air Force favored large men to pilot heavy aircraft because the controls of a large aircraft often required the strength and long limbs of a strong pilot. As a general rule, pilots of smaller stature like me functioned better in the restricted cockpit of smaller fighter airplanes; however, I was determined and certain that I was adequately strong to fly a large aircraft. On January 9, 1944, I was one of the few cadets from my basic training class to be assigned to Blackland Air Force Base, located near Waco, Texas. I packed my bags and moved across town prepared to enjoy my impending birthday and grateful that I would remain near Dorothy during my advanced training.

As we followed our new flight instructor around a parked AT-17 "Bobcat," I thought to myself, this is a large airplane compared to a Primary Trainer PT-19 but not much larger than the basic trainer I had previously flown. Although its 42 foot wingspan and its 33 foot length was not much larger, the AT-17's two engines caused it to weigh about 1500 pounds more than a BT-13. In addition, the two engines expanded the flying altitude and doubled the range of a BT-13. It was first used in 1939 as a Cessna T-50 transport, but in 1940 the Army Air Corps designated it an AT-8 Advanced Trainer, later modifying and renaming it an AT-17. It was equipped with two 245 horsepower engines, retractable landing gear, adjustable pitch propellers, a range of 750 miles and a ceiling of 15,000 feet. This would be the first time our training airplanes were equipped with a retractable landing gear, a control column shaped like the steering wheel of an automobile, and side-by-side pilot seats. In all my previous trainers, the student was positioned in front or behind an instructor.

Lieutenant Baker said as he stepped up into the AT-17, "Come in and stand behind me where you can see the instrument panel as I explain the instruments to you,"

We followed him into the cabin looking over his shoulder as he demonstrated the flight controls and explained the instruments. He demonstrated the use of the throttles and pitch controls, explaining that now we would be using two of everything since we would be flying with two engines rather than one. He explained that the engine propellers must be synchronized or attuned to each other by sound; that one propeller must be adjusted to the speed of the other until all pulsating noises cease. He demonstrated how the landing gear was retracted. He said,

"You are now advanced cadets and our instruction, other than checking you out in this aircraft, will be minimal. You already know how to fly, so flying this "Bamboo Bomber" will be easy for you. It will fly itself if you let it. Advanced training is designed to improve your skills in flying a multi-engine aircraft, your navigational skills, instrument flying, formation flying, and night flying. You will no longer use aerobatics, unless you want to kill yourself. That's for the fighter jockey boys. This plane is made of wood and canvas so if you want to try it, go ahead but don't be surprised if it comes apart. A multi-engine airplane is designed to provide a solid foundation for transporting bombs, equipment, or people. You will complete most of the assignments solo, and then we will give you a flight check. If you pass, you will go on to the next assignment. If you fail, we send you back to practice and check you again. If you fail the third time, you wash out. Is that understood?"

"YES SIR!" We replied.

His remarks proved to be correct, for upon demonstrating to our instructor that we could safely fly the airplane, most of our training consisted of practicing assignments given to us. We would later be tested for our proficiency in executing these assignments.

Soon after I began advanced training in January 1944, the United States and their Allies began pounding Casino, Italy. The Germans had fortified an unassailable monastery built on the top of a steep hill near Casino in an attempt to halt allied armies advancing toward the city. It soon became one of the bloodiest battles of the war and although a victory, it proved to be a costly one for the Allies. A few days after the attack on Casino, the Allies, using Sicily as a base, also invaded Anzio, located on the coast a few miles northwest of Rome. It was January 22, 1944, only seven days before my 20th birthday, and the war was intensifying in both the Pacific and Europe.

"Have you forgotten something, Mister?" My AT-17 flight instructor asked as I prepared for a landing.

I could think of nothing that I had failed to do as he pushed the throttles forward and pulled the column back, gaining altitude for another approach to the runway. With a grin on his face, he said,

"Did you intend to belly-land? You didn't let your landing gear down! The aircraft really lands better with wheels."

I slapped my forehead. How could I do anything so stupid? My only consolation was knowing that I had never before been accustomed to a retractable landing-gear and had not developed the habit of remembering to retract it after takeoff or lower it when landing. A checklist was attached to the instrument panel but we often ignored it for landings. Instructors preferred a dramatic moment like this to impress on their students the importance of remembering to lower the landing gear. I discovered later, that this was not an unusual occurrence whenever cadets were first introduced to the AT-17. During landing procedures, instructors seemed to enjoy waiting until the last moment before informing their student that his landing gear remained in the "up" position. It was an effective training technique.

During advanced training we were introduced for the first time to the famous Link Trainer. It was an anchored miniature aircraft containing a cockpit with flight instruments attached to a system of hydraulic controls. Whenever the trainee moved one of the flight controls, the Link responded in the same fashion as an airplane in flight. The movement of the Link Trainer caused the trainee to feel almost the same sensations that he would feel in actual flight and the panel instruments would accurately indicate the attitude of the aircraft. An instructor sat outside the craft controlling flying conditions while communicating with the trainee by radio. If the student over-controlled sufficiently to cause a stall or a spin in a real aircraft, not only would the instructor inform the student of his mistake, the trainee would sense the feeling of a spin or stall. We practiced simulated night and poor-weather flying many hours during advanced training.

There were few "wash outs" or failures in advanced training, for most of those who displayed poor flying ability had been eliminated earlier in primary and basic flight training. I dared not, however, assume that I would graduate until I had passed the rapidly approaching final flying test. The graduating ceremonies for class 44C were scheduled for March 12, 1944. I was to have my final flying tests on March 9th but unfortunately, I contacted a case of the flu a few days before the tests. I was acutely aware that if I was unable to take the final tests on the scheduled date, I would be reassigned to the following class of 44D and my graduation delayed a month—a tragedy I refused to consider.

I therefore ignored the flight surgeon's recommendation that I report to the medical clinic for rest and treatment and continued to fly. Sustained with determination, despite a cough and high fever, I could only pray that I would be well enough to report for the final flight test.

On the day of my flight test, I continued to run a high fever but I repeatedly reminded myself that I only had one more flight check to go before graduation. Upon arriving at the airplane, the test pilot looked at me and immediately asked if I was well. I replied that I was OK and although I did not feel well, I wanted to complete the test. He said,

"OK, let's go."

I will never understand how I passed the test. I was weak from fever, poorly coordinated, my eyes unfocused; yet, I was determined to fly. I made several mistakes as the test progressed, but I have no doubt that my test pilot understood that I was impaired by illness and respected my determination to graduate. At the conclusion of our flight, he assured me that I had passed and said,

"Lieutenant, go home and go to bed. You look awful."

This was the first time anyone addressed me as Lieutenant, although in a few days I would indeed become one.

GRADUATION AND FIRST ASSIGNMENT

THE GRANDEST DAY of my life finally arrived—Graduation day, March 12, 1944. It was celebrated with squadrons of marching soldiers proudly hoisting flags, a marching band, a general to deliver the ceremonial speech, and a group of happy cadets wearing brand new officer uniforms. For the first time, we were permitted to wear officer uniforms without insignia during the graduation ceremony. My mother and Dorothy were present to complete the final rite of the ceremony by attaching my lieutenant bars and pilots wings to my uniform. It seemed unreal that I had completed all the requirements to become a pilot for I believed that I was incapable at one time. As the graduation ceremony progressed, I could only revel in the contemplation that I had exceeded all that I believed I was capable of achieving and in addition, had met and conquered the rigid requirements set by the Air Force. It was for me a grand day indeed, and on this fine day, 12 March 1944, two months after my twentieth birthday, I took the oath of an United States Air Force Officer.

War creates unusual circumstances. I was a teen-ager and ineligible to lawfully purchase beer only two months before my graduation to officer status. As a military officer, I was delegated the responsibility of commanding and protecting the lives of other men, yet I remained ineligible to lawfully purchase beer until I turned 21 years of age. Fortunately, military Officer's Clubs ignored this law.

We had been notified that after graduation ceremonies, our new assignments would be posted on the bulletin board in the orderly room. I had been granted a well deserved weeks leave and was anxious to leave for Nacogdoches where I could proudly display my new officers uniform; however, I was more curious about my new assignment. As I read through the assignments of my squadron, I noted that most of my classmates were assigned to either bomb or transport groups. I had no desire to be assigned to combat duty because I wanted more time to enjoy the good life of an officer nor did I have any desire to be a target for enemy aircraft guns; life was just too beautiful. I was elated when I discovered that I had been reassigned to Blackland Air Training Command as an advanced flight instructor. I was required to only move from the cadet barracks to a shared private room in the bachelor officer's quarters (BOQ) on the same airfield. I was overjoyed! I had been granted my two wishes: to delay a combat assignment and to be stationed near Dorothy. In addition to this pleasant change of assignment, my military salary would increase $100 per month, allowing me to afford a life style appropriate for an officer of the United States Army Air Corps.

"Second Lieutenant Jesse Pettey, age 20."

While on leave visiting my family I discovered that an insurance company had employed my mother. She had been hired to sell life insurance and collected insurance premiums from existing policyholders living in her debit area. A debit was a term used by insurance companies to describe a territory assigned to an agent. Debit insurance was created early in the history of life insurance to enable low-income families to purchase small amounts of life insurance and pay premiums each week. My mother had assumed the duties of an insurance agent who had been called to war with the agreement that she would surrender the job to him when he returned from military duty. She had not worked for about 20 years but with her children no longer dependent on her and a war creating many opportunities for employment, she had decided to reenter the work place. I was stunned upon learning that she was an insurance agent but I admired her determination and courage to take on such responsibilities. I was very proud of her. During the war women filled many jobs vacated by men enlisting in the armed forces; they drove trucks, built airplanes, automobiles, ships, and performed many tasks formerly believed to be too strenuous for women. They made it possible for the economy to continue through out the war without interruption. When the war was over, patriotic women all over the country surrendered their jobs to returning veterans, returned to their homes, and resumed the duties of full-time wives and mothers. Without this heroic effort, it is doubtful that the needs of the vast U. S. military machine could have been fulfilled, but there was an unexpected reward from this mighty effort. For the first time, I believe, women discovered their true worth and found that they were capable of doing things they had never imagined possible. This was also a benefit for men serving in the military. An entire generation of my contemporaries found their potential greater than they had ever dreamed. Indeed, it was a generation that had overcome incredible adversity during a depression and a war— a generation that discovered that while meeting and overcoming these great hardships, they had created the greatest nation ever.

During my leave, I purchased a beautiful black 1938 Plymouth Coupe. It was the first automobile I had ever owned, and although it was six years old, it seemed new to me. My father cosigned a note with me guarantying repayment of a loan from First National Bank of Nacogdoches of $400.00. At that time, $400.00 was a great deal of money and represented almost two months of my salary as a military officer but my satisfaction with life was complete. I was an officer, a military pilot, stationed near Dorothy, and the proud owner of an automobile. Indeed, the two months following my graduation were one of the happiest intervals of my life. Life was so sweet! I wanted it to last forever—but it was not to be for new orders had been posted in the orderly room. I discovered my name on a memorandum ordering me to report May 5, 1944, to Hammer Field, San Francisco, to join crew #144 as a B-24 copilot.

My happy world crashed and shattered at my feet. As an officer and instructor, I held an important position and was a very important person to my students. I was convinced that I had become a "hotshot" pilot and one who had been selectively chosen to instruct student pilots. Surely this had earned me the right to be a commanding pilot. My young ego was not prepared to accept the reality that I would only be a copilot! I did not consider my young age and inexperience to be a handicap, although I was to discover later that it was a significant factor indeed. The decision to place me under the command of an older pilot, trained and experienced in flying B-24s, would prove to be the best thing that could happen to me. A ten-man crew relies on the skills and experience of a command pilot to survive air combat. I was nearer a teen-ager than an adult and still unable to legally purchase beer. While I had been enjoying an ego-inflating assignment as an AT-17 instructor, my future first pilot and crew had been training in a B-24. On the other hand, I had never been inside a B-24 cockpit. After a tearful farewell to Dorothy, I boarded a train bound for San Francisco and my new assignment. Military service creates many love affairs as lonely servicemen seek female company while serving assignments in far-away locations; yet the same military service terminates almost as many love affairs as it creates when one lover is assigned to another location. And so it was with Dorothy and me. After an exchange of a few letters, we never heard from each other again.

"Aircrew—Standing L to R: David Thomas and Author"

B-24 TRAINING

WITH THE LATEST orders in hand, ten airmen, Crew #144 met for the first time in an orderly room at Hammer Field: First-pilot Second Lieutenant Dave Thomas, copilot Second Lieutenant Jesse Pettey, navigator Second Lieutenant Richard Krall, bombardier Second Lieutenant Robert Cline, flight engineer and waist gunner Corporal John Ribovich, radio operator and top-turret gunner Corporal Russell Westaby, nose gunner Corporal John Masterson, tail gunner Private John Tighe, waist gunner Corporal Earl Williams, and belly-turret gunner Sergeant Kenneth Melton.

First pilot and commander of the crew, Dave Thomas, was a tall, good-natured 23-year-old from upper New York who was designated to command our B-24 crew and to be my flight instructor. Dave had been studying engineering at Columbia University when his education was interrupted by the war, resulting in his enlistment in the Air Corps. After graduation from pilot training at Pecos, Texas, he was sent to Albuquerque, New Mexico, for three months of intensive B-24 transitional training before joining us at Hammer Field, California. Flying day and night, his three months at Albuquerque was equal to about six months of ordinary training. When one is only 20 years old, a 23-year-old seems a great deal older and wiser. So it was with me, and due to our age difference, Dave ultimately became a substitute older brother. Without his mature tolerant attitude, our relationship would have been stormy. Like most jealous younger brothers, I attempted to resist and compete with him at every occasion. I was certain that I was an equal, if not better, pilot than Dave, and my immature ego would not allow me to consider that his age, his experience, his physical size and his training perhaps better qualified him to command our crew. Radio operator Russell Westaby and I were both 20 years old and the youngest members of the crew. The oldest member of the crew was flight engineer John Ribovich, who at age 27 seemed indeed old to me. We would ultimately meld together as a team, with each member depending on the skills of the others to survive, but in the beginning, we possessed nothing in common except our youth, skin color, and desire to survive. We came from diverse sections of the United States: Texas, California, Washington, Pennsylvania, Massachusetts, New York, Indiana, Iowa, and Kentucky. We represented varied cultures from farming communities or rural small towns to large urban cities, and our ancestors were Polish, Irish, Scottish, German, and who knows what else. Crew #144 was indeed a diverse combination of backgrounds, viewpoints and attitudes.

After a night on the town, we prepared to board a train the following morning bound for Tonopah, Nevada, with orders to begin combat training, learning the skills of a bomb crew and how to survive in air combat.

. . .

After three days of paper work and orientation, we prepared for our first high altitude training flight. Dave began by demonstrating an outside inspection with the use of a checklist. We walked around the airplane to note anything unusual and to make sure everything was fastened securely beginning at the right wingtip. The checklist instructed us to:

1. Check wing panels and running lights for dirt or breakage.
2. Look at de-icer to see if there are any cracks.
3. Inspect No. 4 engine for oil leaks or foreign matter.
Look over the propeller for cracks and nicks.
4. Inspect No. 3 engine the same way.
5. Look at de-icer between engine and fuselage.
6. Check right pitot tube to make sure cover is removed. The pitot tube measured airspeed. Without it, the pilot was dangerously

handicapped during landings or takeoffs and the navigator or
bombardier could not make accurate calculations.

7. Check that the nose turret is locked in forward position and free of
damage.

8. Check left pitot tube.

9. Look over the nose wheel assembly for damage.

10. Check the right wing and engines as the left.

11. Look over the main landing gear beginning with the tires.

Dave said,

"A good pilot never permits the ground crew chief or flight engineer
to persuade him that everything has been inspected. He would like to
think that he is the third crewmember to inspect the airplane and be
assured that nothing is overlooked."

He emphasized that the safety, or even the life of crew members,
may depend upon this inspection; however, I learned that it was extremely
rare for us to find anything amiss, for most ground crews were very
protective of their airplane.

As we walked around the Liberator, I was stunned by the size of
the aircraft. Dave and I would be sitting 18 feet above the ground and
67 feet from the tail. The wingspan of a Liberator is 110 feet and it can
lift 65, 000 pounds into the air including 8,000 pounds of bombs. Its
range is about 3000 miles at 275 miles per hour and 28,000 feet
altitude—about 10 hours' flying time. Four Pratt & Whitney engines
powered the Liberator, each producing 1200 horsepower. When fully
armed, two .50-caliber machine guns protrude from the nose turret,
two from the top turret, one from each side of the waist, two from the
belly turret, and two from the tail turret, totaling 10 heavy caliber guns.
A B-24 was a formidable arsenal of weapons, but when several B-24s
were in formation, the combined firepower was so great that enemy
fighters could rarely attack the formation without incurring some damage
to their aircraft. Even so, the enormous load of bombs, crew, and

ammunition was of great concern to us on take-off. Sometimes, we could barely lift off the far end of the runway due to the weight, but we somehow always managed to struggle off the runway. Others were not so fortunate and crashed with a full load of bombs.

Upon completing our inspection, we donned our flying clothing for high altitude flying: sheepskin-lined leather boots, sheepskin-lined leather trousers held by suspenders, a sheepskin-lined leather jacket, and a sheepskin-lined leather helmet with attached goggles. Along with the heavy clothing, we wore a "Mae West" inflatable vest to keep us afloat in the event we bailed out over water. Later we were issued an electrical wired jump suit that could be plugged into an electrical outlet like an electric blanket to provide more heat beneath the sheepskin clothing. This arrangement usually worked well, but occasionally a hot spot would develop within the wiring system causing the wearer discomfort or even a skin-burn. It was amusing to observe a crewmember suddenly begin to squirm while struggling to disconnect his electrical suit. The Liberator was neither pressurized nor heated. An open window on each side of the fuselage allowed the waist gunners a clear view from which to fire their machine guns. The bomb bay was also opened so that bombs could fall clear of the aircraft during bomb-run over the target. At 20,000 to 25,000 feet, where we most often practiced flying formation, the temperature was frequently 30 to 50 degrees below zero. At that temperature, my breath would condense inside my oxygen mask forming icicles under my chin. We often had the appearance of icemen. Unfortunately, for most of the crew, there was little room inside the Liberator to change flying clothes; therefore, it was necessary for us to don most of the sheepskin clothing before entering the airplane and suffer from the heat until we reached a cooler altitude. Located in the desert, Tonopah was often over one hundred degrees at ground level in August and minus thirty degrees at our practice altitude.

In order to enter the aircraft cockpit, it was necessary to bend from the waist, stoop and step inside the bomb bay; then step up into the radio compartment located behind the pilot and copilot's seats.

Dressed in heavy sheepskin clothing, a .45-caliber pistol strapped under my arm, carrying extra boots with an extra parachute, I found it physically difficult to enter the cockpit. On the other hand, during an emergency evacuation of the airplane, it was even more difficult, if not sometimes impossible to quickly exit the aircraft burdened with these items. This difficulty was compounded when it became necessary to overcome centrifugal forces created by the airplane plunging out of control. We were instructed to fasten an extra pair of boots to our parachute harnesses in the event we were forced to parachute. Boots wear out rapidly when one walks long distances over rugged terrain. Those who had previously bailed out advised us that an extra pair of boots would seem a luxury in such circumstances. In the event that our regular parachute failed to open, we wore a second harness to which a chest parachute was fastened. The .45 pistol was presumably for protection if we found ourselves in enemy territory. We were advised, however, that the pistol was worthless most of the time and might even get us killed. I suppose it was issued more for a sense of security than practicality, for certainly the sound of a gunshot would instantly alert any enemy troops within hearing distance and identify our location. Despite the precautions taken for our safety in combat, few were able to safely parachute from a damaged B-24 because the aircraft often exploded from fire, or the crew was helpless to overcome the centrifugal force created by the bomber spiraling out of control.

I was ready to take my place in the copilot seat for the first time. Dave showed me how to adjust my seat and make sure it was locked in place before takeoff. Immediately after taking my seat, he explained that one of my responsibilities, as co-pilot was to unlock a lever that secured all flight controls in a locked neutral position. All flight controls were securely locked after each flight to prevent strong winds from moving them about and damaging them. Before starting the engines, I was instructed to read aloud a checklist near my seat that was attached to the right side of the instrument panel. I was to read it in a loud voice so that Dave or John, the engineer, could understand the questions and respond. I began reading by the numbers:

"Number 1. Form 1A?"

The form was a written report from the chief engineer of the ground crew describing all repairs that had been completed and any that remained to be completed. From this report, the pilot could decide whether the aircraft was airworthy or not.

Dave responded, "Form 1A checked."

"Number two. Loading checked."

This form was always left in the cockpit to inform the pilot of the location and the weight of items loaded in the aircraft. The pilots would know from this information if the airplane would be tail-heavy or nose-heavy during takeoff and flight.

Dave answered, "Loading checked."

"Number three. Wheel chocks?." I shouted.

The pilot would look out his left window and the copilot out the right-side window to verify that both chocks were in place. Chocks, or blocks, were placed in front of the wheels to prevent the aircraft from creeping forward because of wind or idling propellers.

The pilot called out, "Chocks in place left."

I responded, "Chocks in place right."

"Pitot covers?"

Both pilots looked out his side and responded, "Removed left" and "Removed right."

"Gas-tank caps?"

The flight engineer, John Ribovich, sat on top of the airplane with his legs dangling through a hatch just behind our seats. This position gave him unrestricted vision of the various parts of the airplane that were invisible to us.

He answered, "Gas caps checked and safe tied."

"Number six. Flight controls?"

The pilot then called out the name of a flight control as he pushed or turned it to its maximum position.

Dave shouted, "Elevators?"

From his position, John could see the flight control move and called out the name of each control as the pilot continued moving them until he was sure they were all working correctly.

Our flight engineer, Corporal (later Sergeant) John Ribovich, developed into a very good flight engineer, and except for the pilot, was the most important member of our crew—even more so than me. John was from Pittsburgh, deeply religious, very knowledgeable, and the most mature member of the crew. He was respected by all of us. His responsibility, as flight engineer, was to make certain that the airplane was in a safe condition to fly and to keep it flying when it was in the air. While we were in the air, he was constantly in motion, climbing over the airplane checking generators, fuel consumption and countless other items as well as serving as one of the waist-gunners during combat. He was the first crewmember to be consulted whenever an emergency occurred.

There were 21 items to be read aloud and checked before starting the engines. In order to not overwhelm the reader with a long list of procedures that may prove monotonous, I will assume that the six illustrations given above will enable the reader to better appreciate the meticulous attention given to every detail, however insignificant it might appear. Airline crewmembers complete these checklists while the passengers are waiting in the terminal, and are, therefore, mostly unobserved. Along with flying the airplane, reading aloud the checklist was one of my most important responsibilities as copilot. I was also responsible for supervising the storing and care of oxygen for the crew, the containment of any fires that may occur during flight, replacing our flight-engineer if he were incapacitated for any reason, and assisting or replacing the pilot if he were incapacitated in any manner. In addition, I was a co-commander and shared the responsibility of supervising the entire flight crew. These were important responsibilities for a twenty-year-old and ten lives often depended upon their proper execution.

After finishing the "Pre-start" checklist, Dave instructed me to begin reading the "Start engine" checklist.

I began reading aloud,

"Number one. Clear engines and fireguard posted."

Dave looked from his window to make certain that no one was near the two propellers on the left side and shouted,

"Clear left!"

Upon observing that one of the ground crew members held a fire extinguisher and was in position to observe the engines, I said,

"Clear right!"

I then held up three fingers to alert the ground crew member that we were about to start the number three engine and replied,

"Guard posted!"

I read aloud, "Number two—Ignition switches all on!"
I then switched all four ignition switches to the "on" position.

"Number three throttle?"

Dave moved the throttle to 1/3 position and called out,

"Number three throttle cracked."

"Booster pump?"

I turned on the booster pump for engine number three and responded,

"Booster pump on."

Dave had taught me to prime the engine. When fuel pressure was over four pounds, I pressed the primer switch for one second and released it, repeating if it was needed. This operation caused fuel to be pumped into the engine. I shouted,

"Start engines."

While priming with one hand, I pressed the starter switch with the other until the engine fired and then eased the mixture-control lever back to auto-rich. With a puff of smoke the engine started and the propeller began rotating. As I observed the oil pressure rising, I again said aloud,

"Oil pressure coming up. Number three engine is started!"

Initiating the number three engine also activated the electrical system that provided electrical power throughout the aircraft. Before boarding the aircraft, the engineer always turned on a temporary generator that created sufficient electrical power to light the cockpit and start the number three engine; however, the generator was powered with a limited supply of gasoline and it was no longer needed after the number three engine was activated.

After starting the three other engines, we continued to follow a checklist procedure that activated the flight instruments and radio before we were ready to taxi.

Upon receiving permission to taxi from the tower, Dave gave a thumb up signal to a ground crew member who removed the wheel chocks and signaled us with another thumb up indicating we were clear to taxi. Dave then released the brakes and began easing the throttles forward while Ribovich, the flight engineer, positioned himself with his head outside the top-hatch. He could observe and warn us of any obstacles that we might not be able to see. With a combination of throttles and brakes Dave maneuvered the large airplane out of the parking area along the taxiway toward the end of the runway. A few minutes after we had received permission to taxi, the tower said,

"874, you are clear to use taxiway 16 and runway 22. Wind is northwest at 7 miles per hour and visibility is 10 miles, over."

I replied,

"Roger, I read you. Will wait your final instructions."

Radio communication with the tower was another responsibility I had been assigned by Dave, although later I usually taxied while Dave spoke with the tower. Upon arriving at the end of the runway, we moved off the taxiway and stopped so that I could read another checklist.

"Trim tabs?" I read from the checklist.

Dave set the tabs at desired position for takeoff and answered, "Trimmed for takeoff."

"Mixtures?"

I checked to make sure everything was set at auto-rich and announced,

"Mixtures in auto-rich."

We continued to examine each item listed on the takeoff checklist. Dave then "revved" (throttled) each engine to its maximum power as we checked the instruments. Upon completion, Dave nodded and I activated my microphone to radio the tower,

"Tower, 874, ready for takeoff, over."

"Roger 874, you are cleared for takeoff" the tower replied.

Dave turned the B-24 onto the runway and slowly moved the four throttles forward as I observed Dave's every movement. My assignment during takeoff was to follow his right hand with my left as he pushed the throttles forward. Whenever he removed his hand from the throttles to adjust other controls, I tightened the friction lock that prevented the throttles from creeping back and causing us to lose power during takeoff. I had been instructed to observe the airspeed indicator and call out our airspeed during take-off so that Dave could focus his attention on maintaining proper alignment of the aircraft as we thundered down the runway. Because of its tricycle landing gear, I discovered that a B-24 would easily fly itself off the ground during takeoff. Moments after we had lifted off the runway Dave called out "Gear up" while signaling with a thumb pointed upward. I pulled up the lever that raised the landing gear and eased back the superchargers and throttles into a climbing position. I proceeded to read from the checklist each remaining item that should be raised or lowered to reduce air drag and trim the aircraft. I soon discovered that it was necessary to use flight instruments, even in clear weather and daylight, while flying a Liberator. Restricted visibility and the weight and size of a B-24 did not permit the pilot to fly "by the seat of his pants"—a term used by pilots meaning flying by sensations. A slight raising or lowering the nose, or one wing rising slightly will send a equilibrium message to the brain of a pilot flying a light aircraft, but the same pilot will not sense these messages while flying a heavy aircraft such as the B-24.

Navigator Krall came on the intercom to give us the desired compass heading, airspeed, cruising altitude, and estimated time of arrival (ETA) over Phoenix and our return flight to Tonopah. Richard, from Pasadena, California, had graduated from college as a chemist a short time before entering the service and was two years older than I, in spite of his youthful look. He had baby-like facial skin, and like a teen-ager, grew fuzz instead of whiskers. He was the most excitable member of the crew when under pressure, and I feel sure that he suffered a nervous breakdown before completing his tour of missions, although it was never medically diagnosed. He would wake up shouting in his sleep and often became hysterical while speaking over the intercom in the midst of an air battle. He was intelligent, a fine navigator but pensive and aloof. His responsibility was to navigate—to know where we were at all times, to calculate compass headings, headwinds, airspeeds, distances, to keep the pilot informed of our location and to make needed corrections. He also would operate the nose turret if the nose gunner was incapacitated and be the backup bombardier if the bombardier became incapacitated. He made his calculations on a tiny table located in the cramped Plexiglas nose of the aircraft that he shared with the bombardier. They had an unobstructed view of the ground underneath. This view allowed the bombardier to better observe his target during bomb runs, but it also allowed them an unrestricted view of exploding anti-aircraft shells and enemy aircraft.

Our bombardier, Bob Cline, was responsible for the loading, storing, arming and releasing of bombs. During the bomb run, he was in command and by sighting through the Norden Bomb Sight, he actually controlled the aircraft before releasing the bomb load. Upon announcing, "bombs away," the pilot resumed control of the airplane. Bob was a very mild-mannered, quiet person and was liked by other members of the crew. Unfortunately, he spent only three months with us while training in Tonopah. When we departed Tonopah for Italy, he remained behind because of illness and none of us ever heard from him again. A replacement bombardier was assigned to us upon arriving at our new base in Italy.

We flew an assigned departure pattern away from Tonopah Air Base and headed toward Phoenix. I had never before witnessed such a barren desert landscape. I had grown up in East Texas where I was accustomed to panoplies of green forest, grass and streams of water. The desert was so displeasing to me that I could not comprehend why anyone would live there and vowed that I would never voluntary return again. My dislike of the desert grew even more intense during the hot days that followed and when added to my dissatisfaction of being a copilot, a prescription for depression and rebellion was created within me. As I matured, I would learn to accept circumstances over which I had no control, but then I was too young, immature and impatient. How surprised I would have been to know that many years later I would be blissfully residing in the Las Vegas desert valley; as a consequence, I have learned that one should never say, "never."

Dave began a gentle turn to our desired compass heading and continued to climb until we reached our assigned altitude. There was little for us to do after takeoff but to activate the automatic pilot. When activated, the automatic pilot controls the airplane, and by employing a spinning instrument called a gyro, maintains it in level position. With the automatic pilot in control, we could relax, but it was necessary for us to remain alert for extreme turbulent air or other aircraft flying nearby. If either event occurred, we promptly turned off the automatic pilot and resumed control of the airplane. The automatic pilot also occasionally drifted slightly off the desired heading and required a delicate adjustment. Dave informed me that, if possible, the automatic pilot might be used while parachuting. When pilots abandon control of an airplane, it often goes into a spin and can create a centrifugal force with sufficient power to prevent a person from moving about the aircraft. The automatic pilot allowed the pilot to move from his seat to the bomb bay and parachute while the aircraft is in level flight. This, of course, would not be possible if the airplane lost power because of damaged engines. Like a sea ship captain, the pilot was the last to leave the airplane.

It was a short round trip flight from Tonopah to Phoenix, but it was an important one to me. I had never before been inside a B-24, flown at such high altitude or controlled a B-24. Dave disconnected the autopilot several times so that I might manually fly and become familiar with the controls of a Liberator. I turned, climbed, dived and slowed almost to a stall. Although the controls were much more resistant because of its size and weight, there was little difference in flying this bomber and flying previous training planes. I did, however, begin to understand why the Air Force favored larger and stronger men as bomber pilots. Several incidents would later occur that confirmed the need for long strong limbs while flying the Liberator under adverse conditions. For instance, I would experience landing a B-24 in an extreme strong crosswind, when my arms and legs were extended to their limits, as I wrestled the controls to maintain control of the airplane.

We had climbed to 9500 feet when I ordered the crew to don their oxygen masks. As Oxygen Officer I had been assigned the responsibility of ordering the crew to connect their oxygen masks at 10,000 feet and remove them when we had descended below 10,000 feet. I also had been assigned the duty to periodically verify that each crewmember had a sufficient supply of oxygen and insure that none had silently dozed into unconsciousness from a lack of it. Above 10,000 feet most persons require extra oxygen to maintain alertness and good job performance. At higher altitudes oxygen starvation becomes a surreptitious killer; following a brief feeling of euphoria, one becomes lethargic and dozes off into a deadly sleep.

The high altitude round trip mission to Phoenix was uneventful. We had reached an assigned altitude of 20,000 feet only moments before the navigator announced that we were directly over Phoenix. Climbing at 100 feet per minute at a speed of 180 miles per hour, a B-24 requires approximately 200 minutes or a little over three hours to reach 20,000 feet. On the other hand, descending at 200 feet per minute, the B-24 requires only 100 minutes or less than two hours at normal cruising speed to descend to landing traffic altitude. Dave began a decent approximately one hour and 50 minutes from Tonopah. He informed me that delaying a descent could cause a pilot to carelessly reduce power and descend at a faster, unsafe rate in order to arrive at a destination at a correct altitude for landing. Rapid loss of altitude can result in over-cooling the engines and may cause them to fail when power is restored. Dave continually reminded me that a B-24 was not a fighter airplane, nor was it built to withstand violent maneuvers and speeds; instead, it was constructed to carry a heavy payload a long distance at a high altitude. I discovered that landing at airports located at higher altitudes also requires a longer landing roll after touchdown due to less air resistance; that Tonopah, at 6300 feet above sea level caused an airplane to stall more readily while landing. Dave pointed out that we would be landing at a faster airspeed and a longer landing roll than normal. He said that the B-24 always uses power to land due to its weight and that without power, it drops like a "lead balloon".

"Tonopah tower, this is 874 requesting landing instructions, over."

"Roger 874, you are cleared to land on runway 12. Wind is from the northeast at 20 miles an hour, visibility is unlimited and barometer setting is 29.34."

With this information we understood that we would land in the opposite direction of the wind, which would be a north direction, and that the wind of 20 miles an hour and unlimited visibility would pose no serious problems. Desert winds of 20 miles per hour or more were normal at Tonopah. I reset the barometer instrument at 29.34 so that it would indicate our correct height as we flew in the traffic pattern before landing. Dave throttled back to 155 miles per hour as he entered the traffic pattern, and I began reading aloud the landing checklist so that it would be completed by the time we turned on our downwind leg, parallel to the runway. I read aloud,

"Altimeter set at 29. 34!"

Dave responded, "Altimeter set and landing instructions received."

"Crew to stations?" I continued.

After checking the nose section to make certain that there were no crew member inside, checking to be sure the ball turret was in the up position, and the trailing antenna was retracted, the engineer responded,

"Crew in landing position."

"Auxiliary hydraulic pump on?"

The flight engineer turned it on and signaled that it was on.

"Brake pressure and parking brake?" I read out loudly.

Dave pressed the pedals to read the pressure gauges, checked the parking brake and said,

"Brake pressures checked and parking brake off."
(it would be a disaster to land with the brakes on)

I read, "Automatic pilot off?"

And so I continued reading from the long landing checklist as we made sure that our equipment was in a position that prevented damage to the airplane and assured our safe landing. When one wingtip was pointing in the direction of the end of the runway, we began the first of two gentle 90 degrees turns. The second turn aligned us in a direct approach toward the runway. After a few moments, Dave called out,

"Flaps down."

I lowered the flaps and said to him,

"Flaps 20 degrees."

He reduced power and lined up with the runway as I began calling out the last checklist before landing.

"Propellers?"

"High rpm," Dave called out.

"Superchargers?" I called out.

Dave set the superchargers full forward in case we must take-off again and said,

"Full superchargers."

"Gear down" I called as I lowered the landing gear.

"Full flaps?"

I lowered the flaps, slowing the aircraft to about 125 miles per hour and forced the airplane into a steep descent toward the end of the runway.

"Airspeed!"

I began to read the airspeed to him every few seconds so that he could keep his eyes focused on the runway without the distraction of being forced to look at the instrument panel. Dave began to gently pull the nose up about 30 feet above the runway. At the same time he moved the throttles back, reducing the power until the giant airplane began to drop like a rock; however, our forward speed allowed the main wheels to gently touch the runway and roll down the runway. Dave held the nose off the runway as long as was possible, but as the speed decreased and the aircraft slowed, it became increasingly difficult to hold it off the ground. The nose wheel then dropped and contacted the runway, creating more friction that slowed our forward roll. Dave began to apply the landing brakes until we had slowed sufficiently to begin taxiing toward the nearest runway exit. It was necessary to clear the runway as soon as possible so that the aircraft behind us could land.

The tower had instructed us to follow taxiway 21 when we exited the runway. As we began to taxi to a near exit, I began reading the checklist again:

"Superchargers?"

Dave turned them off while taxiing and said,

"Superchargers off."

"Booster pumps?"

I turned off the booster pumps and said,

"Booster pumps off."

"Generators?"

Generators off." the engineer responded.

"Wing flaps?"

I raised the wing flap control lever to the "up" position and looked out my window to see them rise. "Wing flaps up." I said.

"Cowl flaps?"

The cowl flaps were window-like shuttered openings surrounding the engines that allowed the engines to cool when open or retain heat when closed.

I opened them and said, "Cowl flaps open."

I continued to read the landing checklists as a jeep driven by a ground crew member appeared and signaled for us to follow him. He led us to a parking space, directed us into the parking space, and signaled for us to cut our engines. I again read from the checklist,

"Cut Engines!"

Dave opened the throttles until the propeller speed was 1000 RPMs. I placed the mixture controls in idle cut-off and Dave moved the throttles forward slowly until the engines died from lack of fuel.

"Mixtures in idle cut-off" I said.

Dave responded, "Throttles full open."

"Switches?" I began turning off switches until all were in the off position and said,

"Switches off."

We continued until the checklist was completed and all controls were locked. Instructions to the ground engineer, Forms 1 and 1A, were the last items to be completed before we were free to exit the aircraft. I had completed my first flight in a B-24 and although it was more complicated, the Liberator was not vastly different from the training airplanes I had flown previously. I was confident that I would have no problem flying this Liberator-monster and that I was equally capable as Dave. This thought again fueled my indignation that I was only a copilot. For some time, David would find himself the innocent target of my immature resentment, even though I liked him and would grow even fonder of him in the future.

COMBAT FLIGHT TRAINING

SAFELY FLYING A huge machine, such as the B-24, required profound coordination of the skills previously acquired by each member of our ten-man team. We had achieved these individual skills before coming together as a crew. Now our training objective would be to coordinate these skills so that our actions would become automatic and routine under combat conditions. While Dave and I flew in close formation with other airplanes, the bombardier operated his bomb sight, the navigator made continual calculations, the engineer was available at all times during flight to adjust various mechanical gadgets, the radio operator communicated with those outside our aircraft, the waist, tail, nose and belly-turret gunners were alert and all were assigned gun positions. We trained continually under extreme tension, as if we were in combat—sometimes under unimaginable chaos.

Our day usually began with formation flying. In order to protect each other, it is very important that slow flying bombers remain in a compact formation when encountering enemy aircraft. A group of armed airplanes flying tight formation increases their fire power by several times that of a lone aircraft and becomes almost impenetrable. Enemy pilots, therefore, concentrated their attacks on straggling airplanes in preference to attacking the formation. Indeed, the sure way to attract the ire of a flight commander was to lag behind an assigned slot in a formation. With few interruptions, we practiced formation flying continually. While Dave and I flew formation, the gunners improved their accuracy at other locations. Some days we practiced bombing over dry lakebeds marked with a bull's-eye. Bombs filled with white flour were used so that we could observe the results from our aircraft at high altitude. The flour formed a small white cloud above the bomb crater when it impacted the ground and the bombs could be reused since they did not explode.

. . .

Tonopah, Nevada 1944, was a mining town consisting of less than two thousand people, an air base with several thousand airmen, and two hotels: the Mispa and the Tonopah which yet exists at the time of this writing. The hotels, each containing a casino and bar, provided the only entertainment in town. Airmen would often say, "Tonopah has ten thousand airmen and two single girls." Since meeting girls and dating were not viable options, we were left with the choices of either attending a movie on base or spending an evening in a casino gambling and drinking. The latter, as one would expect, resulted in an occasional fight between bored and drunk soldiers. Indeed, the only fistfight in my adult life occurred while stationed at Tonopah. I am not proud to acknowledge it, but on the other hand, we lived in unusual times. I was teeming with youthful vigor, bored for lack of more fulfilling activities, full of resentment because of my assignment as a copilot stationed in an unsightly hot desert city. I also fully understood that our next assignment would place us in air combat from which I might not return. There was in all of us a philosophy of, "live today, for tomorrow you may be dead". We certainly lived!

To occasionally escape from what we considered our 'hellhole' in Tonopah, we could only visit Reno, Las Vegas, or Bishop, California; each about a six hours drive from Tonopah. We were indeed isolated at a desert airfield without automobiles. For me, there was nothing of interest in these towns since they offered little more entertainment than Tonopah. Being desperate, we devised a plan to visit Los Angeles over a weekend. Five of us agreed to share the expenses of hiring a taxi driver to drive us to Los Angeles on a Friday night and return to Tonopah the next Monday morning in time to begin our day of training. The driver planned to remain in Los Angeles until it was time for us to meet him for the return trip to Tonopah. The entire expense for the taxi was one hundred and twenty-five dollars, which amounted to forty-five dollars each. We would also incur addition expenses of a shared hotel room and other activities; a total amount that would almost equal our monthly salary.

Somewhere in the California desert, the taxi had a flat tire. Rubber and automobile tires were scarce, even non-existent during the war. In order to extend their use, tires were recoated with a synthetic rubber employing a method called retreading; however, improper processing or driving at high speed frequently caused the retreaded tire to fail and disintegrate. The taxi driver did not possess a spare and the hole in the tire was beyond repairing. With Joshua trees standing guard, we slept and waited until daylight for traffic to resume so that we could hail a ride into the next town for tire repair. We arrived in Los Angeles the next afternoon eager to see and experience all that our time would allow. We prayed that the tire would withstand the remaining trip and deliver us to the air base early Monday morning. Fortunately, our prayers were answered. With four bald tires, the taxi delivered us to Tonopah before training exercises began Monday morning, a tired but happy group of airmen.

. . .

On 4 June, 1944 German troops retreated from Rome, allowing Allied roops to enter the Eternal City while we trained for combat in Tonopah. In the early morning of June 6th, 7000 American and British ships landed the greatest invasion ever to be recorded on the beaches of Normandy, France. These dates marked the beginning of the end of the European war. Within one year the war would end, although there yet remained some of the most intense battles to be fought. As the end of combat training in Tonopah drew nearer, I was aware that a terrible war waited for me just over the horizon however, I could hardly imagine just how terrible it really would be.

We continued practicing formation flying, cross-country flying, bombing and firing at targets almost every day. At various times we would practice firing twin .50-caliber machine guns from a simulated

Plexiglas turret attached to the ground, shooting at clay pigeons with a shotgun, and flying while the crew fired at a tow-target pulled by another airplane. I often thought about how dangerous it must be to fly an airplane towing a target with inexperienced gunners shooting at me from a short distance away. The tow pilot could only hope and pray that the neophyte gunners would be accurate. With so many inexperienced crews flying training missions at that time, almost every sort of accident that one could imagine occurred.

On July 10, 1944 we received new orders to report to Hamilton Field, California. Although the orders did not state our final destination, we were aware that our combat training had ended and that our skills would be needed in some war theater. Bets were placed between crewmembers on our ultimate assignment, but I refused to think about it. I tried to live one day at a time.

JOURNEY TO WAR

NONE OF US had the slightest clue as to our destination. That we were assigned serial number 42-51336, a B-24 Liberator, to fly to our next assignment came as quite a surprise; however, we were informed that our destination was secret and would be revealed at a later time.

After three days at Hamilton Field processing and test flying our new airplane, we received "restricted" orders dated 14 July 1944. "Restricted" appearing at the top of any communications was a warning that the contents were secret and to be shared only with authorized personnel. The penalty for revealing restricted material to any unauthorized person was a possible court marshal or a trial in a military court for treason. The orders instructed us to fly our new B-24 to Harvard, Nebraska and then to Grenier Field, New Hampshire. The aircraft was modified, during our stay at Hamilton Field, by installing large gasoline tanks in the bomb bay. The added gasoline capacity was an indication that we would be flying long distances without refueling—in all likelihood, over an ocean. We were informed that new orders would be issued at Grenier Field.

The flight to Grenier Field was uneventful, and upon arrival, we were presented orders dated 17 July 1944, stating that the next day we would fly to Gander Field, New Foundland, and that we would receive additional instructions there. The secrecy became more exciting with the release of each new set of orders and with the realization that I would soon leave the United States for some mysterious assignment. From the direction that we were being routed, I could only conclude that we were destined for Africa or Europe.

As we flew toward New Foundland, the weather began to change.

Almost from the time we departed New Hampshire, we encountered huge dark clouds extending up to twenty-five thousand feet. After a discussion with the navigator and consulting our weather maps, Dave and I made a decision to try to fly under the clouds rather than turn back to Grenier Field. Although we were trained to fly with instruments, we preferred to fly beneath the clouds and maintain visual contact with the ground and water. After we passed the coast of New Brunswick and onto the open Atlantic, the weather worsened and the ceiling became so low that we were forced to fly less than one hundred feet above the water. Flying only a few feet above the waves required intense concentration. We must be prepared to react immediately to a sudden gust of wind that might suddenly force us down into the ocean. Using the automatic pilot or relaxing, even for a moment, was out of the question.

After hours of grueling flying, the ceiling suddenly lifted. Ahead I could see steep cliffs rising out of the ocean supporting vast level fields of green grass. It reminded me of a withered prune that had been cut in half, laid in the ocean with the rounded edge above the water, covered with fields of brilliant emerald green. Dave and I breathed a collective sigh of relief, as we perceived how near the cliffs we had been when the clouds lifted a few moments earlier. The weather scarcely improved, but visibility was sufficient to view the ground, and we were soon able to find Gander Field. As we approached the airfield, I could see that the architectural design of the buildings differed from those I had been accustomed to seeing in the United States. They appeared to be more British, as I remembered English houses in the movies. We were already in a foreign country.

Upon landing at Gander Field, we were presented more sealed instructions. We were scheduled for takeoff at 0300 the next morning, and the sealed orders were not to be opened until after takeoff.

It was raining at 0300 hours, and low clouds had reduced visibility to almost zero, but we were cleared for an instrument takeoff with a northeast heading. Because of the darkness and a thick fog of rain, we could barely discern the taxi strip ahead of our wing lights as we taxied toward the runway. After a prolonged slow taxi, the end of the runway was finally sighted, and preparations were made for takeoff. I had concluded reading aloud the checklist when Dave said over the intercom,

"Prepare for takeoff".

Despite the bright wing lights, we could see no more than thirty feet ahead of us, but with the confidence of youth and faith that our instruments would guide us, we pushed the throttles forward and began rolling down the runway gathering momentum. I could barely see the runway beneath us as we lifted up into a world of pitch-black darkness with only our instruments eerily glowing in the cockpit to guide us. We headed northeast and proceeded to climb for the next hour and a half. Suddenly we broke through the overcast into a world of cold blue light and gray clouds. The contrast was startling. There is nothing more breathtaking than flying near huge billowing clouds. We were surrounded by pearly white mountains of clouds, interspersed with lavender valleys and gray hills of smaller clouds splashed with wispy shadows. A morning sky illuminated by a bright blue moon gave ample light to read a newspaper in the cockpit, but we had more important things to do. We must now open and read the package of instructions that would reveal our destiny and sooth our speculative fever. I could hardly contain myself as I waited for Dave to open the package. After attaining our assigned altitude, carefully checking all instruments, turning on the automatic pilot and the cockpit lights, Dave pushed his seat back and reached for the package.

As our B-24 flew toward an unknown destiny and Dave opened our orders, an event was taking place in Germany that almost made our orders invalid and our participation in the war unnecessary. A group of high-ranking German officers had determined that getting rid of Hitler offered the last remaining chance to end the war before

Germany would be forced into a disgraceful surrender. Led by Colonel Claus Schenk von Stauffenberg, the group included two other distinguished German officers, General Karl Heinrich von Stuepnagel and General Rommel who had distinguished himself in the African campaign and had led the counter-assault against the allies on Normandy. Their plan called for a time bomb inside a briefcase to be placed under a table used by Hitler during a meeting of officers and high ranking civilians at the Rastenburg in East Prussia 20 July, 1944. The bomb exploded as planned, but Hitler had moved from a position next to the bomb and was only injured. Several other members of the group attending the meeting were killed. The Gestapo hunted down everyone suspected of complicity in the plot, and Colonel Stauffenberg was executed the night of the explosion. General Stuepnagel and General Rommel were later allowed to commit suicide. Had the plot succeeded, the war would have concluded before I ever reached the battlefield. Unaware of this event, I waited anxiously for Dave to open the package.

"You are hereby ordered to fly via the Azores, Marrakech, French Morocco, and Tunis to Gioia, Italy, where you will be assigned to a Bomb Group of the 15th Air Force".

Dave and I read the orders before notifying the crew over the intercom. We were on our way to Italy! My knowledge of Italy was indeed limited. It consisted of the knowledge that Rome was where the Pope lived. I had seen movies depicting Italians as people who speak funny. I had viewed movie clips of Mussolini making speeches and strutting about in his comical posture. I had heard some news reports about the allied landing in Anzio and I understood that Italy was our enemy. Despite the fact that they were allied with Germany, the public impression of the Italian soldiers was that, because most had relatives in the U. S., they had no stomach for fighting and would surrender at the first opportunity. A year before my arrival, Mussolini had been dismissed by King Umberto and forced by the Germans to set up a government in Northern Italy.

Dave called the navigator on the intercom and requested that he plot a course to the Azores. A few minutes later, he called to give us a corrected heading for our destination. By that time, the adverse weather was behind us and we could enjoy a clear view of the Atlantic. I had never before flown over such a large body of water so far from land. I was suddenly aware that we were completely dependent on our navigator. There were no landmarks—a vast ocean without anything in sight as far as one could see.

The flight to the Azores was rather boring. We were over water after leaving New Foundland until we arrived at the Azores Islands. There are few tasks to be performed when flying over water, and the days seem incredibly long. Dave and I would take turns napping while the other observed the instruments and watched for other airplanes in the area; however, I fear there were moments when we both dozed at the same time. The navigator was busy throughout the flight checking his maps, taking readings of the sun and stars to calculate our position, the engineer was busy checking fuel gages and verifying that all engines were running smoothly while the other members of the crew napped or read.

After refueling and remaining overnight in the Azores, we spent another boring day over the ocean anticipating the sight of the coast of French Morocco. Although we finally arrived over land, the monotonous desert was not much more interesting than the ocean, but upon arriving at Marrakech, the scenery became more interesting. Descending to the runway, I observed a man in Arabic clothing seated on the rump of a tiny donkey, his feet dangling a few inches above the ground, while an Arab woman followed him with a bundle on her head. The sight was bizarre and unlike anything I had ever witnessed before. It was like a scene right out of the movies. My overnight stay in Marrakech was filled with surreal images of bearded men in undulating robes moving in and out of traffic blending with silhouetted figures covered with black garments and strange face masks. We had been warned at the air base not to stare, photograph or talk with Moslem women because

Arab custom forbids it. This was quite a new experience for an East Texas boy.

The flight next day to Tunis was equally uneventful with another day filled with monotonous views of unchanging desert sand. The evening again proved to be quite different. After landing Dave and I were assigned a double room in the officer's bachelor quarters. I could hardly wait to visit the downtown area of Tunis but Dave had little interest in accompanying me. He preferred to lounge around the officer's club and retire early. Always the explorer, I was determined to see and experience all that I could, even if I must go alone.

. . .

Tunisia was a French colony at that time, providing a potpourri of French military uniforms, Arabic robes, a few English military uniforms caught up in a vortex of veiled Moslem women, bazaars, camels and military vehicles. The city of whitewashed buildings is located on the coast of Lake Tunis connecting the city to the Mediterranean and partly surrounded with distant mountains covered by downy, silken clouds. I selected a sidewalk cafe to absorb the exciting environment around me and to experience a milky anisette; a native drink made from the anise plant.

After the anisette and a cigarette, I decided to walk the streets to soak up some of the breath-taking scenes around me. I soon heard dance music combined with loud voices issuing from a second story windows above me. My curiosity awakened, I found a stairway that seemed to lead to the activity above. After a brief discussion with myself about the dangers and rewards of entering a strange place in a foreign land, my inquisitiveness prevailed—I began climbing the stairs. Once inside and encountering no hostility, I soon found an attractive young military female soldier in my arms as we danced to the music of a French military dance band.

"No, me—vous—est vous!"

She pointed her finger at my chest emphasizing her words, "No me,—you—it is you!" A petite blue eyed French soldier in military uniform was teaching me a few French words. I began learning French words from her during our first dance, although she found it difficult to teach an untalented, but eager student. By the second dance, I had learned, "Venez avec moi", repeating it several times. Translated, I said, "come with me", each time adding some pantomime. She spoke no English, I spoke no French, but we laughed and enjoyed our dances together, proving that youth can ignore language barriers—it merely slows communication, never halting it. I would repeatedly ask her, "Venez avec moi?" She would repeatedly answer with a wag of her finger, "Non, ce n'est pas possible", "No, it is not possible." We would then convulse into laughter.

I had curiously opened a door at the top of the stairs, revealing a gathering of French soldiers dancing to the music of a band. I could see at a glance that there were many unescorted female soldiers sitting at tables patiently waiting and hoping for an invitation to dance, but I was also suddenly aware that I had walked uninvited into a private French military party. Immediately the entire group had recognized me as an American by my uniform, and I was the only American in the room. It was too late to turn back. I could only square my shoulders, act as if I had been invited, and walk to a table occupied by unescorted females and ask one to dance with me. It proved to be the correct decision. By the end of the evening, I had danced with most of the French female soldiers, learned a few French words, and had been offered drinks by many of the male soldiers. It had been a grand evening. During my return trip to the air base, I thought about Dave and the party he had missed. I could barely wait until morning to tell him about it.

The following day, our flight was the most scenic one of the entire journey. We departed Tunis 23 July 1944, flying north over the

Mediterranean Ocean, Sicily, and the mountainous regions of Calabria to the small town of Gioia near the Adriatic Sea. As we flew over mountainous terrain, I thrilled to the sight of many ancient walled villages perched on the crest of mountains. Apparently, medieval builders made an effort to build as high as possible in order to defend themselves against marauders. Gioia is a small city located southwest of Bari in Southern Italy where a large military air base was located. All bombers flown from the U. S. to southern Italy landed there in order to be modified for combat. The ground crews installed .50 caliber machine guns in the nose, top, waist, bottom and tail of our airplane, and removed the bomb bay gasoline tanks to install bomb racks. We were advised that a sergeant attached to the base would paint a logo on the nose of our aircraft for a fee of fifty dollars. We discussed it with the enlisted men but they seemed to have little interest in the project. For that reason, the other two officers and I decided to select a logo and pay for it. The selected nose art was a painting of a scantily clad lady sitting before the words, "Shady Lady" and painted on both sides of the fuselage. Thereafter our airplane would be called "Shady Lady".

"Shady Lady"

The first night in Gioia, I was eager to go into the city for an Italian experience. Again, Dave and Richard preferred to remain on the base. I began to understand that both had girl friends back home and had no interest in meeting Italian girls. In addition to meeting girls, I was curious about Italian people, their culture, their historical sites and wished to learn their language. I later became aware of the reality that many American soldiers possessed a fear of anything different from that which they were accustomed to back home. Most of them felt more comfortable spending their leisure time on the base rather than exploring sites in a foreign country. I quickly discovered that I was one of the few military youths who relished the prospects of being subjected to new situations and sights. At the same time, my outlook created a dilemma for me, for I must decide whether I would remain on base with friends or investigate alone. My curiosity usually won the decision.

. . .

I encountered an odor unlike anything I had ever known as I jumped from the back of a truck used to transport military personnel. The smell was a mixture of pleasant odors from restaurants and home cooking intermingled with unpleasant ones emerging from open fish markets, pools of stagnant water and open sewers. It overwhelmed me in the beginning, but I later learned to ignore it. We had been briefed about the conditions we would encounter outside the air base and warned not to drink the water. Italian cities had been partially destroyed from allied shelling and bombing attacks and even though they were beginning to rebuild, they suffered from a lack of facilities that I had always taken for granted. There were few civilian jobs, the Italian economy was devastated, and citizens were compelled to survive by any manner that they could devise. To add to their hardships, it was often necessary for residents to obtain their drinking water from a fountain in the main piazza of the city and to devise temporary sewer drains. Their sewer and water plumbing had been mostly destroyed. In order to replace a ruined economy, the people had developed a system of barter and black market to replace their lost incomes and to provide them with basic necessities. Italian citizens frequently traded whatever they possessed, sometimes even their bodies, for food and other essential items; as a result, venereal disease was abundant. In cellars of downtown buildings, military medical personnel pragmatically installed prophylactic stations, called pro stations and identified them with a flashing red light to announce their location. These stations provided free prevention treatment of venereal diseases for servicemen who had experienced a sexual encounter within the past hour, the limit for effectual treatment. There were also free prophylactics for those who anticipated such activities. Not by choice but by orders, we attended lectures and training movies about preventing venereal disease that were designed to turn our stomachs. In an effort to impress on our young minds the horrors of venereal disease, the medical staff exhibited photographs of various parts of the human body infected with VD.

As I walked about Gioia, I observed signs posted around the city which read, "This Is A Malaria Area, Do Not Drink The Water" and "Pro station, straight ahead".

INTRODUCTION TO ITALIAN LIFESTYLE

A SMALL CRUDE sign soon attracted my attention. Scrawled on a small piece of cardboard was printed, "Two cooked fresh eggs 50 cents", with an arrow pointing down the street. Military mess halls rarely, if ever, provided fresh eggs. Occasionally we were served various dehydrated foods but powdered eggs and potatoes were served almost daily. Italians soon understood that American GIs yearned for fresh home cooked meals, and since they desperately needed money, some began providing fresh food cooked in their homes. The sign caused me to salivate as I thought about fresh eggs, buttered toast, bacon and coffee. I smelled, either imagined or real, an odor of bacon, and like a bee drawn to honey, I began walking in the direction the sign had indicated. At last I detected another small sign with an arrow pointing to a staircase leading to an apartment on the second floor. I hesitated a moment as I listened to animated voices within, then resolutely knocked on the door.

A matronly woman opened the door and asked, "si?".

Since I spoke no Italian, I could only say, "Eggs?"

She understood and opened the door wide. "Entrata" she said as she motioned me to enter.

Five people arose from a table to shake my hand. I stammered,

"My name is Jess Pettey."

The lady introduced me to each person in the room, pointing to them and saying,

"Cio e mio sposo, Alberto, mio filia, Rosa, mio padre, Favlio, mio madre Anna, sono, Maria."

I understood that her husband's name was Alberto, her daughter's name was Rosa, her father's name was Favlio, her mother's name was Anna, and her name was Maria. She began setting a plate for me while Alberto poured a glass of wine for each person. He raised his glass and said,

"Saluto".

"Salute", we responded before taking a sip of the wine.

Maria asked me, "come lo desirata cucinare le vostre uova?"

She motioned palms up and palms down with her hands. I responded with the palms of my hands down, indicating that I preferred the eggs cooked over. While she cooked the eggs, the family continually replenished my glass of wine causing me to feel as though I was a celebrated guest rather than a customer. The party grew more animated with each glass of wine. I was intrigued with this family who seemed to joke and laugh endlessly. There seemed to be no "generation gap" between the youngest and oldest members. Arguing, teasing, the young daughter participated in the conversation, while older family members extended her the same respect as other adult members. I was to discover that most Italian family members treated their children with the same deference, unlike most American adults who believed a child was only to be seen, not heard. By the time Maria had finished cooking, I felt as though I was also a member of the family.

They intensely and curiously watched me while I dined as if they were waiting for approval of Maria's cooking. With every bite, I was offered more bread and wine until I pantomimed that I could eat no more. The family then began teaching me some Italian words. I pointed to the lamp and they responded, "lampada". I pointed to the floor and they responded, "pavimento". I pointed to the wall and they responded, "parete". I pointed to the table and they said, "tavola". Each time I pronounced the words in my Texas accent, they would convulse with laughter, but I learned many words that I would never forget.

Upon giving the mother a generous tip and indicating that the time for my departure had arrived, I was introduced to the Italian custom of saying goodbye. As I prepared to exit the door, each member of the family warmly embraced me as if I was a family member. That first night in Italy spent with this lovely family instilled in me a cordial regard for Italians, their food, and their customs. Despite war propaganda portraying Italy as our enemy, I found it difficult to regard this kind family as an adversary—to the contrary, after spending an evening in their home, it was more comfortable for me to regard them as a loving family who had been betrayed by their leader.

Because of a curiosity that prompted me to journey into a strange city alone, I had enjoyed an unforgettable evening, a visit with a lovely family, a 50-cent freshly cooked meal, an Italian language lesson, and an introduction to Italian culture. Remaining on base to watch an American movie proved to be a poor exchange for my exciting evening.

CERIGNOLA, ITALY

With our papers processed and the "Shady Lady" modified and ready for war, we received an order dated 30 July 1944, attaching us to the 766th Bomb Squadron, 461st Bomb Group, 15th Air Force. We were ordered to fly our B-24 from Gioia to our new assignment near Cerignola, Italy. From studying a map, Cerignola is a small city located just below the spur of the boot of Italy near the Adriatic Sea. It was a small impoverished town surrounded by numerous B-17 and B-24 bomber groups located on numerous farms in the area. We were informed upon our arrival that tents were temporarily unavailable and that our crew would be billeted in a building that had at one time been a barn. The 766th Squadron had converted farm buildings into operations offices, mess halls, and recreational clubs. The barn that served as our temporary home was a huge building with concrete floors that had formerly housed cattle. Farmers in Italy maintain their cattle in huge buildings where they are fed and milked. There are no open fields of grass for them to graze since all the land is used for farming. Without water inside the barn, it was necessary for us to shave and bath outside with cold water. Our steel helmets served as a water basin filled with water supplied from an outside cattle trough. Farm laborers generously saw to it that our water canteens were constantly full of wine that was fermented in huge tanks located in a building only a few feet from our barn. Since the water from the cattle trough was not potable, many of us used this wine to rinse our mouths after brushing our teeth. I was only beginning to understand that there was no beauty in war—as Emerson said, "one must carry beauty if it is to be found".

On August 3, 1944 Dave flew his first mission as copilot to Friedrichafen, Germany.

Operational headquarters lost little time putting him with an experienced crew so that he might acquire some familiarity with combat flying before leading our crew on our first bombing mission. While waiting for Dave to fly his first two missions, I read, played cards and loafed at the officer's club during the day. At night, flight officers slept in sleeping bags on the concrete floor next to their enlisted crewmembers. The barn soon became uncomfortable—its novelty had long since worn off while we impatiently waited for a tent.

"Lieutenant, I want to see you outside," a major snapped.

He had walked into the barn on an inspection tour and observed me playing cards with some of my enlisted crewmembers. Once outside, he began reprimanding me for fraternizing with enlisted men. He growled in my face,

"Lieutenant, don't you know that you are not to fraternize with enlisted men? Don't you know that?" He paused for a second and continued,

"I should report you to the commanding officer and place you on OD for the next two weeks. You know that don't you?" He paused again for effect as I answered,

"YES SIR!"

I was completely bewildered. Because of a military custom that forbids one from making excuses, I politely listened and withheld an urge to ask him how I might avoid fraternizing with the enlisted members of my crew. We worked together in a confining airplane and slept together in a barn. At the conclusion of his harangue, he saluted and smugly walked away satisfied that he had properly censured me. I did not ask, nor did he offer any suggestions about how I might properly distance myself from my crew—nor do I know today. It is a tradition of long standing that military officers do not live or fraternize with enlisted personnel; however, after the introduction of the military airplane, flyers regarded this custom as rather antiquated because of the need for officers and enlisted airmen to work together as a crew. The safety of each crewmember in an airplane is contingent on the abilities of the other crewmembers to coordinate their tasks together. As a result, after graduation, officers on flying status generally ignored all but the most basic military customs. That was not, however, the disposition of officers in other branches of the military service. Some could be very rigid in their interpretation of military customs, particularly those who had graduated from ROTC (reserve officer training corps) and other military academies. The major I encountered that day was not an officer on flying status.

A few days later we were notified that our crew would be issued two tents: one to accommodate the officers in an area reserved for offices and the other to accommodate the six enlisted men in a location reserved for enlisted personnel. We were assigned a space in a virtual city of tents and told that it was our responsibility to make the tent habitable. To show their willingness to help, the 766th Squadron supply depot issued each of us a folding cot—without mattress, blankets, sheets or pillowcases. The floor beneath the tent was earth, which would soon turn to mud when the rains came and there was no electricity. We were also without heat to counter the cold, fans to relieve us from the heat, or running water. Located in the center of this tent city was a central latrine tent. It was a huge tent containing rows of wooden boxes, each with a hole carved into the top and placed over a deep hole dug into the ground. Showers were located in another tent. In order to shower, we stood on a wooden floor beneath a showerhead constructed of aluminum tubing that had been liberated from a wrecked B-24 and connected to a large water tank above. Aluminum tubing also was used to convey water from a water tank to a trough made from tin and used for shaving and dental hygiene. Urinals were made from a number of ten-inch wide pipes driven into the ground with two or three feet remaining above ground—they were located in an open area, uncovered, and unprotected. We were unconcerned about our privacy for there were no females nearby, but we were concerned about the cold winter winds. The latrine tent and urinals were located only a short walk from our tent but during a cold rainy or snowy winter night, they seemed much, much further.

Dave, Richard and I had moved into our new tent only one day before 1st Lt. James Sullivan entered and announced that he had been assigned to our crew as a replacement bombardier. He was thirty-one years old, a veteran combat officer and a first lieutenant, which made him the ranking officer in our tent. We found it unusual for him to outrank Dave, our first pilot and commander of the crew. I thought at the time that he was a strange bedfellow and my intuition proved to be prophetic, inasmuch as he later proved to be a difficult personality for the crew to accept. He brought with him, however, a large number of classical records that allowed us to spend many pleasant hours together. Our love of classical music created an esoteric union between us that he was unable to share with other members of the crew.

We were eager to begin making a floor of concrete blocks for our tent but our intentions were temporarily postponed—war came first and foremost.

"Suiting up for War"

MISSION #1

Imasfuzito, Hungary

8 August, 1944

O N THE EIGHTH day of August, my name appeared on the operations headquarters information board. Orders stated that I was scheduled to fly a combat mission the following morning, 9 August 1944, as copilot with Dave Thomas and that we were to report for briefing at 0500 hours. All other information about the mission was a secret and would be revealed only at briefing the following morning.

I was struggling from a deep sleep as I heard a voice say,

"Wake up Lieutenants! First and only call for breakfast!"

The Officer of the Day sergeant seemed to call from far away. I crossly reacted to his annoying voice that was propelling me into an awareness of a dark musty canvass tent and a hard cold uncomfortable cot. One of the responsibilities of the duty sergeant was to wake officers on stand-by status two hours before flight briefing. We must have time to shave, dress, eat breakfast and be transported to headquarters where briefing would take place. It was 0300 hours, two hours before a 0500 briefing.

After breakfast we were transported by truck to the briefing room at headquarters. We sat crowded together on benches in the back of a canvas-covered truck and despite the rough road and uncomfortable seats, most of us fell asleep during the ride. Most often, I was only partially awake when I entered the briefing room, but I was jolted fully awake whenever the briefing officer began describing our target. The briefing area was a room large enough to accommodate fifty or more chairs for pilots, and a stage sufficiently large to display several covered maps and a blackboard. Bombardiers and Navigators were briefed at separate locations.

Often the commanding officer would make a brief introduction about the importance of the impending mission; however, the briefing officer stepped up to the maps with his pointer and without delay announced,

"Today, your primary target will be to destroy the oil refinery at Almasfuzito, Hungary".

He uncovered a large map with pins and red markers indicating the route we were to fly. Maps disclosing the secret target of the day were covered as we entered the room but uncovered when the briefing officer was ready to reveal the target. Colored markers represented the route we were to fly to and from the target while colored pins represented locations of anti-aircraft gun emplacements and fighter bases. The briefing officer announced the altitude we were to fly, at which check-point on the map we were to turn toward the target, and the heading we would fly over the target to drop our bombs. He announced that the mission would be led by Lt. Colonel Knapp, Captain Strong, Lt. Coles and Lt. Sullivan. Although they shared the same name, the leader, Lt. Sullivan, was not our bombardier, Lt. Sullivan. It was to be the final mission with the Fifteenth Air Force for Lt. Coles and Sullivan.

"We do not expect heavy flak or fighter attacks today and the weather will be mostly clear for the entire flight. Lt. McCain will later brief you on the weather."

The word, "flak" was often used to describe the explosion of an anti-aircraft shell that produced a small black cloud of smoke. The expression originated in Germany as an abbreviation of the German words, flieger-abwehr-kanone (FLAK), translated as "airplane defense gun". It was introduced into the vocabulary of the Allied Air Forces and used extensively during the war.

A moment before the target was announced, we became alert and leaned forward in anticipation of the briefing officer's announcement of the target. If it were a well-known dangerous target, the room would be filled with groans. If it was an unknown one or a previous 'milk-run', as easy targets were called, the room would remain silent as the officer continued his remarks. I felt relieved that our target of the day drew only silence; however, one could never be certain that any target would be a 'milk-run'. Enemy fighter groups or heavy flak often appeared where there had been none before.

Our briefing officer continued to brief us on our secondary or alternative target that would become our target if we could not reach the primary target, usually because of poor weather. He instructed his assistants to distribute copies of maps, takeoff time, rendezvous point, the serial number and location of the airplane we were to fly, and other essential information. Takeoff time was to be 0700. We were dismissed with instructions to gather our equipment and that a jeep was waiting to transport us to meet our crew at a designated airplane.

We had about an hour remaining before takeoff to assemble and organize our equipment when we arrived at the aircraft. I arranged my flying clothing and gear on the ground in the order that I would employ them. First I zipped a pair of electrically heated coveralls over my khaki uniform. Then I attached my .45 caliber pistol and holster under my right arm. I stepped into leather sheep-lined trousers as I slipped the suspenders over my shoulders, placed my feet into sheep-lined boots sufficiently large enough to cover my shoes, and slipped into a heavy leather sheep-lined jacket. Over this layer of clothing, I buckled a seat-cushion parachute and harness. I would later place a spare chest chute behind my seat which could be snapped onto my harness if a need arose to bail our of the aircraft, but the main parachute was designed to be used as a seat cushion and was permanently attached to the harness. Finally, I placed a sheep lined cap with an attached oxygen mask and ear phones over my head. I would later place a pair of leather sheep-lined gloves behind my seat to be used at colder altitudes. Next, I placed an extra pair of boots, a spare chute, gloves, metal helmet, and flak vest behind my seat. The helmet and flak vest was to be employed whenever we encountered enemy fire. The pilot and copilot seats were encased in iron and called 'coffin seats' because they suspiciously resembled an iron coffin. In order to protect the pilots, thick cast-iron plates about one foot wide had been attached to each side and above each seat. Another plate was installed behind and underneath the seat so that we were virtually seated inside an upright iron coffin. It might have been good protection from flying fragments of anti-aircraft shells, but observing a coffin each time we entered the cockpit did little to buoy our spirits.

While I made an instrument check inside the cockpit, Dave made an outside inspection of the airplane. Flight engineer, John Ribovich, checked to see that all equipment was in order and securely stowed away. He started the generator to provide power for instruments and interior lights until the engines were started and the generator was no longer needed. The navigator crawled into the nose section to arrange his navigational tools while the bombardier examined the five hundred-pound bombs hanging in the bomb bay. Russ, the radio operator, was tuning his radio bands and the gunners checked their guns. Dave and I began a pre-flight engine checklist in time to start the engines and begin our taxi a few minutes before 0700.

At the completion of a pre-flight checklist, we began to start the engines. I turned to look out my side window and thrilled to the sight of sixty B-24s around us, creating a landscape of over two hundred turning propeller windmills. The noise was deafening. It was almost 0700 as we quickly went through a taxi checklist before moving into line for takeoff. Sixty huge bombers taxiing from every direction must patiently wait in a traffic jam for a signal to move onto the taxi strip. I had never before witnessed such a huge traffic jam but when we were finally allowed onto the taxi strip behind our formation leader, we moved rather briskly toward our takeoff position. We were instructed to complete the takeoff checklist before we reached the end of the runway and to accelerate our forward movement as we turned onto the runway. It was imperative that we move quickly in order to conserve fuel for those aircraft waiting behind us for takeoff and those in the air waiting to rendezvous with us before heading toward the target. To launch and assemble sixty airplanes in the air was a very complex operation and sometimes required an hour or more. We consumed about ten percent of our 2750 gallons of fuel while taxiing, waiting for takeoff, and rendezvousing.

Our formation leader lifted from the runway ahead of us when I observed a control officer standing beside the runway on a command jeep holding a flag. Waving the flag, he signaled the airplane waiting for takeoff to begin rolling forward as the aircraft ahead cleared the runway. When our turn came for takeoff, he signaled us to start our roll. Dave replied with a traditional thumb and first finger forming an O before pushing the throttles forward. The control officer responded with a raised thumb in a "good luck" signal as we slowly gained speed down the runway. With five thousand pounds of bombs, twenty-seven hundred gallons of fuel, a full supply of ammunition, and a crew of ten airmen, our overloaded B-24 laboriously shuddered off the ground the last few feet of the entire runway.

During briefing, we were instructed to fly an assigned heading and to rendezvous with the group over a designated site on our map. Upon joining our formation, our leader continued to circle over the area waiting for our formation to be completed by those who were delayed. The group leader also continued to circle waiting for all squadron formations to form into a larger group. Bombers covered the sky like a cloud of disturbed bees from a honeycomb. We had been assigned the number four slot that was directly behind and below the formation leader. Positions number two and three would fly off the right and left wing of the leader. Number five and six would fly just above our right and left wing, and number seven, would fly behind and below us. Poor weather was an impediment to locating the formation leader after takeoff. We could keep our leader in sight as he left the runway under normal visual conditions, but with many airplanes in the sky and poor visibility, we could only circle the rendezvous area searching for him until some crew member was able to recognize the numbers painted on his aircraft. It was important that we find our leader, but it was even more essential that we avoid crashing into other aircraft. The sky was a dangerous place to be in those days, and not entirely because of the enemy. We lost almost as many airplanes in air collisions or hurried overloaded takeoffs as we lost in enemy encounters.

Subsequently we found our formation leader, snuggled into position, and waited for our group leader to turn in the direction of our target. As we climbed toward our assigned bombing altitude of twenty-five thousand feet, we maintained a loose formation. Sustaining close formation for six or eight hours would exhaust even the super-strong. Flying the number four slot was exceptionally tiring because we were exposed to propeller turbulence created by the lead plane in front of us. The turbulence made it difficult to maintain a stable position so that our wingmen could fly near us. Many times the weather would create additional turbulence.

Soon after leaving the rendezvous area, an order was given to clear all guns. All too often, machine guns jam from extreme temperatures and from other causes; consequently, it was judicious to test-fire them before flying deep into enemy territory. The entire formation fired several bursts from each gun sending a cascade of shell casings tumbling into the air below. Our slot in the formation, below and behind the three leading B-24s, made our airplane more vulnerable to colliding with shell casings ejected from above; consequently, we lagged behind the leader until the firing ceased.

We headed over the Adriatic Sea to the coast of Yugoslavia and deeper into enemy territory. Germany controlled the military defenses of Yugoslavia, and although we avoided flying over known gun emplacements, we were occasionally surprised. I ordered the crew to their gun stations after crossing the Yugoslavia coast in preparation for any surprise fighter attacks. When we approached our IP (initial point) and prepared to turn onto our designated bomb run heading, weather conditions ahead were ideal. There were only scattered clouds and the ground was plainly visible to our bombardiers while they adjusted their Norton bombsights. We saw some flak at a distance but no German fighters were in sight. To protect us from enemy fighters, a group of American P-51 fighter planes had greeted us over the coast of Yugoslavia, and like a swarm of flies, they were nervously scurrying in every direction. Nothing was more pleasing to me than sighting a group of American fighter planes waiting to escort us into enemy territory. Dave and I began to don our flak vests and metal helmets. Flak vests were made with overlapping metal strips sewn into canvas and tailored into a vest. Barely impeded by the thin aluminum covering of a B-24, shrapnel from exploding anti-aircraft shells was an ever-present danger to a bomber crew. A flak vest offered some body protection and our flak helmets somewhat shielded our heads. The iron coffin seat also partially protected the pilots' back and sides, but our legs and face were completely exposed. Whenever flak was exploding nearby, I would pull the vest up over my nose and the helmet down over my eyes leaving a small opening from which I could see ahead; nevertheless, I received little comfort. I felt as if I was naked.

As we approached the target, waist gunners scattered bales of chaff out the waist windows. We deployed chaff, narrow strips of metallic foil that deflected enemy radar, in an attempt to interfere with the accuracy of their anti-aircraft guns. After our gunners had dispensed the chaff, the entire sky seemed to sparkle like diamonds from the sun reflecting from dancing floating strips of foil.

Dave said to the bombardier,

"Pilot to bombardier, you're on PDI."

PDI are initials for Pilot Directional Indicator, an instrument that connects the autopilot to the bombsight and allows the bombardier to control the airplane with each adjustment of his bombsight. As he maneuvers the cross hairs of the bombsight to the center of the target, every adjustment moves the controls of the airplane, inexorably moving it to the precise spot that will send the bombs to the enter of the target. The pilot may override the PDI at anytime and always resumes control when the bombardier releases the bombs. Bombardier Sullivan had been ordered to release the bombs by "sight" but Dave suggested they pretend that he was controlling the airplane while he practiced sighting through his bombsight. Flying in close formation, it was necessary for the pilot to be in constant control of the aircraft. Only the lead bombardier normally employed the bombsight and other bombardiers released their bombs with a toggle switch the instant they saw the bombs drop from the lead airplane. This method of bombing was known as "pattern bombing".

Bombardier Sullivan made small adjustments to his bomb sight while he practiced maintaining the crosshairs of the bombsight centered on the target, but shortly before we arrived dead center over the target, he abandoned his bomb sight and concentrated on the bomb bay of the lead airplane. When he saw the bombs appear in the bomb bay of the lead plane, he released our bombs with a toggle switch and said,

"Bombs away!"

The moment the bombs were released our aircraft, 5000 pounds lighter, lifted as if a burst of air had pushed it upward. It was the first time I had been in the immediate area of bursting anti-aircraft bombs, and although we encountered what was considered light flak, numerous small black clouds appeared around our airplane. Because of the noise from aircraft engines, they seemed soundless and harmless, but an experienced pilot once said to me,

"You should not worry about the black clouds you can see. The ones you cannot see are the ones that will get you."

Nevertheless, I flinched each time I saw a puff of black smoke appear near us.

An instant after "bombs away", the formation leader made a steep vertical turn to the right while losing altitude and gaining speed. Maintaining a close formation, we locked our airplane onto his airplane as he turned and dived away from the target. The maneuver said to me, "now that we have dropped our bombs—it's time to get the hell outa' here!" By rapidly changing altitude and speed we were no longer a stationary target, as we had been during the bomb run. While turning away from the target, I had an unobstructed view of the target beneath us. The oil refinery was sending up black smoke from burning oil almost to our altitude—a billowing, twisting, gray mushroom cloud that looked like a tornado in reverse.

Enemy anti-aircraft gunners ceased firing at us as we turned away from the target. We could then relax and level out for an uneventful return flight. This had been my first mission; one that was called 'a milk run' with few casualties and little damage to our bombers. During our peaceful return journey, I contemplated the difference between a 'milk run' and a 'big one', a term used for any mission that encounters heavy flak, enemy fighters, and suffers many casualties. I concluded that to the dead, there was no difference between these missions. One is no less dead if killed during a "milk run".

Our formation leader flew directly over the runway at an altitude that allowed each pilot to peel away from the formation into a landing pattern. I did not see flares fired from any aircraft that signaled a request for landing priority because of wounded crew members; however, emergency staffs were always on standby to meet us upon landing. There was ever present the danger of landing accidents. I would later see much of this.

We taxied to our parking hardstand where a truck was waiting to take us to a building where we could be debriefed and stow our equipment. While waiting for debriefing, a flight surgeon sat a table in the center of the room with a stack of paper cups and bottles of rye whiskey. He called the name of our crew and signaled for us to advance and receive a shot of whiskey as he scratched our names from a list. We had several non-drinkers among our crew who offered their shots of rye to others; consequently, I enjoyed a pleasant debriefing. By accumulating information from returning crews and viewing aerial photographs, group intelligence could evaluate the success or failure of the mission. They tallied the number of planes lost, how many enemy fighters were observed, and the number of casualties. With photos of our exploding bombs during the raid and photos of the target after the smoke had cleared, they were able to draft a report to headquarters. A report that sixty-two per cent of our bombs had exploded in the target area severely disabling the Almasfuzi oil refinery was sent to headquarters, who in turn released the report to the news media. I was to learn that this was an exceptional score and that most bombing missions were not as successful. The American Air Force had adopted a strategy of utilizing heavy bombers flying at high altitudes to destroy targets that manufactured or supplied material needed by the German military. 'Strategic bombing' would ultimately severely damage the German military machine by depriving it of fuel and other supplies.

The next day headquarters released the following summary of the mission:

"The veteran team of Lt. Colonel Knapp, Captain Strong, Lt. King, Lt. Coles, and Lt. Sullivan came through with their second superior mission of the young month when they scored 62 per cent on the oil refinery at Almasfuzito, Hungary. Conditions for the attack were ideal—CAVU, (clear and visibility unlimited) weather, no fighters, and not too much flak."

Upon returning to our tent, we discussed how we might begin the next day upgrading our home. We were eager to begin making it more livable and comfortable, but alas, it was not to be. That night, our names appeared on the operational board announcing that we were to fly another mission the next morning.

MISSION #2

Ploesti Xenia Oil Refinery, Rumania

10 August 1944

"FIRST AND LAST call for breakfast! Sir! Lieutenant Thomas are you awake? Lieutenant Pettey! Breakfast in thirty minutes!"

The rasping voice of the duty officer jolted me into consciousness from my dream of the Almasfuzi oil refinery mission the previous day. It was 0330 hours; a 0530 hours briefing and a 0730 takeoff had been posted on the board. I could hear the jeep drive away as I struggled to sit upright on my canvas cot.

At 0530 hours, we waited in the briefing room. A soft rumble of muted conversations drifted over the briefing room as I sat staring at covered maps located on a stage. If I could only see through the covers:

"Attention!"

We lurched to our feet in a rigid brace.

"As you were!" The commanding officer said as he marched to the stage. He paused at the podium and silently glared at us while we resumed our seats. When order was restored, he said,

"Today, we will be visiting the Xenia oil refinery, at our old friendly target, Ploesti."

A loud groan arose from the audience as the briefing officer removed a cloth covering a map that revealed our route to the target, Ploesti,

Rumania. I understood instantly why the commanding officer announced the target rather than the briefing officer. Ploesti was a 'BIG ONE', and most of the pilots in the audience had previously flown a mission over this target or had heard about it. Among airmen, Ploesti was a famous saga of low flying Liberators and dreadful losses. All had watched movie scenes of the famous original low altitude mission and many books would be written in the future describing this awful raid. For the reader who may be unfamiliar with the 1943 mission, I will attempt to provide a brief description of the famous raid.

. . .

Ploesti is a city located forty miles north of Bucharest and is a center for oil refineries. On August 1, 1943, one hundred and seventy nine B-24 Liberators lifted off the dirt runways at Benghazi, Libya headed for an eighteen hour, 2400 mile round-trip bombing mission to Ploesti, Rumania. If properly executed, the low level mission, named "the tidal wave", would surprise the Ploesti defense by flying beneath their radar warning system permitting little advance warning, and allow the Americans to destroy the Nazi supply of oil with a minimum number of casualties—so it seemed.

The first tragedy, a portent of things yet to come, struck before the group had cleared the field. One of the Liberators from the 98th Bomb Group experienced engine failure on takeoff and crashed into a telephone pole in a dust storm created by the many Liberators taking off on unpaved runways. Carrying 600,000 pounds made up of 1000 and 2000 pound bombs, the B-24 Liberators successfully formed into groups over the Mediterranean heading for Ploesti. While planning the mission, it was decided that the bomb sight would be of no use while flying at thirty to one hundred feet above the ground at a speed of 225 miles per hour; therefore, in addition to the bombs, crews were given incendiary explosive sticks to be thrown by hand out of the airplane to start fires.

After three hours, near the coast of Albania, the groups began climbing to 10,000 feet when the second tragedy struck. The lead B-24 became unstable, plunged into the sea out of control with full crew aboard, exploded, and immediately sank. The deputy lead plane dropped out of formation and began to look for survivors. Overloaded, it was unable to regain sufficient altitude to rejoin the formation and was forced to turn back to Bengazi taking with it the only surviving navigator who had received a special briefing for the mission.

The climb proved also to be difficult for twelve other Liberators who, for various emergencies, were compelled to abort the mission.

As the remaining planes reached land, they encountered yet another problem that was soon to bring about the failure of the mission. A front had produced huge cumulus clouds from below the peaks of the Pindis Mountains up to 17,000 feet. Not able to break radio silence, the leader of the 376th Bomb Group, Colonel Keith Compton, followed by the 93rd Bomb Group, began a steep climb over the top of the clouds.

By the time the trailing three bomb groups encountered the clouds, the other two groups were out of sight. Not sure whether the leading groups had flown through or over the clouds, they chose to fly through them at 12,000 feet—high enough to avoid the mountains. The flights were now divided into two groups sixty miles apart and neither knew where the other group was.

Still another mishap was about to plague the ill-fated bombing mission. The two leading groups, the 376th and the 93rd, mistakenly turned early toward Bucharest rather than Ploesti, thirty-five miles south of the target. The succeeding groups correctly turned north toward Ploesti. Realizing their mistake, the leader of the two groups, General Ent, broke radio silence and verified that a mistake had been made. Making a steep turn to the left, the two groups were then on a correct heading traveling north to Ploesti. When they arrived at Ploesti, the flak was so intense that General Ent changed directions again believing they would attract less fire if they approached from the north. He again broke radio silence and ordered the pilots to abandon their original plan and bomb 'targets of opportunity'. This order subsequently caused chaos when one group bombed targets assigned to another.

Meanwhile, the three groups behind and separated, searched unsuccessfully over the Danube for the two lead groups. The realization that they were separated caused more confusion and delay, which in turn caused them to miss their IP before turning on their bomb run toward Ploesti. Some even flew to Bucharest before turning back toward Ploesti.

Despite the chaos, the two leading groups mounted a bomb attack on Ploesti at altitudes from thirty to one hundred feet, and although most bombs were released, only a small number hit their intended targets. The liberators were met with such intense flak and small arms fire that, "airplanes were going down left and right" as one crewmember described it. Some even found it necessary to gain altitude to fly over buildings.

When the later groups arrived, they did not know that those ahead had already initiated an attack. It was impossible for them to know if other Liberators were flying hidden in the smoke and fire, where cables, hidden chimneys were located, or how many forty-five second delayed action bombs would be waiting thirty feet beneath them. Although it would have been justifiable to turn back, the leaders maintained their bomb run into the inferno. For this courageous action, they were awarded the Medal of Honor. Altogether, there were five Medal of Honor awards granted to participants of the 'Tidal Wave' mission that day.

Of the one hundred and seventy-nine Liberators which began the mission, only one hundred and sixty-five attacked Ploesti, forty-three were lost to anti-aircraft or fighter planes, and twenty-three were forced down in Turkey or other emergency fields. Only ninety-nine returned to their base and of those, fifty-eight had heavy damage. Of the original one hundred and seventy-nine bombers, there were only forty-one indeed fortunate B-24s that escaped with little or no damage.

. . .

Our commanding officer continued,

"These circles indicate where one thousand anti-aircraft guns are located around Ploesti. This will be our sixth bombing mission of Ploesti and as you already know, it is a heavily fortified target. Our job is to destroy Hitler's source of oil and shut down his air force, tanks, and the transportation of his supplies. The briefing officer will now give you more information on gun emplacements and what you may encounter over the target. Good luck and God bless."

Upon finishing his briefing, the colonel turned away from the podium and walked toward the door as we jerked to attention.

Orientation continued with more target information and expected weather conditions, but I was unable to remove the voice of the commanding officer from my mind as he said,

"These circles indicate where one thousand guns are located."

Although this was only my second mission, I understood that one thousand guns arranged around a small target area would result in heavy and deadly fire. It would be later that I fully understood just how much the phrase, "heavily fortified", was an understatement when describing Ploesti. The briefing concluded with a prayer by the group chaplain. Our crew then assembled at the 'Shady Lady', to prepare for a 07:30 takeoff and a group rendezvous that would lead us to our destiny with Ploesti.

The flight to Ploesti in good weather, with no sign of enemy fighters and only an occasional burst of anti-aircraft smoke in the distance, was uneventful. We gradually climbed to our bombing altitude of 22,000 feet and closed our loosely spread formation as we drew nearer to our IP for our bomb run. The entire flight had been so repetitive that I had relaxed and the thought of one thousand guns had almost lapsed from my consciousness. Far away I began to notice something that looked like a dark storm cloud. As we drew nearer I could see that indeed it was some sort of a storm cloud rising from ground level up to our altitude of 22,000 feet. As we approached even nearer I was able to see that it was more akin to black smoke from burning oil. There were several groups ahead of us flying into the smoke when I suddenly recognized the distinguishing characteristics of flak, a sudden puff of black smoke following a dull flash of orange. The sky contained such a mass of these individual wisps of smoke that they assumed the form of one great, flat, black cloud—flat because the shells were exploding at our altitude. Beneath this high cloud of flak smoke, columns of black clouds created from previous bombings, curled upward to join the cloud of flak. Dave and I put on our flak helmets and began helping each other with our flak vests. In spite of the iron coffin seats, helmet, and flak vest, I suddenly felt hopelessly exposed.

At the time we reached the IP, we had entered the cloud of flak and began witnessing several Liberators in flames. We had previously been instructed to count the number of parachutes and identify all crippled aircraft; however, I was doggedly engrossed in assisting Dave fly our aircraft. I had little time to count survivors. Momentarily, I glimpse out my side window and observed enough to convince me that it was impossible to fly unscathed through such a maelstrom of exploding flak. I saw small orange flashes of fire followed by varying jolts and bumps to the "Shady Lady" as the shells detonated around us. Puffs of smoke would appear an instant before we flew through them, like the bow of a boat breaking through water. Many of the explosions were so near I flinched and waited for the imminent blast that never came. I again recalled something an experienced pilot had once said to me, "if you see the puff of smoke, you are already out of danger. It's the flak that you don't see that gets you."

Almost immediately after our bombs were released, our flight leader turned the formation away from the target into a precipitous turning decent in an effort to evade the anti-aircraft shells being fired at us. Usually enemy gunners continued firing barrages at our former altitude intended for following formations, but gunners at Ploesti were so numerous and accurate, their puffs of black smoke followed us like a swarm of bees while we dived away from the target. Anti-aircraft artillery employed two methods of firing at enemy planes: aim at individual airplanes, or fire a pattern, called a barrage. Ploesti employed both. A barrage of fire discharged from 1000 guns created such a voluminous pattern, evasive action was almost impossible but it seemed that fusillades of explosions followed us regardless of our direction or altitude. It was only after we were out of their range that we could relax and assess the damage to our aircraft.

By intercom, I called each member of the crew to inquire about injuries and if they could observe any damage to the aircraft. Fortunately none of the crew was injured and none of the aircraft controls were damaged; however, after landing we were able to count over fifty small holes in the "Shady Lady". The debriefing procedure was the same as described before—the good news was that the jiggers of rye whiskey were not depleted.

The following is the official report released by the 15th Air Force:

Mission #79
10 August 1944
Target: Ploesti Xenia Oil Refinery, Rumania
"Back again to the guns out in the fields at the old familiar target, the Xenia Oil Refinery, Ploesti. Back again to the smoke screens, high towering black clouds from the burning oil, and to pathfinder bombing. The results: no score:

photographs which show nothing but smoke; thirteen planes with holes in them. Crewmembers who had become accustomed to results like those at Blechhammer and at Ploesti frequently wondered how much or how little damage they were really inflicting on these targets."

"Our Home"

MAKING A "HOME"

AFTER TWO STRESSFUL missions, the crew had been granted a free day. We could now concentrate on making our tent more comfortable. Since moving into our tent, I had slept inside a sleeping bag on an empty mattress cover placed on an uncomfortable folding cot. The damp ground served as our floor. We had no heat and were informed by those who had experienced a winter season in Italy that winters can be very cold. My tent-mates and I agreed that we should first install a floor and that we should begin by inspecting tents of our neighbors in order to learn how to make one. We found that they had built their floors with what they called "tufee brick", a concrete brick that was plentiful on the air base and best of all, free. I never discovered the significance of the word tufee but I was grateful to the Air Force for making them available for any who might want them. An armload at a time, we carried and stacked the bricks outside our tent where they would be available to lay side by side and end to end on the dirt floor of our tent.

My next objective was to make a comfortable bed. Our neighbors slept on a straw mattress made by filling a mattress cover with dry weeds growing in a field bordering our living area. Pulling the weeds by hand, I filled my mattress cover and placed it on my folding cot before covering it with a sleeping bag. The comfort of the bed was limited but it was somewhat cushier than the bare cot and it would prove to be much warmer in the cold winter. Sleeping on it, however, dispelled any notions I might have entertained about a straw mattress being a comfortable bed. It proved to be a scratchy, lumpy, and uncomfortable bed that smelled of dust and weeds. The weeds pricked my skin through the thin mattress material until they became compressed. The mattress then became firm and hard but my sleeping bag offered some relief.

Our Next objective was to install electrical wires and replace the temporary extension cords we were using. Bomb Group headquarters had installed light poles and electric wires over most of the living area; consequently, we were able to place an electric line into our tent within a short time. We were then able to walk on a dry brick floor, sleep on a warm uncomfortable bed, and enjoy the amenities of lights and radio. Our next important task was to prepare for the cold months by furnishing our tent with stove and brick walls to warm it. The following night our names again did not appear on orders and allowed us additional time to make improvements to our home.

We had inspected our neighbor's stoves and found that they had without exception installed the same type of stove: one half of a metal barrel set on a brick foundation with the open side down. A small opening was cut near the floor to serve as a door and a stovepipe was inserted into the top of the barrel. The end of the stovepipe extended outside the top of the tent so that it could funnel smoke outside. Aluminum tubes from disabled aircraft served as a plumbing system, channeling 100-octane gasoline by gravity from a 50-gallon drum mounted on an elevated platform behind the tent. The flowing gasoline was controlled by a petcock located inside the metal drum. The petcock was essentially a valve to increase, decrease or block the flow of gasoline. In order to light the stove, one held a match at the end of the tubing inside the drum and released a tiny drip of gasoline by slightly opening the petcock valve. If executed slowly, skillfully, and carefully only a small flame would ensue. As the petcock was opened, the fire increased and heated the drum. If one allowed any gasoline or fumes to collect in the stove before inserting the burning match, the risk of an explosion was imminent. Often on a cold night, a "whomp!" sound could be heard as some neighbor lit his stove; nevertheless, we understood the enormity of the danger and acted with caution. There were several tents destroyed by fire as a result of carelessness, however.

It soon became evident that we did not possess the skills needed to install a stove, and that it would be reasonable to pay someone to install it. We found a sergeant willing to hook up the stove for a price and upon returning from a later mission, found it installed in our tent. The necessary aluminum tubing had been fitted into place, and a 50-gallon drum filled with gasoline had been mounted on a platform behind our tent. Our only remaining chore was to build a brick wall before winter set in. This endeavor must wait however, for we found our names on mission orders the night of 12 August.

MISSION #3

Genoa Gun Positions, Italy

August 13,1944

WE WERE INFORMED at briefing that our target for the day was a gun emplacement south of Genoa, one of the most important Italian Mediterranean harbors that provided anchorage for ships supplying German and Northern Italian armed forces. As the briefing officer informed us that we could expect light flak over the target, there was a sigh of relief from the pilots. There were rumors that another allied invasion of Europe was imminent. Upon being assigned the tactical mission of bombing gun emplacements on the Mediterranean coast, we were sure that the invasion would soon take place near Genoa. Later, as our crew assembled at the aircraft preparing for takeoff, we discussed the forthcoming invasion of Northern Italy. The rumor of an armed invasion was accurate, but the location of the invasion proved to be incorrect.

Our formation of bombers encountered no enemy fighters and little flak during the flight to Genoa. The weather was ideal, but when we arrived at the Initial Point and began our bomb run, flak increased. A moment before releasing our bombs, a B-24 piloted by Lt. Crain in the formation ahead of us exploded and embedded bits of the airplane into other nearby B-24s. Upon returning to their air base, pieces of the B-24 were found lodged in engine cowlings, wings, and fuselages of the formation. It was believed that an anti-aircraft shell had exploded directly on the fuse of one of the bombs prior to its being released from the airplane. Despite the clear weather, only 6.4 per cent of the bombs found the target. We approached the gun emplacements from the landside rather than from the sea and the bombardiers experienced difficulty locating the emplacements.

Our return flight from the target to our base was routine and uneventful. The day after headquarters had studied our debriefing statements and reconnaissance photographs, the following caustic announcement was released:

"Target: Genoa Gun Positions, Italy"
"Having failed to knock out its target on the 12th of the month, the Group tried again on the 13th with even poorer results. It seemed impossible for the Group to identify the assigned gun positions."

Although the mission had been described as a "milk run", it was a disaster for Lt. Crain and his crew. It was also a failed mission.

. . .

As I thought about the results of my first three missions, I began to question if the small amount of damage we had inflicted on the enemy merited the loss of lives I had witnessed. I had been led to believe that in war, lives were exchanged for winning a noble conflict against dark forces for a noble cause. When I weighed the cost of ten lives with the gain of only six-percent of 480 bombs finding their target, I could only conclude that war is a horrid extravagance—that both lives and materials are expendable and insignificant. To add to the tragedy, there was no evidence that the few bombs that found their way to the target inflicted any damage to the gun emplacements. This conviction would only become stronger as I observed more tragedies of war.

However, strange things do indeed happen in war as we discovered many weeks later. After the allies had captured Genoa, one member of our bomb group visiting Genoa reported that the gun emplacements had disappeared, leaving only a huge crater. There was no evidence that our 28 bombs had inflicted any damage—but who will ever know?

MISSION #4

St. Raphael, France

14 August 1944

WE WERE ADVISED during our 0500 hours briefing that we were to again bomb gun positions at Genoa near Frejus, France. I was convinced that the landing of the second invasion of Europe would take place at Genoa soon, because today was the third consecutive day that our group had bombed gun emplacements at Genoa. The missions seemed to indicate that we were attempting to destroy gun emplacements along the beach area in preparations for an amphibious landing of allied forces. We did not know how much damage we had inflicted in the preceding missions. Weather forecast predicted clear unlimited vision over the target area and the briefing officer estimated limited enemy defensive anti-aircraft fire.

The rendezvous and flight to the target indeed occurred in perfect weather and without event. When we arrived at the IP, I saw miles of beaches and an occasional burst of flak as we engaged in the bomb run. It was a "milk run", even sometimes boring, but considering the last "milk run" and the disaster to the Lt. Crain crew, I was happy to receive credit for another combat mission with such little danger. I had begun to count off each of the 35 missions we were expected to fly— this mission was number four—31 missions to go.

Headquarters released the following report the next day:

"14 August 1944
Target: Genoa Gun Positions near Frejus, France
When the Group was assigned its third consecutive tactical

mission against coastal gun positions, speculation ran rampant as to when the invasion would start, and as to whether or not it would be aimed at the Genoa area of Italy or at the Marseilles area of France. Lt. Colonel Knapp, flying this mission with a new flight leader crew, turned in his third consecutive superior mission of the month when 64.5 per cent of the bombs were dropped within 1000 feet of the assigned coastal gun positions on the beach near Frejus, France. Conditions for this mission were ideal."

TARGET #5

St. Raphael, France

15 August 1944

A SPECIAL BRIEFING was called for the afternoon of 14 August for all staff officers and lead crews assigned to fly a mission the following day. We were notified of this unusual activity when we landed, leading to speculation that something big was about to happen. I found my name on flying orders the evening of the 14th with instructions to attend a briefing the next morning at 04:30 and to be prepared for takeoff at 06:30.

It was a very subdued and tense group of pilots that waited for the briefing officer and commander to begin the briefing. Our commander casually sauntered to the stage, turned and allowed a dramatic moment to pass before saying,

"Gentlemen, you are about to participate in one of the most important events of this war, the invasion of southern France. At daylight this morning, troops landed at the beach of Frejus, France, and my reports indicate that things are going well. I will now let Major Seagraves give you more information."

This was it! We had speculated for some time about a second invasion of Europe, and now it was here, only it was not Genoa; it was southern France at Frejus south of Marseilles. Major Seagraves began the briefing session,

"I must begin by saying that today you will participate in one of the most difficult and dangerous bombing missions that you will ever have assigned to you. You will be supporting troops already on the beach, dropping bombs that must land more than 100 yards from them or you will be aiding the Germans by killing our own troops. You can see areas of the beach marked on the map where you will be expected to drop your 100-pound general-purpose bombs. Our troops will be here in this marked square, and you will bomb here in this colored square. At the top of your bomb rack are two bombs containing propaganda leaflets addressed to German troops telling them to surrender—that they are defeated."

While I read and executed the checklist for takeoff, somehow in the excitement created by our participation in the invasion of southern France, I had failed to call on the engineer to make sure the controls were properly working. All flight controls are locked in the neutral position when the aircraft is parked so that wind will not damage them. Sometimes, while taxiing in severe winds, we would temporarily lock the flight controls as a protection against the wind until we reached the end of the runway. Because flight controls do not interfere with other controls used to taxi, the pilot may not even be aware that they are locked during taxi. As Dave ordered full throttles for takeoff, I saw the control lever in the up position and immediately released it as we rolled down the runway. Dave, concentrating on the takeoff, was unaware that the controls were locked. If I had not instantly released the lever, Dave would have discovered that he was unable to fly the aircraft from the runway. It was a tense and embarrassing moment for me as I thought about the crash that surely would have followed, but we safely lifted from the runway and joked about it later.

The following bulletin was released the next day. Although it was well written and an accurate description of the mission, I must believe that the writer had another agenda in mind. Did the lavish praise for certain people speed their promotion to the next higher military rank? I suspect that a "good old boy" network might have been in place.

"Mission #83 461 Bomb Group

15 August 1944

Target: Frejus Beach, France

During the afternoon of the 14th, the "hot information" on the big push came down through channels. "H" Hour of "D" Day was to be the break of dawn the morning of 15 August. The invasion was to be aimed at the southern coast of France. Missions of the Fifteenth Air Force in the support of the invasion were four in number: (1) To cause maximum destruction to enemy coast and beach defenses within the assault area; (2) To isolate the battlefield by destruction of remaining rail and road bridges across the Rhone River up to its junction with the Iser River as well as those across the Iser and Durance Rivers; (3) To block defiles and rail lines running through the Alps from Iser River Southward; and (4) To drop propaganda leaflets from the water's edge to about 30 miles inland. The field order for the mission revealed that many of the Groups were scheduled to hit their targets at the break of dawn. This was the explanation of why the planes of the Groups of the 304th Wing had been for weeks disturbing the sleep of the 461st bomb group with their constant night takeoffs, formation flying, and landings. Target time assigned to the 461st was 1210 o'clock. The target was a section of beach in front of the town of Frejus and just to the left of a concentration of friendly troops that were scheduled to be ashore.

As soon as Colonel Glantzberg saw the field order and the annexes which accompanied it, he made his decisions rapidly. The Group would attack its target with five boxes staggered to the left. The Colonel would lead the first box and a squadron commander would lead one of each of the other four boxes. All Group and Squadron Operations Officers, Navigators, and Bombardiers would fly. Lt. Hawes, the Deputy Group Commander, would be the only flying officer of the Group or Squadron Staffs not to fly. Captain John Specht, probably the most outstanding original flight leader left in the group, would be the Lead Pilot; Major Marian Pruitt, long believed to be without equal in the Fifteenth Air Force, would be the Lead Navigator; 1st Lt. Jack H. King, formerly the Bombardier on Captain Strong's outstanding crew and currently the hottest Bombardier in the Group as well as acting Group Bombardier, would be the Lead Bombardier; 1st Lt. John W. Coles, a Squadron Navigator and a veteran of many missions on which he had done pilotage from the nose turret of the lead plane, would be the Pilotage Navigator; 1st Lt. Leonard C. Gizelba, the prima-donna of the Mickey operators, would fly in the Lead Pathfinder plane.

The decision of the Commanding officer to permit all but one of his flying staff officers to participate in this mission was an outstanding example of the methods he continually used in making every deserving officer and man feel that he was an important personage in this Group. Special Briefing was held in the afternoon, which was attended by all flying staff officers, as well as by all of the Flight Leader crews who were to participate in the mission.

Conditions for the mission could not have been better. In the complete absence of enemy fighters and flak, with CAVU weather, with all Flights in formation, with many friendly vessels in the water near the target, and with many friendly troops on the ground near the target, the Group did an excellent job of spraying the assigned section of landing beach with 100 pound general purpose bombs. On the top rack of each plane were two bombs which carried propaganda leaflets addressed to the enemy personnel.

All crews returned to the base without incident."

. . .

When the mission orders were posted that evening, I was heart-ened to know that I would not be flying the next day. Flying under normal conditions is somewhat tiring but combat flying in formation while remaining alert to other aircraft who may be dangerously near, and intently looking for enemy fighters is particularly exhausting. We had flown five missions in seven days and I was beginning to feel the strain. During the war, pilots were expected to fly so long as they were needed and airplanes were available. As a result, many suffered combat fatigue: a decline in judgment, poor memory, careless mistakes, inat-tention and poor judgment—a lethal combination for a pilot. Later, airlines would recognize that flying under these conditions can be dan-gerous to passengers and crew; consequently, they restricted the num-ber of hours pilots may fly each week. During the war however, pilots and airplanes were expendable and disposable. Our only recreation was to read, listen to a radio, play cards, and drink at the squadron officer's club. I have never cared for playing cards, and the city of Cerignola had little to offer. Drinking became the diversion of choice for most of us. In order to protect our crew and ourselves, we honored the unwritten rule that a pilot refrain from drinking alcohol eight hours before flight time.

The officer's club was part of the operations building that at one time had been a farmhouse. The Air Force had appropriated many farms in southern Italy to use as air bases. Runways were built in open fields, barns were used as storage facilities, farmhouses were converted into headquarter offices, operation offices, mess halls, recreation clubs and various other uses. Our squadron had converted a farmhouse near our tent into the 766th Squadron operation offices, officer's mess and officer's recreation room. The second floor was remade into several operation offices where orders were posted and squadron business was conducted. The first floor had been changed into an officer's dining room and recreation club and bar. Other farm buildings had been converted into similar squadron operation offices and all together, made up the 461st Bomb Group. Headquarters for the 461st was located in yet another group of farm buildings. The airstrip used by the 461st Bomb Group was named Torretta airfield, located about seven miles south of Cerignola.

Cerignola was a dusty, dirty little city that American airmen avoided when seeking excitement. As a result of heavy damage from bombs and the 15th Air Force occupation of most of their farmland, the prewar farmers and city businessmen of Cerignola had largely disappeared. The remaining inhabitants were either without a place to go, were too poor to leave or too uneducated to be resourceful. As a result, the remaining population attempted to maintain a meager existence by maintaining small shops and businesses or working as menial laborers for the Air Force. Some were so desperately impoverished they resorted to begging and stealing from soldiers. After one trip into town I vowed that I would only visit the city when en route to another destination. The Air Force provided transportation for airmen by scheduled trucks equipped with wooden benches from each air base into Cerignola. The road into town was unpaved, full of potholes and dusty. We were forced to hold onto the side of the truck to avoid being thrown out and my kidneys received a terrible beating from the back of the benches during each trip. When we arrived at Cerignola, we were instantly surrounded by poverty stricken Italian children begging for gum or candy. They had learned to say, "Hey Joe! Got any candy?" Italian children called all American soldiers "Joe". The populace of the city appeared to be disheartened, listless, and I suspect, resentful of us for many very good reasons. We had bombed them, destroyed their city, destroyed their economy and caused suffering though out their countryside; nevertheless, Italians favored us more than the Germans. The German soldier had generally treated their Italian allies with disdain, whereas most Americans treated them with more compassion and friendliness. I believe another cause of their fondness was because almost every Italian family could boast of a relative living in the U. S. Most other soldiers and I bought candy at the PX before visiting an Italian town and distributed it to the children. By giving out candy, the American soldier not only fed the "sweet tooth" of children, they also impressed the population with their generosity—an image that many Italians remember to this day.

Rather than spend our rare off-days in Cerignola, we thought it best that we build the walls of our tent. Not knowing when we would be ordered to resume combat flying, we could only work one day at a time and leave the work unfinished when we were ordered to fly a mission. We began by stacking bricks beside our tent, mixing cement, and laying a foundation for the walls. We planned to build the walls about three feet in height so that the canvas flaps or walls of the tent could be attached to the outside of the brick wall forming a shelter from the cold wind. Our labor was interrupted after only one day because our names appeared on orders with instructions to report for briefing the next day.

MISSION # 6

Ploesti, Rumania

17 August 1944

A S THE BRIEFING officer announced our target, a familiar groan rose from the audience. As a Ploesti veteran, I now had earned the right to moan with the others. I had been blessed with a few free days and two consecutive milk runs since my last Ploesti raid and had temporarily forgotten that I was in a deadly war. I think the correct term for such memory is "compartmentalization", or being able to store certain memories and temporarily close the door. The announcement of our target opened the door. The thought of Ploesti flooded my head causing my stomach to tighten, my breath to shorten, and a shadow to engulf the room. I knew there would be no "milk run" that day—rather I would be a sitting target for 1000 guns.

The flight to the IP was temporarily interrupted when the lead airplane was forced to abort the mission because of mechanical problems. Due to inexperience, the deputy flight leader, who had assumed the position of flight leader, flew too fast and several formations behind us were unable to catch up. We were flying the number three slot in the lead formation and as a result, we had accelerated with him and had been able to match his air speed.

At the IP I could see the same ominous black cloud of flak hanging over the target and thought again that it was impossible for any airplane to survive such a cataclysm. I lowered my flak helmet over my eyes, pulled my flak vest up to my chin and pushed my body against the back of by coffin seat. I was hoping to gain as much protection as I could from flying metal that I knew was sure to follow. I could see rivulets of sweat streaming down Dave's face. Our plane shuddered several times from nearby explosions and we seemed to suspend in mid-air as I heard the bombardier calmly announce,

"Bombs away!"

The formation then quickly rolled into an accelerated dive to escape the anti-aircraft guns. Flying beyond the range of deadly fire, the return flight was uneventful.

Upon landing, we counted several holes in the Shady Lady and found a jagged piece of shrapnel about the size of a man's hand. It had pierced the fuselage, traveled between the legs of a waist gunner and struck his ammo-belt; furthermore, several cartridges in the belt were bent and damaged beyond repair. Fortunately the gunner was unharmed.

The 461st Bomb Group Headquarters released the following bulletin:

> Mission #84
> 17 August 1944
> Target: Ploesti Romana Americana Oil Refinery, Rumania
> With the invasion of southern France from the Mediterranean now successfully under way, the Fifteenth Air Force swung back for targets to sources of German oil. The target assigned to the 461st Group was the Romana Americana Oil Refinery at Ploesti, Romania. This target was the largest and most important of all the vital oil installations at Ploesti. This was the target that the Group had failed to reach on 22 July, when the formation was stopped short of its objective by flak.
>
> This mission was the seventh to be flown by this Group to Ploesti. Although no one knew it at the time, this was destined to be the last mission to be flown by this Group

against this first priority target which had long since been recognized by all United Nations as one of the most important and well defended target areas possessed by the enemy. On 30 August 1944, what was left of the Ploesti oil supply and industry was captured by the Russian Army.

Despite the fact that it took a lot of explaining on the part of some of the twelve crews who were early returns from this mission, in many ways the mission was the most successful ever flown by this Group against a Ploesti target. The 19 Planes that made it over the target dropped 45.6 per cent of their 146 five hundred pound RDX bombs within 100 feet of the briefed aiming point. Numerous hits were scored in the tank farm at the northwest corner of the refinery; one string of bombs fell across the center of the refinery with four direct hits on the storage tanks in that area which resulted in large fires; and the distillation units, the boiler house, and some of the administration buildings were also hit.

No fighters were encountered. With CAVU weather at the target, the master anti-aircraft gunners, who had been getting plenty of practice all summer, were up to par with their effort. As a result, fourteen of the nineteen planes over the target were hit and the one flown by 2nd Lt. Thomas C. Moore failed to return from this mission.

Most of the twelve planes which returned early from the mission were those which had been flying in the rear positions of the various flights. When Lt. Colonel Hawes was compelled by mechanical failure to abandon the Lead position in the formation, the lead was taken over by the Deputy Leader, Captain Ryder. This was the first mission that Captain Ryder had led. Due to his inexperience plus the fact that his plane was not accurately calibrated, he maintained too high an air speed en route to the target. As a result, the "tail end Charlie" planes were unable to climb and maintain position in the formation.

. . .

And so the saga of Ploesti ended—I participated in this, the seventh and last of the Ploesti missions which had been launched a year before. On August 1, 1943, 179 B-24 Liberators departed Benghazi, Libya to set in motion a series of Ploesti bombings by first attempting to bomb at tree top level. Since then, airmen who parachuted from disabled bombers during these raids were taken prisoners and placed in a schoolhouse near the oil refinery. They witnessed at close range the daytime bombings of 500 to 700 bombers of the 15th Air Force and the terrifying night missions of the English Royal Air Force. The prisoners of war were never touched by either the American or English bombers but when it became apparent that the fall of Ploesti was imminent, Hitler ordered the bombing of Bucharest. On the 24, 25, and 26th of August thirty German Suuka and Junker bombers dive-bombed the school prison killing five American Prisoners and wounding many others. On August 24, 1944 Romania surrendered and a few days later, August 30, Soviet ground troops entered the ruins of Ploesti. In addition to the 1000 anti-aircraft guns placed around the refinery, a series of pipelines had been cleverly constructed to connect all oil tanks so that whenever any were bombed, their oil could be emptied into other tanks. The most interesting discovery however, was two replicates of Ploesti built to deceive our bombardiers.

. . .

During our two free days between missions six and seven, we were able to finish our brick wall—the task of winterizing our tent was complete! We had installed electricity, a dangerous 100 octane gas stove, a brick floor with an occasional half inch opening between bricks (none of us claimed to be brick masons), and a reasonably level brick wall to our tent. The openings between our floor bricks offered a wonderful ashtray for our cigarettes, but the floor was dry and never muddy. Although we lacked the skills and innovative talent of some other officers, the tent was sufficiently warm and snug. We had observed some examples of exceptional skills used in other tents, but the one I remember most vividly was a mechanical footlocker. A mechanical device that, when activated by an electric switch, would roll a footlocker along a track from under a bed and open. By activating the switch again, the locker would close and return to its original place under the bed. The genius that had created the moving footlocker had also created other devices, but none equaled the footlocker. Both enlisted and officer crewmembers from all over the 461 Bomb Group visited his tent to marvel at his inventions. I do not remember his name or what happened to him; I can only believe that if he survived the war there must certainly exist many patents issued in his name.

MISSION # 7

Szolnok, Hungary

20 August 1944

AT 0315 HOURS on the morning of August 20th, the duty officer woke us to prepare for our takeoff scheduled for 0715. After a breakfast of powered eggs and dehydrated mashed potatoes tasting of sawdust, we climbed into the rear bed of a truck to be transported to headquarters and briefing. The road was unpaved and rough causing us to sway in unison like seaweeds oscillating in a sea current. I sat in the darkness, leaning forward with elbows resting on knees, silent, eyes closed, waiting stoically for whatever fate might bring that day.

The briefing officer stepped to the podium and announced that our target would be Szolnok, Hungary Air Base. The air base stored many enemy airplanes in dispersal areas and hangers that we would attempt to destroy. Our airplanes were loaded with fragmentation bombs that on impact would spread metal fragments over a large area. He informed us that we could anticipate light anti-aircraft activity, but to be prepared for enemy fighter attacks. This was the first time we were informed to expect enemy fighters; although, during every briefing thus far we were warned to remain alert for them.

There was light flack during the mission, an absence of fighter planes and another "milk run" added to my mission credits. That night I was lulled asleep by incessantly repeating, "Seven down and twenty-eight more missions to go".

Headquarters released a bulletin the next day:

20 August, 1944

Target: Szolnok Airdrome, Hungary

"On the frag mission of 20 August against the airdrome at Szolnok, Hungary, Lt. Colonel Knapp turned in his fourth consecutive highly successful mission of the month as Group leader. The bomb pattern started at the center of the south dispersal area and continued southeast across the target with an even pattern of strikes. Seven enemy aircraft received direct hits and near misses were scored on three others. The weather was good except for haze; the flak was light, inaccurate, and heavy; and there was no enemy fighter opposition. Only one plane was damaged. All returned safely from the mission."

. . .

We enjoyed two more free days before our eighth combat mission. There were no urgent tasks remaining to make our tent comfortable; therefore, for the first time since arrival, I was free to explore. My tent mates chose to remain on base, to relax, read, or sleep, but I, the restless one, wanted to see more of southern Italy. Since I was not interested in Cerignola, the next city a short distance away, Foggia beckoned me. A regularly scheduled truck operated between Cerignola and my squadron, but there was no scheduled transportation between cities. There were, however, many military trucks traveling the highways and their drivers willingly offered servicemen transportation. I found that I rarely waited more than fifteen minutes before a military vehicle would stop in response to my hitchhiking thumb.

Foggia, like most Italian cities had been partially destroyed by war, and as a result, there was insufficient money to repair roads, damaged buildings or parks. It was down-at-heel, dirty and depressing. I walked for a while observing the sad state of maintenance and then decided to visit the officer's facilities around the city. I was satisfied that I had seen enough of Foggia.

MISSION # 8

Mardersdorf, Austria

23 August 1944

AT 0500 HOURS on August 23rd, we were awakened for breakfast and transported to the briefing room where we were informed that our target was Markersdorf Air Base, St. Polten, Austria. Our aircraft was loaded with fragmentation bombs to damage and destroy aircraft parked on the airfield. We were briefed to expect heavy flak and enemy fighter attacks—our "milk runs" seemed to have ceased.

After our rendezvous, the formations flew without event from southern Italy to the border of northern Italy and Austria where P-5l fighter escorts were waiting for us. Hairs on my arms stood up as I recognized hundreds of American fighter planes below us with tail markings of every imaginable description and color. I was able to distinguish a group of P-51s, some with red tails and others with a checkerboard design that were squadrons from a famous black fighter group, the only black pilots in the Air Force at that time. They were called the "Schwartze Vogelmenshen" (Black Birdmen) by the Germans who both feared and respected them. White American bomber crews fondly referred to them as "The Black Red Tail Angels" or "Checkerboard Angels" because of the identifying paint on their aircraft tail assemblies. They were our protectors who had gained a reputation for not losing bombers to enemy fighters while providing fighter escort on bombing missions. Known today as "The Tuskegee Airmen", they produced the first black general of the U.S. armed forces and have monuments to their honor in the Air Force Museum at Patterson Air Force Base and the Air Force Academy in Colorado Springs, Colorado.

"Fighters at three o'clock!", someone shouted over the intercom.

"I see them, over the right wing! Here they come!"

At that moment I forgot about the fighter escort and adjusted my comforting flak helmet and vest. The top turret guns began to chatter as the flight engineer fired at an approaching enemy BF-109. An instant later he was joined by the rattle of the right waist guns. We were engaged in the bomb run and unable to maneuver our airplane to evade the fighters; we could only fly in a stable flight path in the direction of the target so that the bomb load could, at the correct moment, direction, altitude and speed, be released. We were sitting targets for both anti-aircraft guns and enemy fighters. The next moment I witnessed an event that made me ill. A German FW-190 suddenly appeared from below the nose of our aircraft and within a few seconds, released two rockets into a B-24 ahead of us. He then rolled upside down and disappeared in a dive underneath our airplane. It occurred so suddenly, our gunners had insufficient time to react or to fire. I could distinguish the German pilot as he rolled over because he appeared only a few yards ahead of the nose of our airplane. Instantly, the B-24 ahead exploded into a fireball and began a downward spiral. Only a few parachutes opened underneath the revolving inferno but even more terrifying, some of the parachutes and clothing of the airmen were on fire.

"Fighters at six o'clock!" Someone shouted over the intercom.

"I see something that looks like a flock of buzzards!" The tail-gunner shouted.

"OK I got 'em covered!" Someone said.

"Here he comes at five o'clock!"

"I think I got that one, did anyone see it go down?" The flight engineer asked from the top turret.

"Yeah, I saw it smoking and going down," replied another.

"Burning B-24 (note: Pilot in Cockpit)"

By that time, the sky was filled with American fighter airplanes. I could also see many German FW-190 and BF-109s fighters, alleged to be the best German fighters of that time. Like disturbed hornets they were locked in mortal combat with our fighter escorts, chasing, diving, and spinning away in every direction.

"Bombs away",

After what had seemed an eternity flying a straight and level bomb run we were now free to depart this anguishing scene. The words had barely left the bombardier's mouth when the formation leader wrenched his bomber into a turning dive away from the exploding target and bursting anti-aircraft shells. We followed him closely and began regrouping a few miles from the target. Because they were busy defending themselves against our fighter escort, enemy fighters did not follow us. After releasing our bombs and returning to safe territory, the gunners usually gathered in the waist of the aircraft for a smoke and a chat, but that day, all remained silently at their station during most of the return flight.

"Ball turret gunner to pilot, there is a bandit B-17 following us. Over."

"Roger, keep me posted on his location. Out."

I was not concerned, nor was Dave. It was not unusual to see friendly disabled airplanes that had been unable to keep up with their formation, limping home alone while discarding equipment overboard. Moreover, we had heard stories about Germans rebuilding American airplanes from crashed airplanes. In order to relay altitude and air speed information to their anti-aircraft guns, they would sometimes fly near a formation of U.S. airplanes disguised as an American airplane.

"Waist gunner to pilot, he seems to be catching up with us. Over."

"Pilot to crew, can anyone see any markings on the nose or tail?"

I could see the black B-17 flying at a distance behind our right wing. It had gradually moved from behind us to a position more parallel but still about a mile away. Although I could not identify any markings other than a white tail, I was reasonably sure that it was an allied bomber. Identification markings were sometimes difficult to interpret because many allied nations used American manufactured B-24 and B-17 bombers. On the other hand, a silver star on the fuselage always identified U.S. aircraft.

I said, "Dave, I believe he is closing in on us."

Dave replied, "Pilot to crew, have your guns ready to fire if I give the order. John, give him a warning shot across his front nose—Over".

"Roger", he said as he fired a burst of machine gun shells directly across the path of the bomber. Other airplanes in our formation began firing warning shots at the same time. We watched intently to determine what effect the warning shots would have on the B-17: would he continue to move in closer, would he retain his position or would he go away? I was troubled with the thought that perhaps the crew was a group of scared, inexperienced Americans who had lost their radio and could not communicate but needed the security of other American airplanes. I did not like the idea of shooting an allied crew out of the sky; however, the airplane incrementally moved nearer our formation.

"Pilot to crew, if he gets any closer to us, be ready to fire on him."

"Black B-17 flying south with a formation of B-24s on your left. Do you read me?" Dave waited for a response.

"Black B-17, if you read my respond wag your wings. Over."

After a few moments, Dave said, "Fire at will!"

Suddenly the B-17 made a steep turn away from us and quickly lost altitude as it disappeared into the clouds. Dave and I were occupied flying our airplane. Neither was aware that it had fired on us, but some of our crewmembers along with other crews in the formation confirmed that they did indeed observe fire coming from the bandit B-17 and had returned fire.

Compared to the excitement we had experienced during and after the mission, the returning flight to our base was tranquil; however, we had a few moments of hilarity when Dave said over the intercom to Tighe, the tail gunner,

"John, you said the fighter looked like a buzzard?"

"Yeah, I thought I saw a bunch of buzzards." Tighe replied.

Dave said, "well, I surely wonder where those buzzards got their oxygen masks. They were flying at 20,000 feet."

We were so exhausted from stress and tension that not a word was uttered for the balance of the flight. I suspect that we were silently reflecting on the horrible deaths we had witnessed that day and offering a prayer of gratitude for surviving the bomb run.

The following account was released to the press the following day:

"23 August, 1944
Target: Markersdorf Airdrome, St. Polten, Austria
The third frag job of the month against enemy airdromes. The target was the Markersdorf Airdrome at St. Polen Austria. The first string of frags started at the Southwest corner of the airdrome and continued northeast to the service apron, the second string fell across the western half of the airdrome. Seven enemy aircraft were hit and three others received near misses. Forty-two enemy aircraft parked on the airdrome can be counted in the Group pictures.

Again enemy fighter opposition was encountered. Upward of seventy Bf109's and FW190's were seen between Lake Balaton and the Target. As a result of repeated attacks, five of these were destroyed, six probably destroyed, and one damaged. The cover provided this Group by the P-51s on this mission was exceptionally good. There was no flak at the target. The plane piloted by 2nd Lt. Gordon W Rosecrans, Jr. was set on fire by enemy fighters. More than half the crewmembers were seen to bail out from the plane.

For the second time since the Group had been operating in the Mediterranean Theater of Operations, a strange airplane joined the bomber formation on this mission. At 46 deg., 25' North and 15 deg., 52' East a black B-17 with white vertical stabilizer and elevators joined the formation and flew a wing position for approximately thirty minutes. At the end of that time it fired upon the formation and then turned away when fire was returned."

Dave Thomas was awarded a Distinguished Flying Cross and Flight Engineer John Ribovich was credited with a downed enemy fighter for their actions under intense fire that day making it one of my most outstanding missions. There was yet to be an event that would make it even more unforgettable. After piloting the SHADY LADY, serial number 4251336, from California across the Atlantic to Italy and bombing eight targets, this mission would to be the last time we would ever fly or see her again. The next day, 24 August, Lt. John A. Wren Jr. flew the SHADY LADY on a mission to bomb a railroad bridge in Ferrara, Italy. Flak was intense over the target and of the 25 Liberators in the bombing mission, 19 were severely damaged, including the SHADY LADY. She crashed near Pesaro. It was reported that the crew managed to bail out but I do not know if all survived. We were to fly the next 27 missions in many different models and versions of the B-24.

· · ·

Again we enjoyed two free days between missions and I was able to enjoy a long awaited swim. Perhaps because I had always lived 200 miles inland from the ocean, I was fascinated with open seas and beaches. Cerignola was located near the Adriatic Sea and on a main highway running from Cerignola to Bari. The beach was only a short walking distance from the highway. Dave and I had hitchhiked a few miles from Cerignola to a small beach that was crowded with soldiers from many nations. Soon after arriving, we were warned that there were strong undercurrents in the water and to be cautious. I waded a few feet from the beach and felt the currents tugging at my feet but inasmuch as others were in deeper water, I ventured further. I considered myself a strong swimmer. When I was in chest deep water, I suddenly realized that the current had moved me further out to sea with each step I had taken. I found it impossible to walk back to shore with the current tugging at my feet; however, by swimming above the current, I was able to return to the beach. I was fully aware by then that the water was frightfully dangerous and that perhaps it was more prudent to enjoy the sun and avoid the water.

"Help!" Someone shouted.

The call originated from a swimmer who was barely able to keep his nose above water. Without considering the danger, I ran toward him and plunged into the water. I began insisting that he remain calm as I approached and assured him that I would help him return to the beach. I warned him not to panic or he could drown both of us.

"I'm OK, Yank. Just help me. I can't swim"

Standing, I could scarcely keep my nose above water. As I held onto him, hopping and pushing away from the bottom like a kangaroo, we were swept by the undertow further from shore. Calmly I explained to him that I wanted to hold him across his chest and swim but that he must remain motionless. I had not been formally trained to rescue a swimmer in trouble but I instinctively understood that explaining my actions before executing them would help calm and reassure him. He cooperated and remained reasonably calm while I held him with one arm and stroked with the other, but I found that I tired quickly fighting the current. I rested every few moments by standing before I resumed swimming. The tide swept us seaward with each step but by alternating swimming and walking, I was eventually able to reach shallow water and wade to shore. I had been so intensely focused on my effort to rescue the British soldier, I had been unaware that no one else had responded to his call or offered to help me. The soldier was grateful and profusely thanked me for the aid I had given him. As I walked away, feeling good about helping someone, I questioned if I had acted courageously or had I been plain stupid?

. . .

While we were enjoying a respite from combat on the 24th and 25th of August, monumental events were taking place in Paris. General de Gaulle led a parade down the Champs Elysees to celebrate the liberation of Paris, thereby assuring his leadership of the French nation for many years to come. Hitler had ordered General Choltitz to raze before surrendering Paris to General Eisenhower. Choltitz, nevertheless, risked his life to avoid the disagreeable task of destroying the beautiful city unaware that General Eisenhower planned to bypass Paris in order to conserve supplies needed for the further invasion of France. After learning that Eisenhower planned to delay entering Paris, General de Gaulle, fearing communist would lead an uprising and control Paris, allowed the Free French forces to attack the city, forcing Eisenhower to discard his plans and assist the French after all. On 25 August, Paris was liberated.

MISSION #9

Bucharest, Rumania

26 August 1944

THIS MISSION WAS rather uneventful since we encountered no anti-aircraft or enemy fighters. Rumanian soldiers had compelled the Germans to concentrate their attention toward them rather than us.

The following bulletin was released a few days later:

"26 August 1944,
Target: Bucharest, Otopeni Airdrome, Rumania
By the 26th of August, Rumania had requested an armistice with Russia and Rumanian soldiers were fighting the Germans in the city of Bucharest. North of that city at the Otopeni Airdrome, the Germans were using the landing strips for two purposes: (1) As a place to set down large transports bringing in reinforcements; (2) As a place from which to launch aerial attacks against the city of Bucharest. The mission of the 461st Bombardment Group for the day was that of post-holing the two landing strips on the Otopeni Airdrome with 500 pound general-purpose bombs.

First reports of the results of this mission clearly indicated that Lt. Colonel Knapp had failed miserably in his effort to lead five consecutive exceptionally successful missions during the month of August. With CAVU weather and in the absence of both anti-aircraft and enemy fighter opposition only 4.6 per cent of the bombs were dropped on the briefed aiming point. Photographs of the mission reveal that two enemy airplanes, one of which was a six engine transport, were destroyed on the ground, but most of the bombs fell across barracks, the administration buildings, and the main highway leading from the airdrome to Ploesti. Only two airplanes were damaged on this mission, but still another crew was lost when 2nd Lt. Howard G?. Wilson, who was flying one of the two damaged planes, was forced to bail his crew out over Yugoslavia when returning from the mission."

I credit this "milk run" to the brave Rumanian soldiers but the Lt. Howard Wilson mentioned in the bulletin was our next door neighbor. He and his crew were rescued by Yugoslavian underground and returned to Cerignola a few months later.

A few days after this mission, the city of Bucharest was completely cleared of German resistance by the Rumanians and the Russians. Shortly thereafter approximately 1100 flying officers and enlisted men were released from prisons in Bucharest and returned to the Headquarters of the Fifteenth Air Force. Among these were part or all of the personnel of four different crews lost by the 461st over Rumania. When these individuals returned to the Group, they enthusiastically reported that our Group had broken the backbone of German resistance in Bucharest on the 26th of August. The bombs from our planes had practically missed their target, but had destroyed German headquarters, transportation equipment, heavy guns, and a great deal of the personnel and munitions concentrated in the area where our bombs fell. We had also heard of the damaging mission from one returning crew attached to our squadron. They reported the bombs had missed the target and exploded in a wooded area nearby where the Germans had established their headquarters. The Germans were furious. After exercising a huge effort to hide the buildings in the forest, they could only assume that the American Air Force had received information about the location of their headquarters and equipment from an informant. We had quite a laugh when we were advised that our lead bombardier had received a low score for his accuracy and more than likely, would be denied a promotion in the near future. To add to the farce, we were never awarded for our excellent bombing either. So go the fortunes of war.

MISSION # 10

Venzone, Viaduct, Italy

August 27, 1944

AGAIN WE ENJOYED another "milk run". We were repeatedly reminded at briefing that anticipated "milk run" missions can turn into "a big one", or "big'on" when pronounced by some Southerners. Germans were very good at hiding gun emplacements and would often send fighters from distant airfields as a surprise for American bombers. Fortunately, this mission held no surprises for us.

The following bulletin was released a few days later:

"Lt. Colonel Applegate, in leading a mission against the Venzone Viaduct, Italy, proved that Lt. Colonel Knapp's accomplishment of leading a formation and hitting a bridge at Avignon, France, on the first mission of the month was not a fluke. The score on the Avignon Bridge had been 73.1 per cent; the score on the Venzone Viaduct was 73.9 per cent."

MISSION #11

Szolnok, Hungary

28 August 1944

ABOUT AN HOUR before we were to turn on our IP and begin a bomb run over Szolnek, Hungary, our bombsight malfunctioned. Without the ability to release our bombs at the precise moment that the lead bombardier released his bombs, there was no need to continue our flight with the group; even more important, we did not want to land with a dangerous load of bombs. We reported our predicament to the flight commander who ordered us to abort the mission and select a target of opportunity before returning to our air base. A target of opportunity is an unplanned target selected at random during a return flight, usually a railroad, river or highway bridge. It is a method of jettisoning the bombs before landing, and at the same time rendering damage to the enemy. Bombardier Sullivan stated that for such an emergency, he had been taught a method of sighting between his bare toes as a substitute for a bombsight. I thought at the time that he was joking but found him to be quite sincere and determined to use his makeshift bombsight. We later labeled his toes, "Sullivan's bare-foot bombsight."

As he prepared his bombsight, we began reducing our altitude and looking for a target of opportunity. Within a short time we observed a railroad bridge spanning a river. If we could destroy the railroad bridge, we could disrupt transportation of enemy troops and equipment; however, a small village located at one end of the bridge complicated our plans. In order to spare injury and death to the citizens of the village, we must accurately release our bombs at the opposite end of the bridge. Bombardier Sullivan was confident that he could avoid bombing the village and so we made a few practice passes over the target. He opened the bomb bay doors, removed one of his boots, and positioned his bare foot over the spot where the bombsight had been removed. By aiming between two of his toes while estimating drift, air speed and distance, he could calculate the estimated moment to release the bombs. This method was something like "Dead Reckoning" in nautical terminology.

"OK, I'm ready. Keep it on 270 degrees", Sullivan announced.

Dave banked until 270 degrees appeared on the compass, then said,

"Jim, you are the skipper now. Give me the corrections."

"Roger."

After a short pause, Sullivan replied, "make that about two more degrees to the right, over."

The new course set by the bombardier seemed to align the nose of the aircraft directly over the railroad tracks as we approached the bridge.

"Bombs away!" Sullivan said. Dave turned into a steep bank.

After what seemed an eternity, I watched in horror as the first bomb exploded at the edge of the bridge near the village. Subsequent bombs exploded about 500 feet apart along the railroad and through the middle of the village. Indeed, it was as if we had intentionally targeted the village. Like colossal footsteps of a behemoth that had crushed everything in its path, the bombs pounded through the village. We had scored a perfect bomb drop! We leveled the aircraft and headed for home in silence.

I was sick to my stomach with shame. During the entire return flight I repeatedly visualized a family sitting at a dining table, secure in the belief that there was nothing of value in the village to bomb. This vision yet replays in my mind. I can only hope that it was one of those unusual events that occur in war, when bombs destroy a mistaken target inadvertently causing enormous damage to the enemy. In retrospect, the blame should not be attributed to the orders of the flight commander or to our fear of landing with a load of bombs; rather the blame should be placed on a war that sponsors such dreadful events. In order to better understand Hitler's officers' plea of innocence during the Nuremberg trials, which was based on the argument that they were merely following orders, one must first experience war. We also were following orders that day. Should we have disobeyed our order and defiantly jettisoned our bombs over the Adriatic Sea? We were taught and believed that one never questions an order. At what point should a military soldier ignore orders that he believes are wrong and will result in the death of innocent persons? At what point does discipline break down, soldiers no longer accept authority, and a war is lost? It is easy for one, in a comfortable secure environment, to answer these questions by applying theoretical and moralistic standards—it is not so easy under actual war conditions. The extent of death caused by the ill-advised order from our flight commander together with our immature judgment will never be known, nor do I wish to know. It will haunt me forever.

Upon arrival at our home base, we were informed that the group had enjoyed a "milk run" but was credited with an excellent mission. Although we did not participate in the raid, we were relieved to know that something worth while had occurred despite our inglorious results.

The bulletin read:

"28 August 1944
Target: Szolnok/Szajol Railroad Bridge, Hungary
On the 28th of August, Colonel Glantzberg took his turn at leading the Group on an excellent mission against a railroad

bridge. The target was the Szajol Railroad bridge at Szalnok, Hungary. The Group Bombardier, now Captain King, continued to demonstrate his ability to knock down bridges. The score on this mission was 55.1 per cent."

. . .

This was to be our last mission for the month of August, our first month of combat and a month of deadly raids over Ploesti and Markersdorf. We were indeed war veterans after surviving eleven missions in only one short month. Although some were "milk runs", all should be classified as deadly. Today a "milk run" over a target might have been a hazardous mission the day before or the next day when enemy flak and fighters attack with ferocity. For some reason unknown to us, the Germans would decide not to send fighters on a certain day but would release them the following day. We always prepared for the worst. Our information officers informed us that our bombing of enemy oil refineries and railroads was creating a shortage of gasoline for the German armed forces. Perhaps they were conserving gasoline when they failed to send fighter planes to attack us.

Between missions I had visited two or three small Italian cities near Cerignola because it was essential that we return to our air base each evening to read daily orders. Unless informed differently, we were on standby to fly every day. If we failed to report for an assigned mission, we were considered AWOL (absent without leave). During wartime, AWOL was a serious infraction of the rules that could result in the death penalty; although I was not aware of any such penalties during World War II. Nevertheless, I had no wish to risk a serious AWOL charge and thought it prudent to restrict my sight seeing ventures to areas only a short distance from Cerignola.

Early the next morning, after our ill-starred mission to Szolnok, I hitchhiked to Bari, a nearby city, and began walking the streets seeking places of interest. There were few travel brochures printed in English then but I often hired an English speaking local Italian to accompany me to places of interest in order to explain the sites I would view. I am yet puzzled why so few American soldiers in Italy were interested in learning about the country. I usually visited cities and historical sites alone because I could seldom find interested friends to join me. On off-days, most officers and enlisted crewmen relaxed around their tents, reading, sleeping or loafing at their squadron club. When they ventured into town, they most often visited a military recreational club. Although I understood their distaste for wretchedness and squalor, a result of the war, I found it difficult to accept their lack of interest in a nation rich with history and culture. In order to appreciate the country, it was necessary for one to overlook the depressing sights of debris, disagreeable odors and the sad plight of the people. When I first arrived, I considered Italy an enemy until I understood that its citizens were caught up in a terrible predicament not of their making. In time I grew to understand that Italians had never wanted war with the United States. They detested Germans and most admired the United States. Unfortunately, many military soldiers never bothered to look deeper than the appearance of an impoverished populace, their roads, and their buildings. Because Mussolini had allied Italy with Germany, many U.S. soldiers considered Italy a defeated enemy and regarded the people with contempt. Walking on a crowded street in Naples, I observed an American soldier purposely forcing Italian pedestrians off the sidewalk and aggressively colliding with those who failed to give way to him. I remember the word "wop", often used to describe Italian people.

The city of Bari was a port city and like all port cities, there were dangerous sections to avoid. The old city was interesting but the Basilica San Nicole was the most fascinating of all. Saint Nicholas was reportedly the original Santa Claus. Sailors had stolen his bones from Myrrh, now part of Turkey, and brought them to Bari where they are buried under the altar of a church built over 1000 years ago. Since that time I have found so many churches and chapels in Italy that claim to possess the bones of San Nicole, that I reached the conclusion there was indeed more than one San Nicole or Santa Clause. When I was an innocent child, I believed in one jolly Saint Nick and I am grateful that I did not know there were so many. After searching a few more hours for interesting places, I returned to Cerignola. It had been an interesting day despite losing my wallet. It had slipped from my back pocket while climbing aboard a truck bound for Cerignola.

MISSIONS #12,13, 14, AND 15

1, 2, 3, and 5 September 1944

MISSIONS #12, 13, 14, AND 15 were rather uneventful; consequently, for the sake of the reader I will only reproduce official bulletins that describe each sortie. Although we encountered some light flak, we considered the missions "milk runs", and the round trip flight to each target was routine. Our group, however, did receive a commendation from General Twining, commander of the 15th Air Force for our mission to Smederovo Ferry Slip, Yugoslavia on the third of September.

> "1 September 1944
> Target: Ferrara Railroad Bridge, Italy
> On the first mission of the new month the Group failed again to seriously damage or destroy the railroad bridge North of Ferrara, Italy. Seven of the planes became separated from the formation and bombed a bridge at Boari Pisani, Italy."

> "2 September 1944
> Target: Mitrovica Railroad Bridge, Yugoslavia
> On Mission No. 95, veterans in the lead plane, Lt. Colonel Appelgate, Captain Specht, Captain Murphy, Lt. Prien, and Major Pruitt, came through with the mission that was scored at 57.3 per cent against a railroad bridge at Mitrovica, Yugoslavia. The photographs of the mission show a closely concentrated pattern of bombs on the west approach to the bridge with six direct hits on the tracks."

> "3 September 1944
> Target: Smederovo Ferry Slip, Yugoslavia

Against the Smederovo Ferry Slip in Yugoslavia on 3 September, Major Goree, Lt. Garrett, Lt. Herold, Captain DeWitt, and Lt. Littel led a formation which made the highest bombing score ever achieved by this Group. Under ideal conditions the bombs were dropped on and around the ferry slip in such a concentration that 92.2 per cent were plotted within 1000 feet of the briefed aiming point."

Commendation
From : Twining
To : CO 49th Wing
A study of reconnaissance photos taken after the attacks by the Four Nine Wing on 3 September on the Smederovo Ferry Docks reveals that both road and rail terminals are almost completely destroyed. The excellence of the bomb patterns of these two pinpoint targets by the 461 Group is highly commendable."

. . .

5 September 1944
Target: Sava East Railroad Bridge, Belgrade, Yugoslavia
The assigned target for this mission was the Sava East Railroad Bridge, Belgrade, Yugoslavia. Because of a ten-tenths cloud coverage at both the primary and the one assigned alternate target, the planes were forced to return to Base."

I had completed 15 missions and with crossed fingers, I repeated each evening before drifting into sleep, "Fifteen down and twenty more missions to go".

MISSION # 16

Lyon, France

10 September 1944

AN ANNOUNCEMENT BY our briefing officer that we were to fly supplies to an American fighter base in Lyon, France was joyfully received because it would likely be another "milk run." We were informed that the fighter base had been chaotically and hastily established a few days before to support the advancing allies as they stormed their way through Lyon to liberate southern France. Eight days before this mission, on the second of September, the 36th division had entered Lyon, and a fighter air base had been quickly established. The allies had met little resistance and had moved more rapidly than expected, leaving their rear bases with little organization or supplies. We were diverted from combat to ferrying gasoline and ammunition to Bron airdrome, Lyon, France where a group of American P-47 fighters had been based.

After briefing we boarded our airplane loaded with .50 caliber ammunition, empty gas barrels, and tanks filled with gasoline installed in the bomb bay. We had been instructed to wait at the Lyon airfield while ground crews filled the empty barrels we delivered with gasoline from our extra tanks. They were then to remove them to storage after they were unloaded. It was quite an unusual sight for me to observe empty barrels and gas tanks where bombs had formerly hung from bomb racks in the bomb bay.

It was an extraordinary flight beginning with a late 0800 hours departure, an individual unaccompanied climb to our assigned altitude, and no rendezvous or formation flight to our destination. We flew to Lyon secure in the knowledge that we would not encounter enemy fighters or flak over the Mediterranean and southern France. After landing, we encountered a congested and slow taxi along the one remaining taxi strip that had survived previous bombings. Before reaching the unloading docks, one of our B-24s burst into flame. The large amount of volatile high-octane gasoline loaded in each bomber made such an explosion almost inevitable. We were fortunate to be some distance from the fire and none of the other airplanes caught fire; however, the pilot jumped from the top hatch and broke his feet. A detour lane was formed away from the burning aircraft and ground crews quickly unloaded our ammunition and empty gas drums as we arrived at the unloading area. Each B-24 patiently waited its turn to be unloaded and then taxied to the end of the runway where we again waited our turn to takeoff.

The following bulletin was released the next day:

"Target: Lyon/Bron Airdrome, France

The first supply mission to France, which was Mission No. 99, was flown on September 10th. Colonel Glantzberg flew the first of thirty-six planes to take off individually on this mission. As a result of this mission one plane was lost to the group. The plane, which was piloted by 1st Lt. Robert K. Baker, developed a fire on the taxi strip at Lyon after the C-10 generator had been started. The flames spread rapidly through the plane compelling the crew to abandon it. Lt. Baker made his exit through the top hatch from where he jumped to the concrete taxi strip. The bones in both of his heels were broken in this accident.

The following supplies and materials were delivered on this mission: 432 five hundred pound general purpose bombs; 57,600 rounds of .50 caliber ammunition; 648 empty fifty-five gallon drums; 25,000 gallons of 100 octane gasoline."

MISSION # 17

Lyon, France

13 September 1944

W E AGAIN RECEIVED at briefing, a pleasant announcement that we were to fly supplies to the same fighter base in Lyon. Our group had been delivering gasoline and ammunition daily for the past week and the missions were like holidays for us—no flak or enemy fighters.

As we taxied to the unloading area at the airdrome in Lyon, I could see a group of people by the side of the taxi strip who appeared to be digging a huge hole. I was curious and at one of our numerous halts, I climbed out of the airplane to question one of the Frenchman about what they were unearthing. He informed me that they were uncovering some 20 underground fighters, called Marque, who had been executed and buried in a common grave by the Germans before retreating. The hostages had been executed in retaliation for an underground attack that had killed several German soldiers. Executing hostages seemed to have been standard procedure for the Nazi. In many European countries one may find memorials placed at locations where war prisoners were executed by the Nazi. Years later, I lived near one in Vicenza, Italy.

With the exception of this horrible sight, it was a routine mission. The following is an official bulletin issued the next day:

"13 September 1944
Target: Lyon/Bron Airdrome, France
On 13 September nineteen planes delivered 26,676 gallons

of 100-octane gasoline; 1350 gallons of 120-grade oil; 297 empty fifty-five gallon drums; and 54,000 rounds of .50 caliber ammunition."

. . .

The day after our second ferrying mission to Lyon, Dave and I received a notice that we were to report the following day for a flight-check. We had completed one check-flight shortly after being assigned to the 766th Squadron but because we had completed about half of our tour of combat missions, another check-up had been scheduled. Pilots can acquire poor habits over time and need to be reminded frequently of these habits and the dangers of complacency. One might question how we could become complacent during combat, but there is an ever-present temptation to shorten safety procedures because of boredom or to save time. Many crews were lost due to "Pilot Error", a term used to explain accidents caused by overlooking safety procedures or by using poor judgment. We were to fly with a Captain who had earned a reputation for being a "cowboy pilot"; one who enjoys taking risks and feels that he is impervious to danger.

The Captain ordered me to take the pilot's seat while he occupied the co-pilot's seat to observe my landings, takeoffs, instrument procedures, and general proficiency in controlling the airplane. He repeated the test with Dave at the controls while I stood behind the copilot's seat. I was observing and listening to his instructions to Dave when suddenly he said,

"Have you ever seen what a B-24 can do?"

We shook our heads indicating that we had not.

"Never believe that a B-24 is a flimsy airplane and cannot take stress."

Before he had finished speaking, he pulled up the nose, lowered one wing and pushed forward the column causing the aircraft to plunge from a steep climb and reverse itself into a diving turn toward the earth. I had no time to be concerned about anything but holding onto anything available to prevent me from crashing into the top of the cockpit. I was standing without a safety belt but with knowledge gained as a seasoned flyer, I was certain that my stomach would catch up to me. I was even more concerned about the position of the wings when he pulled out of the dive. Our air speed had almost doubled. The air speed needle had passed the red line indicating the maximum safe speed, and stress from excessive speed had caused the wings to flap up and down like a bird's wing in flight. I was concerned that they were about to tear away from the fuselage and take our four engines with them. Much to my relief, he discontinued his exhibition and instructed us to return to our air base. Soon after our check-flight, the captain crashed into a mountain at night in bad weather taking the lives of all on board. It was rumored that he had disregarded a warning about the dangerous weather conditions and confirmed our speculation that he believed himself invulnerable. While walking to the Officer's Mess Hall for breakfast the morning after the crash, I was confronted with the sight of the 10 frozen bodies, stacked like pieces of firewood, waiting to be transported to the Graves Office that accounted for the dead. I elected to skip breakfast.

MISSION # 18

Lyon, France

17 September 1944

A T BRIEFING, WE received the pleasant information that we were again returning to Lyon with more supplies; however, the weather briefing officer drew us abruptly back to reality with the somber announcement that the weather condition at Bron Airdrome was less than desirable.

After another uneventful flight to Lyon, we descended to land only to find the airfield "socked-in" and without instrument landing devices to help us. While circling the field, tower radioed us that a decision had been made to divert us to Marseille, France where we were to land and await new orders. Landing with a full load of highly explosive gasoline was not one of my favorite pastimes but we managed to land and roll to a halt at the end of the runway without harm.

Upon parking the Liberator, we were instructed to remain at the Marseille airfield over night and return to Bron Airdrome the next day to deliver our cargo. I was excited to have the opportunity to visit a city in France that had been liberated from the Nazi only a few short weeks before. After we were conducted to our overnight quarters, I eagerly boarded a bus that would transport me into town.

As I walked the streets of Marseille I approached a crowd of people shielding their eyes from the sun and observing a tall building. Being curious, I stopped and also began scanning the building. I finally detected a man with a rifle strapped to his back scaling a wall of the building and another person emerging from a nearby window also preparing to climb the building. They employed ropes to secure themselves much like a mountain climber would use while rock climbing. At first I thought it was some sort of entertainment but a Frenchman standing next to me explained in English that they were Maquet, Free French underground fighters, pursuing a nazi collaborator trapped inside the building. The military newspaper, Stars and Stripes, had published several articles about the Free French underground rounding up German collaborators and arbitrarily executing them on the spot. Soon the men entered another window, which I assumed led to where the person or persons were trapped. A few minutes later I heard gun shots and the crowd calmly began to disperse as if they were satisfied that justice had been rendered. I will never know what transpired inside the building but obviously I had witnessed part of a French historical event.

The following morning, after a struggle to lift our over-burdened airplane off the runway, we departed Marseille and completed the delivery of our cargo to Bron Airdrome. The day after our return to Cerignola, the following bulletin was issued:

> "17 September, 1944
> Target: Lyon/Bron Airdrome, France
> On September 17th the load of eighteen planes was as follows: 21,366 gallons of 100 octane gasoline; 1450 gallons of 120 grade oil; 288 empty fifty-five gallon drums; 30 five hundred pound general purpose bombs; and 16,000 rounds of .50 caliber ammunition. Due to adverse weather conditions at Lyon all of the planes were forced to land with their loads at friendly fields and did not reach Lyon until the following day."

. . .

We were always on alert to fly a bombing mission and although our name might not appear on orders during the early evening, there was always the possibility that we might be added to the orders during the night. In that event, we were rudely awakened around four o'clock the next morning by the OD informing us that we were to fly a mission that day. Those not on orders were free to spend the day in any manner they preferred. As noted before, I enjoyed visiting near-by cities— near enough that I could return to the squadron area before dark. Some days were spent merely reading, sleeping, listening to records, visiting friends or hanging around the officer's club. After the 17 September mission to Lyon, I was to spend the next seven days waiting to be notified that I had been assigned to a mission. Some impertinent knave described Air combat flying as,

"Day after day of absolute boredom interspersed with moments of utter panic."

"Primitive Hygiene"

MISSION # 19

Athens, Greece

25 September

"TODAY YOU WILL bomb this submarine base at Athens, Greece. We expect some submarines to be in dry dock and many others to be moored in docks as you can see from this photograph."

The briefing officer was pointing to a projection screen displaying a large photograph of a submarine base. I had bombed every type of war-craft, from trains to airplanes, but this would be the first time that I would target any type of watercraft. The Germans operated a large submarine base located near Athens, just across the Adriatic Sea, and a short distance from Southern Italy where we were stationed. The officer stated that it was crucial to the allied war effort that they are destroyed for they were silently stalking and attacking our ships like wolves—they were even named "the wolf pack". The briefing officer concluded the briefing session with a warning that we could expect heavy flak and possible enemy aircraft attacks.

It was only a short distance from our air base to Athens and to the nearest target we had bombed to date. We rendezvoused over the Adriatic coast of southern Italy and immediately began flying formation in the direction of Greece. It seemed that we had barely climbed to our bombing altitude when the bombardier announced that we were on the Initial Point and began preparing for the bomb run. There was little flak, and after releasing our bomb load, we enjoyed a brief uneventful descent to our home base in Cerignola.

The bulletin released after the mission was as follows:

"25 September, 1944

Target: Submarines in the Athens Area, Greece

Lt. Colonel Lawhon led the last combat mission of the month which was flown 25 September in attacking submarines in the Athens area. The score of the mission was 24 per cent. The only crew lost to combat during the month was lost on this mission. This plane, piloted by 2nd Lt. Ralph E. Nelson, left the formation before reaching the target, but failed to return to Base."

. . .

By the end of September I was eligible for R&R (rest and relaxation) leave. I had participated in 19 tiring missions during the months of August and September and looked forward to temporary relief from the hot, dusty, dirty tent in which we lived. Our headquarters allowed combat crewmembers a one-week leave about every two months. If the stresses of combat flying were allowed to continue without a periodic break, we were susceptible to mental and nervous disorders. Every crewmember reacted differently to this affliction; some could cope for only a short period of time while others seemed to be invulnerable. All suffered to some degree however, and were encouraged to take eligible leave time. The Air Force Command had confiscated most of the Island of Capri and designated it an R&R facility. The island met almost every criteria one could ask for when seeking a place to relax: beautiful beaches, a picturesque setting, a Mediterranean climate, beautiful hotels, many night clubs, but few girls were available as dance partners. Because the U.S. military had occupied most of the homes and hotels, there were few Italian civilians living on the island. I believed that Capri was selected as a rest area because there were few young women residing on the island. Capri held no interest for me, I wanted to see the ancient city of Rome and girls; consequently, Lieutenant Larry Weimer, Lieutenant Jack Schwartz and I applied for a leave of one week to visit Rome. Jack was a bombardier, Larry and I were co-pilots on different crews who had become "buddies" and traveled together when possible. As I reflect on my experiences in World War II, I am struck by the remarkable ease with which young military people, particularly war comrades, bond together. When reporting to a new assignment, I would immediately select two or three individuals who appealed to me and within a short time, we would be close friends. Some of my most distinct and vivid memories of the war are about the happy times I shared with those friends. It is my opinion that war or other major disasters not only eliminate barriers produced by selfishness, wealth, social status, or race, it creates an intense feeling of camaraderie; a sense of friendship that cannot be produced by lesser circumstances. It seems to me that in order to survive a war or any great disaster, our necessities, motives, and requirements must interlock and become indistinguishable. The terms "them" and "me" merge into one. Since we have the same needs and desires, there is no longer a need to make an effort to recognize or love "them". I only need to love "me". When I love "me", I also love "them". The plural "them" becomes the singular "me", and like Siamese twins, we are one. War produces comrades—much different from friends.

"Jack Schwartz, Larry Weimer and Author"

We hired local guides, joined tour groups and toured as a trio while endeavoring to visit as many historical sites of Rome that our time would allow. Since I had only visited small, partially destroyed rural towns in Southern Italy, Rome presented a stark contrast to my early impression of Italy. It contained ancient historical relics, sites, and cultures that had no only survived the war, but had been cared for and preserved with amazing attention by Italian curators. From the moment I first saw a tourist souvenir representing the legend of the abandoned infants Romulus and Remus, founders of Rome feeding from the udder of a female wolf, the mystery and charm of Rome captivated me. Because of their unique place in history, the allies declared the city of Rome and the Vatican City "International Treasures" and great efforts were made to protect them from destruction. Only buildings on the outskirts of Rome and those purposely demolished by the Germans before retreating were damaged; otherwise, the city was virtually untouched by the war.

On the morning of 5 June 1944, only three months before our visit, Americans had marched into Rome behind the retreating Germans. Releasing long suppressed anger brought about by their fascist leaders and arrogant German troops, crowds of Italian citizens joyfully gathered to greet and celebrate their liberators. Unaware that this day would change her life forever, a pretty 16 year old Italian girl stood amid the cheering crowd curiously watching American soldiers being showered with wine, flowers, and kisses from the populace. Nothing would lead her to believe that, fifteen months later, she would wed one of these American victors, an American Lieutenant aviator who had been sent by his government to make war with her nation. Her life would change forever. She would become a U.S. citizen, spend 44 years in the United States, raise a family, and would be laid to rest in 1989 at Nacogdoches, Texas, the birthplace of her American husband. Such are the inexplicable divergences of war and life.

I also never imagined that my future wife was in Rome as I strolled through the ancient streets used by Roman Senators 2000 years before. I could only remember movies of Roman Senators walking to their senate chambers, sitting with the emperor observing an arena filled with gladiators and Christians fighting for their lives. We walked through catacombs that had provided sanctuary to Christians as they secretly worshipped their God, we viewed works of Michael Angelo in the Vatican City where laying on his back he had painted breath-taking scenes on the ceilings of the Sistine Chapel. Back in Nacogdoches, one could only review these events in history books but I was there, seeing, feeling, sensing, and imagining it all. The war seemed far away but all too soon, it was time for us to return to our air base.

MISSION #20

Castelfranca, Veneto, Italy

10 October 1944

THE BRIEFING OFFICER pointed at a location on a large map and said,

"This morning your target is the railroad junction at Castelfranco in the region of Venito (Venice) in Northern Italy. Our assignment is to destroy railroad tracks, station, loading platforms and any trains unlucky enough to be there when we get there. You will be loaded with four 1000-pound general-purpose bombs. Flak should not be a major problem nor do we expect enemy fighters, but be alert, you never know. We think weather could be a problem. I will let Major Smith brief you on that."

"Good morning, gentlemen. I'll walk you through the weather but it doesn't look good. You can expect_____."

We had been handed a weather report map with charts of wind currents, high and low pressure fronts and various other information needed to form a complete a weather forecast. Indeed, it did not look good. The briefing office informed us that we could expect cloud conditions during most of the flight to northern Italy, and that we would experience icing conditions along the way. Under certain conditions, ice forms on the leading edge of aircraft wings at higher altitudes; it may also occur at low altitudes with freezing temperatures. Ice was, and still is, one of the most insidious and treacherous flying hazards that a pilot will encounter. It may be hidden from sight and can gradually increase until it creates a stall, resulting in the pilot losing control of the airplane. A heater device, called a de-icer, was installed in the leading edges of the wings of a B-24, but it was often inoperative due to damages inflicted during combat.

Soon after takeoff, we were concealed in thick clouds. We often said that flying in clouds was like flying in "pea soup". Formation flying in ideal weather can be tiring, but flying formation in cloud cover becomes both tiring and dangerous. We could barely see the airplane just off our wing. At times even the nearest airplane would disappear momentarily behind a thick patch of clouds as we climbed toward our bombing altitude of 21,000 feet. We had been assigned a bombing altitude of 20,000 feet during briefing but just before takeoff, it was changed to 21,000 in an attempt to break out of the clouds before beginning our bombing run.

At 20,000 feet we were in the clear and as we prepared for our bomb run, we could see ahead that the target lay beneath a total blanket of clouds. I have never understood why an order to abandon a target and return to base is ever justified, but about an hour after turning away from our obscured primary target, our flight commander radioed ordering us to jettison our bombs over the sea. It seemed such a terrible waste when the bombs could have been released over or near a target; however, a policy to avoid bombing cities and killing civilians was sometimes followed. Nevertheless, as the reader will recall, my crew was previously ordered to bomb a target of opportunity. By the time we reached the coast, we were able to find a temporary hole in the cloud cover that enabled us to see water and eject our bombs. Many other flights were not so fortunate and were forced to land with a full bomb load. Landing a B-24 with a bomb load added a new dimension to the stress of an ordinary landing. The simplest accident during a landing can become deadly. A faulty bomb rack jolted during a landing may release bombs onto the runway resulting in an explosion, even when disarmed. A hot fire most certainly would cause an explosion. Although bombs were never armed until a few minutes before a bomb run and always unarmed during a flight, there was always the uncertainty of whether an unarmed bomb would explode on impact if accidentally dropped on the runway. Indeed, none of us wanted to find out, but all flights landed safely and although the mission was a failure, no one was lost. We were awarded credit for a combat mission, even though we did not encounter flak, enemy fighters, or bomb our target. Nevertheless, it was one of the most dangerous and stressful missions that I ever flew. The following bulletin was released the next day:

> "Target: Castelfranco Veneto Railroad Junction, Italy
> On 10 October Major Word led a formation of twenty-eight planes against the Castelfranco Veneto Railroad Junction in Italy. After fighting their way up through a seven-tenths stratus layer, which extended from 15,000 to 20,000 feet above the Adriatic, the planes arrived at the target to find it completely covered by a ten-tenths layer of stratus. No bombs were dropped on the target; some were jettisoned in the Adriatic and others were returned to the base."

MISSION #21

Vosendorf Oil Refinery, Vienna, Austria

11 October 1944

AN UNEASY MOANING and shifting was heard throughout the audience of pilots as the briefing officer uncovered his briefing map and announced our target. All targets in the Vienna area: railroad yards, oil refineries, aircraft factories, munitions factories were heavily fortified, dangerous and called "the big'on", a contraction for "the big one". There was to be no "milk run" that day. He remarked at the conclusion of his briefing that we should expect heavy flak and enemy fighter action then turned the briefing over to the weather officer. As he had the day before, the weather officer informed us that we could experience dangerous flying conditions with heavy cloud cover up to 25,000 or 30,000 feet—he was correct. We had barely begun our climb to our assigned altitude when we found ourselves again nervously flying formation through thick clouds.

During my flight training, instructors would say, "if you can't fly over it, around it or under it, turn around and go home." I had taken their advice several times, and had witnessed the results of those who had not heeded this caution; but military war does not always allow one to exercise good judgment. Airplanes and crews are expendable, the enemy must be destroyed at all cost, and perhaps more important, no commander wishes to find himself in the position of ordering his group to abandon a mission for fear that he will be censured by his superiors. With 300 aircraft concealed in heavy clouds, we continued to climb to our assigned bombing altitude, disregarding the danger of collision and the reality that we may perhaps be unable to effectively bomb our target because of cloud cover.

Our flight leader continued climbing above our bombing altitude in an effort to break out of the clouds, but at 28,000 feet we were still unable to see sunlight. Because of thin air, the Liberator was difficult to control at higher altitudes. Its reaction was slow, increasing the danger of formation flying and added another dimension of peril to flying immersed in clouds. At all altitudes the B-24, due to its bulkiness, was slow to respond to flight controls, but at extremely high altitudes, it was as if we were flying in a vacuum. As an example: if a pilot wished to turn the aircraft in a different direction, for several seconds there would be no reaction to the applied flight controls. This slow response created an extreme hazard of colliding with other aircraft while flying in formation at a higher altitude and poor visibility.

After our flight leader found it impossible to fly over the clouds, he made a decision to approach the target from a different direction, trusting that we would be able to fly around the clouds. When it became apparent that we could neither fly above or around the clouds and because we had burned an additional precious hour of gasoline fuel, the commanding officer gave the order to abort the original mission. He turned and led us to the target of last resort, an aircraft factory at Kranj, Yugoslavia. Because of clouds, the lead bombardier's sighting was ineffective again but we released our bombs. I think we bombed the target more through fear of landing with them than a desire to destroy the target. The policy to avoid bombing cities was ignored again.

Flying formation through heavy clouds was the most exhausting of all flying and the most dangerous. Anti-aircraft fire or enemy fighter attack usually occurred over the target and lasted a short time but flying through extensive cloud formations could last for many hours. After withdrawing from a heavily defended area in good weather, we often spread our formation and somewhat relaxed, but while flying in cloud cover, there was never a moment free of anxiety. Twenty eyes of a nervous ten-man crew would continually strain to see through the clouds. Many times, after such a mission, I was so exhausted that I would go to bed at first dark.

A bulletin was released the next day:

"11 October, 1944
Target: Vosendorf Oil Refinery, Vienna, Austria
The target for Mission 113 on 11 October was the Vosendorf Oil Refinery, Vienna, Austria. Again bad weather was experienced over the Adriatic. In the Trieste Area there were showers and thunderheads which towered to 30,000 feet. Being unable to get through, around, or above the bank of clouds, Major Goree attempted to lead the formation in attacking the last resort target, the aircraft factory at Kranj, Yugoslavia."

MISSION #22

Blechhammer, Germany

14 October 1944

IT SEEMED THAT unfavorable weather over Europe would never change during the winter of 1944. With few exceptions, every day was overcast with thick towering cumulus and stratus clouds producing rain or snow, and sometimes both. The weather on 14 October was the same. Our weather officer informed us that we could expect cloud cover over most of our flight. I disliked the thought of flying formation in clouds again.

A short time after assembling our group, we plunged into intermittent cloud cover that persisted throughout the flight to our target. When we arrived at the IP, our target was completely covered with clouds, forcing our group leader to again select a target of opportunity. Fortunately, flak was light and inaccurate over the target and no enemy fighters were sighted. Despite the poor flying conditions, I enjoyed the thrill of flying as first pilot while Dave served as my co-pilot. Our orders had stated that Dave would be first pilot, but before taxiing to our takeoff position, Dave asked if I wanted to fly on the left side as first pilot. I am sure that he would have been reprimanded if headquarters had discovered that he had swapped positions without orders. I was a combat veteran pilot with 21 missions to my credit, but this was to be the first mission that I would set in the command pilot's seat. Dave and I had shared pilot time since we first arrived in Italy, and I had often controlled the aircraft from both the pilot and copilot seat. Dave allowed me to log first pilot time so that I might better qualify for a crew of my own. It was also in the best interest of the crew that I continually train as a first pilot because a time might arrive when

Dave was injured or killed and I would then be in command of the ship. A pilot living next door was instantly killed when a piece of shrapnel struck him in the head. Dave was always generous in sharing flying time with me and was like a proud father when I was later promoted to first pilot with a crew of my own. Flying 20 combat missions was more than sufficient to acquire the knowledge and experience that was essential to be eligible for a promotion to first pilot but everything depended on the availability of personnel and airplanes. I could only wait and chafe.

The next day the following bulletin was released:

"14 October, 1944
Target: Bratislava Marshaling Yard and Bridge, Czechoslovakia
As had been the case when Lt. Colonel Lawhon had last led the Group on 7 October, extremely adverse weather conditions again compelled him to abandon the Primary Target and bomb a target of opportunity. The primary target had been the Odertal Oil Refinery, in Germany; the target of opportunity was the Marshaling Yard at Bratislava, Czechoslovakia. Despite a seven-tenths cloud coverage at the target, 61 per cent of the bombs were dropped within 1000 feet of the selected aiming point."

. . .

A few days later, an order was issued by our S2 intelligence office for all flying personnel to assemble at 0900 hour the following day in the operations building. When we were assembled and seated, someone called us to attention as our S2 Major resolutely walked to the podium.

"All right you guys, at ease and knock off the talking. I want you to listen to me."

Before he had finished his opening remarks, he slammed the top of the podium with his hand. The noise, amplified from the microphone placed on the podium, resonated through the room like an explosion, shocking us into a deadened silence. He shouted,

"How many times do I have to tell you dumb bastards that people in Europe do not whistle! People have not whistled in years! They have nothing to whistle about! Can't you understand that?"

He then calmly continued to describe an event that had recently occurred near Vienna. A group of American military fugitives, some from our group, had parachuted into an area near Vienna where they had been rescued by the underground. They were being moved along an escape route through a village, about 30 yards apart but within sight of each other, with instructions to walk slowly, pretend to be inhabitants of the area, and to never speak lest their language betray them. One of the members of the group, attempting to appear casual, began whistling. Instantly, civilians and Germans in the area were aware that the whistler was an American; consequently, the entire group was captured and the airmen imprisoned. The rescuers were executed. The Major made a lasting impression on us that whistling was not a good idea when evading an enemy.

MISSION #23

Ali Pasin Most Marshalling Yard Sarajevo, Yugoslavia

7 November, 1944

AT BRIEFING WE were informed that our target for the day was to be a marshalling yard near Sarajevo which was heavily utilized by trains moving German troops and supplies from Greece. Athens had been liberated 14 October 1944, leading to an exodus of troops and supplies from Greece by rail through the city of Sarajevo, Yugoslavia. It was a most favorable target, offering a rare opportunity to bomb a concentration of enemy troops and equipment, while destroying the railroad yard and rendering it unserviceable for the near future. It would be a devastating blow to the German military might. We were informed that we were participating in a maximum effort mission that would include three large bomb groups, the 461st, 484th and 451st. Also, we were warned that flak could be heavy, based on U. S. intelligence reports, and that large movements of anti-aircraft weapons had been moved into the area in an obvious effort to protect the concentration of troops and equipment. The weather information officer assured us that we could expect clear weather over the target and intermittent clouds to and from the target.

After rendezvous and assembling into formation, the flight to the initial point was uneventful; however, when we were within sight of the IP I observed a dark ugly cloud of flak hanging over the target awaiting our arrival. I said to Dave,

"Wow! Look at that! Let's cover up."

We began to don our flak vests and steel helmets. At the IP we could see small dark clouds erupting all around us and we began to feel an occasional shudder of the airplane as anti-aircraft shells exploded nearby. I had learned to compartmentalize by putting the fear of being struck by an exploding shell into a separated compartment of my mind while I directed my entire attention to assisting Dave fly the aircraft. Although it was almost impossible to block the sight of clouds caused by exploding anti-aircraft shells completely from my sight, I attempted to concentrate on one task at a time. During our bomb run, I observed several B-24s with feathered propellers who had been struck with flak and lost power in one or more engines. When an engine ceases to function properly and loses power, the propeller slows until it only rotates from the force of the wind, called wind milling. This windmill effect creates a restriction that slows the speed of the aircraft. A pilot can alter the angle of the propeller blade, called pitch, so that the blade presents the least amount of its surface to the air current, thereby reducing its drag. The propeller will then cease to rotate, and is "feathered". The intense flak damaged several airplanes in our group causing them to lose speed and abandon their formation. Whenever an aircraft vacated a position in a formation, one of the remaining airplanes moved into the vacated slot. When we began the bomb run we were flying the #5 position, but by the end of the mission, we had replaced damaged B-24s until we were in the #2 slot. Three of the six airplanes in our formation had been damaged and trailed behind us during our return flight.

A bulletin was released the next day:

"7 November, 1944
Target: Ali Pasin Most Marshalling Yard near Sarajevo, Yugoslavia.
The target for Mission 130 of 7 November was the Ali Pasin Most Marshalling Yard near Sarajevo, Yugoslavia. This target was of high priority at the time it was attacked because of the use the Germans were making of it in their

withdrawal from Greece. Because of the military importance of the target and because of the fact the target was bombed visually, it was a great disappointment to the Group to almost completely miss it. The intense, accurate, and heavy flak defending this target hit sixteen of the twenty-four planes in the formation and wounded one man."

A laudatory assessment report for the 49th wing was issued a few days later, specifying that the mission was a success, despite the poor results of our group:

Damage Assessment Report
HEADQUARTERS FORTY NINTH BOMB WING
APO 520

16 November 1944
SUBJECT: Attack on Sarajevo of 7 November 1944
To: S-2, 451st Bomb Group, 461st Bomb Group, 485th Bomb Group.

For your information: Following is a report received from ground sources on results of the attack on Sarajevo of 7 November:

Sarajevo arms repair work shops, gas works, engine house, railway works shop destroyed or severely damaged. At Ali Pasin Most Railway repair shop, six locomotives destroyed and station installations heavily damaged. On road between Derventa and Doboj, three locomotives and one armored train destroyed. Casualties at Sarajevo high with the First Ustachi Regimented wiped out."

MISSION #24

Sarajevo, Yugoslavia

21 November 1944

I WAS INFORMED at briefing that I would return to the same area near Sarajevo where we had bombed a railroad yard on 7 November, but this time it was to be German troops near Novi Pazar. B-24 bombers were seldom used to bomb troops since they were built and designed to fly at high altitudes and employ 500 or 1000 pound bombs. Frag, or anti-personnel bombs, were small light bombs affixed in clusters to the bomb rack for releasing at very low altitudes. They separated, descending in all directions when released, and presented a danger of colliding with nearby airplanes if discharged at higher altitudes. Bomber crews disliked the small bombs because they descended in unpredictable patterns, but they were deadly, breaking into small lethal pieces of steel shrapnel, when detonated in the proximity of troops. We were again cautioned to expect heavy flak from both heavy and medium anti-aircraft guns mounted on railroad cars, and reminded that we would be very vulnerable at our low altitude. The weather officer forecasted partially cloud cover during our flight to and from the target.

Suddenly the sky was filled with ugly dark puffs that seemed to come from nowhere! We were not expecting anti-aircraft thirty minutes away from the target and had been secure in the belief that we were over safe territory. The flight leader immediately reacted by making a sharp turn, leading our formation away from the gun emplacements. I remembered the briefing officer saying that mobile guns mounted on railroad cars may fire at us, but he said nothing about tanks and trucks that also transported anti-aircraft guns. The German military had become quite adept at moving anti-aircraft guns mounted on various vehicles around the country. Many times mobile guns mounted on trains were disguised as box cars with sides that could be lowered at the last moment before discharging their shells at unsuspecting pilots who had unwittingly flown within their range. Because the gun emplacements were not identified on our map, and due to poor visibility caused by the cloud cover, we had been unaware of their presence until they began firing at us.

The balance of the flight to the IP was uneventful, but as we approached the IP, we could see the target almost covered with a thick black cloud of flak. Without a radar pathfinder aircraft in our formation, it was impossible to see the troop encampment or supple dumps; consequently, the lead bombardier estimated the location of the target and released his bombs. Pathfinder aircraft were equipped with a radar apparatus that could penetrate cloud cover, creating an image of the target for the bombardier to view and accurately direct his airplane over the target. The air force was just beginning to install radar pathfinder equipment on B-24s, but there were few available at that time.

Upon returning, we were informed that our bombs had missed the target, and the following bulletin was issued the next day:

> "21 November, 1944
> Target: Troop Concentrations West of Novi Pazar, Yugoslavia
> Poor visibility and flak at unexpected places interfered with a two flight frag formation led by Captain Mixson against German troop concentrations in Yugoslavia on 21 November, 1944. Photographs show that the bombs fell across the railroad tracks and the highway three miles southeast of Cacak."

We were surprised, a few days later, when we received a commendation for flying bombing missions in dangerous weather:

"Commendation
From: Lee, CO 49th Bomb Wg.
To: Commanding Officer, 461st Bombardment Group.

The following message received from General Spaats forwarded from General Twining is passed on to you for your information:

'Highly gratified at the excellent progress you are making in bombing under adverse weather conditions by day and by night.' "

And so, after failing in our bombing efforts, we receive a commendation for making excellent progress. An ancient Italian expression says it best:

"Cosi il guerra" (so goes the war)

MISSION # 25

Vienna Maitzlendorf Goods Station, Austria

11 December, 1944

THE BRIEFING OFFICER with a long baton pointed to an area south of Vienna on a large map and said,

"Gentlemen, your target today will be the Maitzlendorf Goods Station here. At the IP you will begin your bomb run at 22,000 feet altitude. Your mission is to destroy storage sheds containing vital equipment and further cripple German troop mobility. We expect heavy flak—after all this is Vienna—and maybe you will see some fighter activity. I will let Major Hardt brief you on the weather, but we are hoping that you will have a clear target, the first in several weeks. There will be lots of activity around you. Several bomb groups will be bombing various targets in the same area as your target. Good Luck and God speed."

There was little conversation among the crew as we loaded and prepared our airplane for the mission. By now I was a pro with 24 missions to my credit, but even so, I had learned long ago that both experienced and an inexperienced pilots were equally defenseless against anti-aircraft shells that explode and scatter shrapnel in every direction. I could only hope and pray that fate had not written our names on one of those shells. Past experiences had convinced me that my best and sole defense was to focus my concentration on the tasks of flying the airplane and force all other thoughts of danger from my mind. I was aware that the upcoming mission was to be a "big on"—one from which some of us might never return. No doubt, the other members of the crew were having the same thoughts as they silently went about their tasks.

During the flight to our target, the sky was awash with numerous groups of bombers on their way to Vienna. We had been briefed that the 15th Air Force, together with the entire Allied Armed Forces, had organized a maximum effort to defeat the Nazi and expeditiously end the war. It was rumored that in some cases, we were bombing materials stored adjacent to already destroyed sites before they could be used to repair the sites. Saturation bombing, as it was called, enabled us to stay one step ahead of the Germans by constantly bombing strategic locations before they could be rebuilt. Although I did not know at the time, the Ardennes campaign was just beginning and would soon be know as the famous "Battle of the Bulge", another part of the maximum effort plan of the Americans and Allies. The number of bombers I observed in the sky that day was ample evidence of our maximum effort, but as we approached the IP, I could see that the sky ahead was filled with something ominously different from our effort. It was darkened by a menacing black cloud, the product of innumerable small puffs of clouds from bursting anti-aircraft shells! It was unquestionably the greatest concentration of flak I had observed since my last bombing run over Ploesti. I had no time to speculate over a comparison of anti-aircraft firepower; it was time to concentrate on adjusting my flak vest, helmet, and attending to other tasks. Barrages of anti-aircraft were fired to explode at our altitude and in our general direction in an attempt to fill the air with bursting shells. Since we were powerless to evade the anti-aircraft fire, fate alone would determine which airplanes would be hit. Being helpless, my only alternative was to make an effort to block the bursting shells from my thoughts and concentrate on my tasks.

The weather was clear but the target was obscured with smoke from fires created by bombs released by other groups before us and from smoke pots set off by the enemy in an effort to conceal their supplies and equipment. Due to the haze and smoke, it was necessary for us to use the pathfinder method of bombing; consequently, we could not observe the accuracy of our bombs. My crew collectively drew a sigh of relief the moment we released our bombs and dived out of range of the flak. My racing pulse slowed as I offered a silent prayer of thankfulness. Upon landing we discovered several small holes in our airplane caused by flack, but I was thankful that shrapnel struck none of the crewmembers or engines.

A bulletin was released the next day:

"11 December, 1944
Target: Vienna Maitzlendorf Goods station, Austria
Pressing to complete his tour of duty, Colonel Hawes led a formation of thirty planes in attacking the Vienna Maitzlendorf Goods Station on 11 December 1944. With only two-tenths cloud coverage at the target the enemy flak, which was intense, accurate, and heavy, was probably the worst ever experienced by this Group at Vienna. Fourteen of the twenty-four planes over the target were hit.

Several Groups in the Fifteenth Air Force had already hit targets in the South Vienna Area before this Group arrived at the target. Despite good horizontal visibility the Group was compelled to bomb by pathfinder methods due to the smoke screen, the fires, and the haze in the target area. The bomb pattern was a concentrated one but unfortunately most of the bombs fell just short of the target in an industrial area.

1st Lt. Jay M. Garner had his hydraulics shot out and his cables jammed on this mission. He circled the field for nearly two hours using up his gasoline and waiting for his crew to find some way of letting down and locking the landing gear. Finally, when nearly out of gas, he bailed out all but two other members of his crew and successfully crash landed the plane in the darkness on the non-serviceable East runway. The copilot, Lt. Roger Nixon, and the engineer, Cpl. Charles Barnes, rode the plane down with him. None of the three were injured and much of the plane was salvaged. Major Joseph N. Donovan, the 767th

Squadron Commander, led the second section on this mission and became the third squadron commander in the history of the Group to complete a tour of duty."

A few days later a commendation was issued:

COMMENDATION
"From: 49th Bomb Wing
To: 451st, 461st, 484th Bomb Groups. Attention: S-3 Officers.
Recent photographic coverage has proved that our relentless attacks have dealt crippling blows to the Hun and his most vulnerable spot—his sources of oil. Definite information verifying the effectiveness of the tremendous effort the combat and service units of this Air Force have been called upon to exert compensated in measure for the sacrifices entailed. I realize that in ordering deep penetrations into enemy territory with favorable weather adding to the hazards of combat I have required the personnel of this command to exert a supreme effort. It is heartening to know that such an effort has been crowned with success. The devastated refinery of Blechhammer North bears witness to the valor, the outstanding flying proficiency and professional skill of our combat crews and to the determination of their combat leaders. I commend the fighter pilots and their leaders on the brilliant performance of their escort assignments. I congratulate the service units and the maintenance personnel of the tactical units on their excellent response to the arduous demands made upon them. We know that our campaign is progressing favorably and that our successful attacks on the enemy in the recent months will hasten his complete and utter defeat."
　(Signed)
　GENERAL TWINING

. . .

Before continuing an account of my air combat missions, I think it appropriate to stop here, and insert part of a letter I received from a German friend I met while living in Germany, 40 years after the end of WW II. He presently lives in Wingsbach, Germany and his letter was dated 23 August 1987. The following is an excerpt from that letter. He wrote:

". . . . But what I'll never forget is a bright, ice-cold day in early December 1944, when the Russians were approaching the Slovakian-Austrian border. I was then a little soldier of the_?_ generation and was on guard near Bratislava when I heard the noise of planes in the air. Just for fun I began to count the number of LIBERATOR-bombers that were on their way to Vienna. It was incredible. We had seen a few German fighters, every now and then a Stuka Ju 87 and a Messerachmitt 110, but there, over us, I counted exactly 834 planes! I've never been stunned more in my whole life. That is why I know that American bomber Liberator so well. You see,—that plane means something to both of us . . . Perhaps even, you were one of the crewmembers but you couldn't see me, openmouthed and spellbound, a tiny beetle 20,000 ft. below. . . ."

I find his comments about the number of bombers interesting, and a forecast of the defeat of Germany. He commented later, that after counting 834 American bombers, he remarked to another teenager soldier who had been ordered to dig tank ditches with him,

"Karl, gegen diese Macht kann niemand etwas ausrichten!" (Karl, all labor is in vain against this power!)

He was intuitively aware that Germany had lost the war; even so, German was to be a formidable and deadly adversary for yet some time.

Although, Willy did not recall the exact date that he counted the Liberators, and I do not remember seeing a tiny beetle openmouthed and spellbound 20,000 feet below me, it is entirely possible that I was flying one of the 834 bombers he observed. The mission to Vienna just described was 11 December 1944, near the time he remembers as "early December", and the 834 Liberators or B-24s he recalls certain correspond to the maximum effort mission in which I participated that day. If I did pilot one of the B-24s he described, I am grateful that he was not a victim of my bombs for I would have been denied forever the pleasure of meeting and being acquainted with my charming German friends, Willy Hanssen and his wife, Waltraud.

. . .

Six days later on December 17, the Battle of the Bulge began to expand with the American 7th Armored divisions blocking and engaging General Dietrich's Sixth Panzer Army as it advanced along a major road at Saint Vith. The Germans were forced to take another path that slowed their attack plan and allowed the Americans to reinforce their troops. 140 American soldiers were taken prisoner at Baugnez by Colonel Peiper who allowed 86 to be executed in one of the greatest atrocities committed during the war. 43 survivors returned to the American lines to report the event, which spread quickly among American troops causing much anger and a resolve to fight more intensely.

. . .

It seemed that we would ever be flying in the clouds. Would there ever again be fair weather? Northern Europe has few clear days during the winter of 1944 and it rained or snowed week after week. Our half-barrel heater would become cherry red as we hovered around it in a futile attempt to keep warm on those cold winter nights. Explosions from soot-clogged flue vents were heard frequently around our tent area as the crude gasoline stoves were constantly in use to ward off the frigid winter air. Without insulation, our tent offered few warm places.

We sat near the stove and baked the side of our body nearest the stove while the other side of our body froze. We sat with our feet resting on the stove until the soles of our shoes began smoking and our feet burning. Oh, how I dreaded walking to the unprotected urinals a short distance from our tent! From the middle of December until March we walked on snow from our tent to these latrine pipes. We learned to heat water in our metal helmet placed on the stove in an attempt to remain inside our tent while shaving and taking spit-baths. The officer's club was a warm alternate to our cold tent. The officers club offered warmth, music records, books, tables for writing letters, censoring mail and playing cards between missions. I wrote a V letter to my parents almost everyday. My mother saved them but unfortunately, the letters were destroyed in a house fire many years later. V (victory) letters were written on a small folded single sheet of blue paper and later photocopied by the military post office. The photocopy reduced the size of the letter to that of a small post card and reportedly saved money that the government diverted to financing the war. Officers were assigned the task of reading letters written by enlisted personnel and to censor them by cutting or blocking out words or paragraphs that, in the opinion of the censoring officer, contained restricted information. If a letter contained too many names of locations, missions, dates or any other restricted materials, the letter was returned to the serviceman with a note that it could not be mailed. It was, however, delivered with omitted words and sentences if there were only a few. Officers were not censored because an officer was considered responsible and would presumably withhold restricted information from letters.

MISSION #26

Wels, Austria

25 December, 1944

"LIEUTENANT THOMAS, LIEUTENANT Pettey, time to rise sirs! Wake up! Merry Christmas! Is everybody awake?" A duty sergeant shouted as he entered our tent.

Someone grunted, "OK, OK, I'm awake."

I began to arise from my warm comfortable bed. I could hear rain outside and because it was so frigid inside our tent, my breath vaporized. The night before, I had been disappointed to find my name on mission orders commanding our crew to be ready for a 0500 briefing and 0700 takeoff the following morning—Christmas day! A Christmas menu of turkey with dressing, cranberry sauce, yams, mashed potatoes, English peas and pumpkin pie for desert was posted on the bulletin board adjacent to the mission orders. The bulletin board also displayed a notice that a USO entertainment group would perform on Christmas day at 1500 hours (3 PM). Only one with a strange or ironic sense of humor would dare display these notices on the same bulletin board. I had drifted off to sleep the previous evening recalling past Christmas mornings when suddenly someone awoke me. It was dark and raining as we made out way from our tent to the mess hall for a tasteless breakfast of powdered eggs, dehydrated potatoes, grits and toast. The breakfast, weather, and grumbling about flying on Christmas day created a gloomy truck ride to the briefing room.

Upon arriving, the briefing officer announced that our target for the day was to be an oil refinery located near Brux, Czechoslovikia. He continued by saying that we would be releasing 500-pound general purpose bombs in an effort to destroy the refinery and anything unfortunate enough to be caught near it. The weather officer informed us that we should expect terrible weather and many clouds—something we had already anticipated.

At our parked airplane, we found the ground crew also irritable and tired from working all night without sleep. They had been called out at 2200 hours (11 PM) the previous night to remove fragmentation bombs loaded in our bomb bay for a canceled 24 December mission, and to replace them with 500 pound bombs. The mood of the ground crew only added to our already dejected state of mind and was an ominous foreboding of the mission ahead.

With rain and poor visibility, the controllers dared not let us takeoff until the airplane ahead had fully cleared the runway. This decision caused us to wait at the end of the runway much longer than a normal takeoff, when we could begin our takeoff roll before the airplane ahead had cleared the runway. A result of this slow down also caused a delay in meeting at the rendezvous site to form into groups. I had never before experienced such poor weather during takeoff. Visibility was almost zero, and although we had been advised that visibility would be two miles, we were in clouds during and immediately after takeoff. I silently thanked the controllers for their wise decision to slow our takeoff for it would have been impossible to avoid collisions due to the lack of visibility. We broke out of the clouds at about 1500 feet and began assembling at the rendezvous site. Although we were many hours behind our schedule, we continued toward our target.

A short time after our rendezvous, the flight commander changed our original target to the alternative target, a Marshalling yard at Wels, Austria. The long delay for takeoff had hampered our rendezvous to such extent that he believed that we did not have sufficient daylight remaining to bomb the oil refinery at Brux, Czechoslovakian and return to our base. In addition, we had consumed much of our fuel while waiting for takeoff and circling the rendezvous area; consequently, he deemed it prudent to chose a target that required less flying time. The combination of bad weather, a distant target, and low fuel was a guaranteed prescription for disaster. I believe this decision saved many lives that Christmas day; nevertheless, the mission was a debacle.

Flak was intense over the target and I remember thinking that although it was inopportune to be shot down anytime, it would be a special catastrophe to be hit on Christmas day. After completing the bomb run, I observed that our bombs had failed to strike the target. Weather further deteriorated during our return flight. We found ourselves inside dense clouds unable to determine the position of the other members of our formation.

Arriving at our air base just before dark, we found the runways completely closed due to weather and were ordered to land at another airfield. We chose Foggia air base since it was near and we could see the runway through the fading light and clouds. By the time we had landed, parked the airplane, checked in with operations and walked to the officer's mess, night had arrived. Hungry and tired, we eagerly approached the cafeteria expecting to find a cold Christmas dinner; instead, we were informed that the cafeteria was closed and that we were unexpected guests. The mess hall was unable to prepare a special Christmas dinner but they did prepare a cold sandwich for us and a place for us to sleep was found in an unused, unheated barracks. This was indeed my most unremarkable Christmas.

The next morning the weather had cleared, and after a cold and miserable night, we were able to return to our base. The mission was further described in a bulletin released the same day that we returned to our base:

"25 December, 1944
Target: Wels Marshalling Yard, Austria
At 2200 hours on Christmas Eve the officers and men in

transportation, armament and ordnance sections were ordered to the line in a cold, driving rain to change the bomb load from frag clusters to 500 pound RDX bombs. These frag bombs had been left in the planes in anticipation of the possibility of flying the mission of the 24 December that had been stood down.

At 0744 hours on Christmas morning twenty-six airplanes took off to bomb the synthetic oil refinery at Brux, Czechoslovakia. The planes were off in the rain which was accompanied by a visibility of two miles and a ceiling of less than 500 feet. This was the poorest weather in which this Group had ever taken off for a combat mission. The planes broke through the ten-tenths cumulus at 1500 feet and proceeded to the coast of Yugoslavia individually for assembly and rendezvous. From the rendezvous area northward the weather steadily improved with the result that by the time the Alps were reached it was CAVU with haze.

Having been late in taking off and also having been late at the rendezvous, the Group did not have enough daylight hours left in which to complete a mission against the primary target. As a result, the Group bombed the third alternate target, the Marshaling yard at Wels, Austria. The bombing was done visually but the target was missed.

It was long after dark that evening before the bad weather over the Base moved out to sea. Each of the pilots in the five planes which were early returns had difficulty landing because of the low hanging cumulus clouds. Only one plane which was over the target returned to the Base at the completion of the mission. The pilot of this plane circled the field three times to get underneath a 200 foot ceiling. Most of the planes landed at Bari and at Gioia with a few at scattered fields in the Foggia area. During the afternoon of 25 December a warning order for a mission on the following day was received by the Group. This warning order was later canceled when it was learned by the Air Force that the Group would not have enough planes with which to fly a mission on 26 December.

During the day of the 26th the planes came straggling back to the Base. Having missed their target despite the good weather, having been away from the Base for Christmas, and having slept in their clothes in a vain effort to keep warm the crews were a dejected lot."

. . .

I made a vow that, since I had participated in a combat mission on Christmas day, I would compensate for it by celebrating New Years Day to the best of my ability. I would also hope that I would not be scheduled to fly on New Year's Day. My squadron had planned a party complete with an Italian band, entertainers, dinner, and an open bar. The only ingredient missing were girls. The 461st Bomb Group was located on an isolated farm about 12 miles from Cerignola, a small agricultural unattractive town without pretty girls. If there were any, I assume they were never allowed outside their homes because I had yet to observe one attractive girl. One must acknowledge, however, that the Italian population at that time appeared drab due to a severe shortage of clothing and cosmetics. As an immature young man, I failed to fully grasp the importance of nutrition, clothing and makeup to feminine physical beauty. It was not possible for me to foretell that after recovering from the ravages of war, Italy would produce some of the most beautiful international movie stars of my generation and become the fashion center of the world. Indeed, it was also difficult to envision at that time that an unattractive Italian child—a street ragamuffin begging chocolates from passing American soldiers—would later become a famous international actress known as Sofia Loren.

As I lay nestled in a warm bed the night before our party, soldiers of the U.S. Third and First Army, wearing newspapers under their clothing as added insulation against the intense cold, were engaged in a battle called The Battle of the Bulge. Only two days before, Allied Forces had launched a furious counteroffensive against the Germans. The Third Army thrashed northward while the First Army pushed southward, striving to trap the German army in a pincer movement at Houffalize. For the next 10 days, while wallowing through frozen snow, the Americans fervently battled to capture the Germans and retake Saint Vith. The symphony of war was rapidly building to an evil crescendo while distant war-sounds, like trumpets and tympani, heralded a dissonant cacophony of fiery death and destruction. It was a crescendo that portended a climax to the most depraved and malevolent war in history. Although many were yet to die, the finale was near—the curtain was about to fall.

The New Years party was a huge success. Upon concluding their acts, the USO sponsored Italian singers, dancers, and musicians joined our celebration at the officer's club, adding color and femininity to our otherwise barren club. It was a special treat for us to entertain the entertainers, to be able to share drinks with them, to speak broken Italian, to share giggling conversations with the female members of troupe, or just to stare at them. Although many officers had been stationed at the air base longer than I had, I was starved for female companionship after only four months of combat. Of course, we drank too much; but after all, it was a day free from the stresses of combat, a day without duty or responsibility, a time to welcome the New Year, and a day to relieve some of our pent-up tensions. It was only a short stroll to our tents; consequently, there was little concern for our safety for most of us would be able to find our beds after greeting the New Year. During late evening, I walked a few steps outside the club for a breath of fresh air when I noticed another reveler holding onto a young sapling tree while he relieved himself. It was quite obvious that he was tipsy and that he needed the tree for support, but as he leaned onto it, I noticed the sapling slowly yielding to his weight, bending toward the ground. I immediately ran into the club to motion some of my friends outside, urging them to hurry and witness a comical spectacle. Unaware that he had attracted a group of spectators, he continued to relieve himself as the tree slowly lowered him to a horizontal position on the ground. We held our stomachs while quietly suffered agonizing spasms of hysterical laughter. Upon finishing, he arose, zipped his pants and staggered back into the club unaware of his unusual performance or his appreciative audience. I will never know if anyone ever informed him of the comic role he had played during our New Years celebration, but we who witnessed his spectacular act agreed that it was the most entertaining performance of the day!

As we suffered in bed the following morning, at 0800 on 1 January 1945, Hitler unleashed an air attack he called "The Big Blow". It was an all out effort to destroy allied air power. From information I have gathered, 206 allied aircraft and many airfields were destroyed, but by 1000 hours that morning, 300 German fighter airplanes and 253 pilots of the Luftwaffe had also been destroyed. The German Air Force was almost depleted and was no longer a major factor in determining the outcome of the war.

By 8 January, 1944, the Germans had withdrawn from the tip of the Bulge, ending Hitler's offensive and returning control of the original front to the First and Third U.S. Army. The Battle of the Bulge officially ended on 28 January, 1945. In the meantime, we continued to pound the enemy day and night.

MISSION # 27

Klagenfurt, Austria

8 January, 1944

THE WEATHER OFFICER informed us that we would again be flying in clouds during most of the mission to Linz, Austria marshaling yards. We had been briefed earlier to expect concentrated flak over the target, and although I had not flow a mission to Linz, I had heard other pilots talk about the heavy accurate flak there. When the target was announced at briefing, there was a moan of disappointment from the audience.

While circling and gathering at the rendezvous area, I observed many huge cotton cumulus clouds surrounding us. These beautiful, peaceful, pearl-like clouds are dangerously violent in their interior. In most cases, they can be easily avoided by flying around, under, or over them but non-violent low cirrus clouds tend to form in layers and cannot be avoided. We began encountering both types of clouds soon after leaving the rendezvous point. Subsequently, while attempting to evade the violent cumulus clouds, we found our visibility so limited by the cirrus clouds that we were forced to fly into the turbulent air of the cumulus clouds. We soon found a space between them however, and continued our flight toward the target. When we arrived at the IP, we were again in the clouds and unable to close formation for our bombing run. Flight commander, Colonel Lawhon, then led us in a 360 degree climbing circle in a futile attempt to reach the top of the clouds. Concluding that we were unable to reach the necessary altitude to fly above the clouds, he directed us to our first alternate target, Graz, Austria. Because of bad weather conditions, we were again forced to turn to our second alternate, the marshaling yards at Klagenfurt, Austria.

At last, we found sufficient visibility to fly close formation but we soon became aware that our target was obscured under a heavy layer of clouds. Fortunately, German gunners were also handicapped with poor visibility and their fire, although profuse, was inaccurate. Even so, we lost an airplane.

The following bulletin was issued the following day:

"8 January 1945
Target: Linz South Main Marshalling Yard, Linz, Austria
Mission No. 161, which was flown on the 8th of the month, was a briefed pathfinder four flight formation led by Lt. Colonel Lawhon with the South Main Marshalling Yard at Linz, Austria, as the primary target. At the key point the formation was compelled to make a 360 degree circle to get above the high cirrus. In the target area the solid deck of cirrus was so high that the formation could not get above it for a bomb run. After abandoning the primary target, Lt. Colonel Lawhon attempted an attack on the first alternate target, the marshaling yard at Graz, Austria, but there, too, the high cirrus prevented close formation flying. At Klagenfurt, Austria, the formation finally dropped its bombs on the marshaling yard through a solid undercast with unobserved results. The plane flown by 2nd Lt. Thomas R. Wiley became separated from the formation and failed to return from this mission."

. . .

By this time, I was becoming very impatient to be promoted to a first pilot status. To fly as flight commander intrigued me more than a desire for promotion to the rank first lieutenant. Some of my friends had recently been promoted to first pilot and assigned a crew. Their elevated status caused me to become even more impatient. I was certain that I was prepared for the job; I had completed a tour of 28 combat missions and had logged many official hours as first pilot. The strong desire to be a commander was a symptom of my immature young ego seeking fulfillment. Although a desire to be recognized is prevalent in most young men, it burned as a fire inside me. Upon reflection, it was more or less unimportant when compared to more mundane but important issues of the day: surviving a war and learning from experiences those things that would be valuable to me in later life. The position of copilot was essential and important, but I wanted more—in the hierarchy of a ten-man crew, I wanted to be number one. I was no longer content to be number two. Upon reflection, I have found that my competitive nature has always been both a blessing and a curse. There have been instances when I was over aggressive and alienated associates and friends, which I profoundly regret. Sometimes I have been impatient for success and spent a disproportionate amount of time between my work and my family, which I regret even more. On the other hand, it has served me well as a motivator for hard work and discipline, which I do not regret. Although I did not know it at the time, my name was under consideration for first pilot status.

Linz, Austria

20, January, 1945

COMBAT ORDERS AT squadron headquarters stated that Don had been assigned to our crew the following morning, but during the night, the order was changed. He was assigned to the flight commander's crew as lead bombardier and another bombardier was scheduled to fly with us in the number two, or deputy leaders slot. It was an unusual last minute switch, but occasionally crewmembers were honored on their final mission by assigning them to the flight leader's crew. I was well acquainted with Don. I had attended many social events with him and he was also the regular bombardier for a very close friend of mine. I was aware that this would be his last combat mission but I never envisioned that it would indeed be his last and final honor.

A groan arose from the briefing room as our commanding officer announced that we were to again bomb the marshaling yards at Linz, Austria. My last mission had also targeted Linz but due to heavy clouds, the mission was canceled. Of the last eight missions scheduled for our group, six had been canceled because of poor weather. Linz had remained safely concealed underneath a giant blanket of clouds but the weather officer predicted that during the upcoming mission there would be few clouds and good visibility. Visual bombing signified good and bad news. Bombardiers would have a clear view of the target through their bombsights; on the other hand, enemy anti-aircraft gunners would also have a clear view of us through their gun sights. Linz had gained a reputation as a very dangerous target due to the accuracy of their gunners. The city is located in a bowl-like valley partially surrounded by mountains providing an ideal base for anti-aircraft gun emplacements. Anti-aircraft guns were positioned on the peaks of mountains up to one-half of our flying height. This altitude reduced the need for enemy gunners to calculate the trajectory of their shells over great distances. We would be unable to maneuver over the target, we would be near the anti-aircraft guns and due to the clear weather, we would be highly visible, all suitable ingredients for a disastrous mission.

Our takeoff and flight to the target was uneventful but as we approached the IP, I saw formations of B-24s receiving heavy damage from flak. I could only push my steel helmet down over my eyes, shrink into the steel coffin seat, make myself as small a target as possible behind my flak vest, and try to ignore the black clouds of flak bursting around me. It was evident that the anti-aircraft gunners were not merely sending up barrages; they were aiming at specific airplanes. Puffs of exploding shells followed the flight paths of Liberators before us as they plunged into diving turns away from the target. Our aircraft shuddered and bounced from the concussion of exploding shells around us. We were assigned the deputy lead slot in our formation, which is slightly behind and above the right wing of the flight leader's Liberator.

Suddenly the lead airplane exploded into a fireball and nosed upward in a steep climb. Because we were slightly behind and above, our B-24 began to overtake the burning plane as it lost forward speed. I was immediately on the controls with Dave attempting to move downward and away from it. When the explosion occurred, we were within seconds of releasing our bombs over the target. Recognizing that we may need more maneuverability, Dave shouted over the intercom for the bombardier to release our bombs. We forced the column control full forward to nose our aircraft into a steep dive presuming the burning plane would pass over us, but suddenly it stalled and banked toward us from above. Because it was diving toward us and gaining speed, my impulse was then to abruptly reverse our direction by pulling the nose upward, climb in order to slow our forward speed, and allow the burning plane to pass under us. Indeed, there was no time to think about consequences, there was barely time to act. Dave was larger and stronger, but miraculously, I overpowered him and pulled the control back as far as it would move. With a stunned expression on his face, he instantly nodded his approval and began to assist me as the burning plane passed underneath us. Relief and joy quickly changed into sadness when I became aware that no one had escaped from the stricken lead airplane.

The return flight was a nightmare, limping along with two engines threatening to quit, without radio contact, without instruments, and expecting to be forced to parachute from our crippled aircraft at any moment. Further more, our formation had scattered over the target and we could not maintain sufficient speed to fly along with any other formations for protection. We were unsure that the airplane would survive a landing but with the grace of God, an abundance of luck, a good engineer, and patience, we managed to persuade the engines to continue functioning, even though they protested, throughout our return trip to our air base.

After a stressful but safe landing and a long taxi ride to our hard stand parking space, Dave commented that my actions had doubtless saved the lives of our crewmembers. Even so, I never expected to be awarded a Distinguished Flying Cross several weeks later.

After his death, Dave's widow sent me a copy of several letters he had written to his parents. I will let him describe this mission with excerpts from his letters to his parents:

> 1/21/45
> "Hi Folks—
> Scratch off one more, only two to go now. I flew yesterday and if the last two are as bad as that, I'll be ready to hang it up. We only had 45 holes in our ship. 35 of them were from the waist windows back but no one was hit. I never ducked so often and so fast in all my life. The waist gunners had flak pieces bouncing off their heads all during the bomb

run. One went between the right waist gunner's legs and went through a 50-cal. cartridge. We got some of our biggest holes to date. One piece put a 6" hole in my window and knocked my flak helmet over my eyes. We also got several hits up front. One was in our #2 gas cell and another knocked our radio out. We were flying #2 position on the right wing of the flight leader when he got a direct hit and broke into a mass of flames. He went out of control and peeled off onto us. We salvoed our bombs and just about pulled up enough so he passed under us. What a mission. Soon as we were clear of flak three of our turbos ran away, two of our flight instruments were out and I couldn't tell how much to depend on the others. Coming home we went in the soup at 20,000' and broke out at 13,000'. We couldn't see the other ships and there we were with our instruments out. To add to our woes we were sweating out 2 engines because our oil pressures were fluctuating and we were afraid we got hit in the oil lines. We sure were glad to hit terra firma after that. That's a good way to pull your hair out in bunches.

Both Pettey and I were so tired we went to bed at 7 last night. We figured we would sleep until it was time to go to church this morning but they got us up to test hop a "micky" ship. _____.

It was quite chilly yesterday. (during the bomb mission) Just a-50 degrees maybe. I wasn't cold after the window was broken. The inside of the cockpit was covered with frost from our breath condensing and every time a shell burst close, the concussion knocked it loose and it seemed like it was snowing. _____.

As ever, Dave"

A bulletin was released from headquarter the following day after the Linz mission:

20 January 1945
"Target: Linz North Main Marshaling Yard, Austria
For Mission No. 164 Captain Roberts drew the assignment
of leading what turned out to be the roughest mission of
the month of January. The target was the North Main
Marshalling Yard at Linz, Austria. For purposes of destroying
rolling stock in the yard, 100 pound general purpose bombs
were used. With only a four-tenths cloud coverage at the
target the flak was extremely intense, accurate and heavy.
Twenty-one of the twenty-five airplanes over the target were
hit. Two of these were extremely hard hit and exploded
before they could completely roll out of the formation on
the bomb run. These explosions spread the formation with
the result that the bombs were scattered over a comparatively
large area at the extreme northern end of the marshaling
yard. The two planes lost were flown by 2nd Lt. Joseph M.
O'Neal and 2nd Lt. James R. Yancey. Four other combat
crewmembers were wounded on this mission."

Any memory of the 20 January 1945 mission over Linz, Austria
always brings to mind the following incident:

Approaching our air base after a terror-filled day of flak, burning
airplanes, and severe damage to our aircraft, a hesitant quivering voice
with a southern accent came over the intercom,

"See ya'll in Church tomorrow."

Today, in a much different environment and under different
circumstances, I hesitate to recount this event for fear that it may seem
rather childish to the reader. But try to imagine ten young men fatigued,
frightened, taut as violin strings, sickened from observing a friend die
on his last mission, uncertain that our aircraft could safely return or
even survive a landing, and one can perhaps better understand the
comic-relief value of the remark. This simple statement made by John

Masterson, our nose gunner, seems a most appropriate climax to a terrifying day.

. . .

A few days before the Linz mission, my promotion to First Lieutenant and first pilot status had been approved, although I was unaware of it until a few days later. A letter written by Dave to his parents describes my elation:

1/25/45

"Pettey finally got a crew of his own. He has seven more to go and is flying his first mission as 1st pilot tomorrow. He is a darn good pilot too. He's happy as a lark because he received his silver bars the same day they gave him a crew. The more missions he gets as a 1st pilot, the better off he will be when he gets back to the States for reassignment. On our last mission (Linz) he logged first pilot time even though he flew as co-pilot.——I guess that's all for now. As Ever, Dave."

I had many reasons for rejoicing after this mission. That I had merely survived was sufficient cause for rejoicing, but in addition, I had flown my last mission as a second lieutenant and as a co-pilot. Although I was unaware until later, on 8 March 1945, I was awarded a Distinguished Flying Cross. The award would only further invigorate the thrill of having survived the mission of 20 January 1945.

MISSION #29

Moosbierbaum Oil Refinery, Austria

31 January, 1945

I WAS IN such a state of excitement that I could barely sleep the night before my first mission as a command pilot. Even though I had previously logged two missions officially as first pilot, both missions had been with my original crew. Throughout our entire training period and 28 combat missions, I had served as their copilot; as a result, it was somewhat difficult for them to recognize me as their commanding pilot so long as Dave was present. I could now expect to receive this respect from a new crew who had never before known me as their copilot. As I lapsed into sleep, I dreamed: "Twenty-eight down and seven more missions to go, but tomorrow I will fly with my own crew".

"Lieutenant Pettey, Lieutenant Thomas, wake up. Time for breakfast and briefing!"

The voice of a duty sergeant on a dark, dismal, cold morning is about the most disagreeable sound one can image; however, on that morning, I leaped out of bed eager for the new day to begin. Today I would be a first pilot and in command of my own crew! Dave was ordered to fly with a new inexperienced crew and Richard was ordered to fly with me as my navigator and complete his tour of 35 combat missions. I knew he was nervous because lately he had experienced several nightmares causing him to shout so loud that Dave and I had been awakened. By speaking calmly, we had been able to gently awaken him from his nightmares. I was troubled that he had been assigned to my crew because I had recently begun to believe that he was suffering a nervous break down. Contributing to my suspicions was an incident that had occurred during an earlier mission when John, our flight engineer, has smelled smoke during a bomb run. Upon investigating its source, John found oil dripping on a heater in the nose section of the aircraft. The nose gunner could not smell the smoke because he was enclosed in the nose turret and the bombardier could not desert his bombsight during the bomb run. Richard, the lone crewmember that had been free to act, was immobilized with fear. Dave, James and I had expressed a fear that this behavior might effect the moral of our crew but we had not yet informed the flight surgeon or requested his advice. We had grown very fond of Richard and although we were concerned about his health, we were uncertain about how we should confront him about his problem. During another mission, the bombardier had physically struck him in frustration. Fortunately, we were near the completion of our combat tour; consequently, we postponed any attempt to solve the dilemma.

I had attended several briefings during the month of January but all were canceled. The briefing officer informed us that the mission looked promising that day with fair weather forecast over the target. I became acquainted with my new crew while preparing for the flight and found they had varied combat experience. Some, like Richard, were near the end of their tour of combat and some were only beginning their tour. I was pleased to find that my co-pilot had flow enough missions to qualify as an experienced combat pilot.

Long before arriving at our target, Richard shouted over the intercom,

"Fighters at one o'clock! It looks like there are two of them. Here they come!"

I saw in the distance what appeared to be two small specks but they were no threat to us at the moment. I replied over the inter-com,

"Calm down, I see them but they are too far away to shoot at us. Just keep your eye on them."

A few moments passed and he began again to shout over the intercom,

"They're coming! They're coming! It looks like two of them at one o'clock. Can everyone see them? Over there to the right at about two o'clock now. Oh, God they're coming! They're coming! Everyone get set to fire they're coming___".

He seemed unable to stop shouting over the intercom. Until he released the activation button on his microphone, none could use the radio. I began to call over his hysterical voice, hoping he would momentarily release the mike button,

"Richard, get off the intercom. Get off the intercom. This is the pilot, I order you to get off the intercom! Richard_____"

It was extremely important that the all crew members maintain intercom silence at all times so that it could be used to report important information which may be life threatening to the entire crew. When the two specks disappeared, he regained his composure and I was able to regain control of the radio.

This was my 29th mission and I would not allow myself to spend much time contemplating future missions. Common wisdom of the squadron declared the last five missions of a combat tour more nerve-racking than the previous 30. Each remaining bombing mission became incrementally more tense as the end of combat duty drew nearer. This was Richard's last mission and he was "sweating it out", as we would say. He had only one more mission to go and his nightmares would be over.

Soon after the navigator was calmed, we began to experience problems with an engine. The copilot said,

"Engine number two is losing RPMs and oil pressure going down."

I was aware that something was unusual when the sound of the engines changed from a steady hum to a pulsating throb. The propeller of one engine had slowed causing the other three propellers to be out of synchronization. The flight engineer immediately checked the fuel gauges to determine if the engine was receiving sufficient fuel. I instructed the copilot to feather the engine before the oil pressure dropped any further because without pressure, it is impossible to feather a propeller. He pushed the feathering button above us as I cautiously watched to be sure that he pushed the correct one. During moments of excitement, copilots or pilots have been known to push the incorrect button and cause the aircraft to lose an additional engine. The feathering button kicked into the "out" position indicating that the propeller did not feather properly. I instructed him to try again, and to our relief, the button remained in the feathering position that time, causing the propeller to slow. The slow windmilling propeller will not stop until the mixture control and booster fuel pump is turned to the "off" position, completely shutting down the engine. When the propeller is feathered and no longer turns, drag is reduced allowing the other three engines to operate more efficiently. A B-24 will climb on three engines but increasing their power to compensate for the loss of an engine may overburden the war-weary engines and cause them to overheat. This creates a very real possibility that another engine will fail. The copilot skillfully turned off the engine and increased the power of the remaining three engines while I struggled with the rudders to overpower the torque created by the loss of power on one side of the aircraft. I signaled him to help me control the rudders while I turned on the automatic pilot and trimmed the airplane. Within a sort time we were able to trim the flight controls for a level and straight course, but while feathering the engine, our reduced air speed had compelled us to drop out of the formation. I turned back toward our air base.

On 2/1/45 Dave wrote his parents:

"Not much to say so I will say very little and hit the hay as I am multi-tired.

I squeezed another one in so now have one more to go. My radio operator finished up today. We briefed three times and then yesterday my flight flew while I stayed on the ground because my starter broke and couldn't be fixed in time. Pettey got off on what started as his first one with his new crew but he came back early with an engine out. We were both disgusted so we told them to schedule us until we flew, so we got me in today.

I should go tomorrow as a copilot for a new crew. They always send an old pilot or copilot along on the first one. I told them I wanted to finish with my old crew. . . . ."

As Dave had written, I was disgusted. We flew a dangerous mission but because we had lost an engine and was forced to return, despite my plea, we did not receive credit for it. I also felt sympathy for Richard who had suffered a great deal of anxiety during the previous flight only to find it necessary to cope with yet another mission. With the exception of the crew that ran out of fuel, it seemed that I had also lost credit for a "milk run", as noted in the bulletin below.

"31 January 1945
Target: Moosbierbaum Oil Refinery, Austria
Ten briefings were conducted during the last third of the month of January before Mission No. 165 was finally flown. On the last day of the month, Lt. Colonel Hardy led the Red Force in a three flight formation on a pathfinder attack on the oil refinery at Moosbierbaum, Austria. The mission went very well until the time of the bomb run. On the bomb run Lt. Holmes, the mickey operator, had the target in his scope but lost it when the formation was forced off the heading of the bomb run by another Group. He was unable to pick up the target again on a second attempted attack on the target. Most of the bombs were returned to Base.

The plane flown by 2nd Lt. Edward K. Delano ran out

of gas and was compelled to ditch not too far off the coast of Yugoslavia on the return route.

Those killed were the Pilot and 2nd Lt. Frank P. Hower, 2nd Lt. John O. Ungethuem, S. Sgt. Raymond H. Steelman, Cpl. Richard J. Gomez, and Pfc. William M. Gross. After having been soaked in the cold January waters of the Adriatic, the following members of the crew got aboard a life raft where they remained for twenty-two hours before being picked up: Cpl. Robert C. Neel, Cpl. William F. Nourse, Cpl. Wallace D. Olsen, and Cpl. Carl B. Peterson. For nine members of this crew this was their third mission, but S. Sgt. Steelman would have completed his tour of duty on the mission had he lived."

MISSION #29 (AGAIN!)

Regensburg Winter Harbor Oil Storage, Germany

5 February 1945

I HAD ATTENDED three previous briefings for missions that had been canceled because of weather. With only seven missions remaining, I became more impatient with each cancellation but when the briefing officer announced Regensburg as the target for the day, I would have been happy if this mission had also been canceled. A groan arose from the audience. I remembered Regensburg as the most dangerous mission I had flown so far and I had no desire to encounter German fighters, as we had before. Judging from the groan emanating from the other pilots, I had much company. When the room quieted the officer continued briefing us of the projected heading, altitude of the bomb run, and other items of interest. Then, to add to my apprehension, the weather officer forecast cloudy and poor visibility over the target.

After arriving at the airplane and donning our flying gear, my copilot asked if I had ever flown a Regensburg mission. I casually answered that it was only another mission and not nearly as dangerous as Ploesti. The blase answer seemed to satisfy him for he asked no further questions as we proceeded through various checklists and prepared for our takeoff.

We encountered thick clouds all the way from the rendezvous site to the target. As we approached the initial point, I was unable to distinguish the intended target due thick layers of clouds; nevertheless, headquarters had anticipated the cloud cover and our lead plane was equipped with a radar bomb sight, pathfinder. As we turned to the desired compass heading of the bomb run, I observed that there was no flak to be seen in any direction. This was most unusual, for Regensburg was noted for its numerous anti-aircraft guns. We flew the entire bomb run without encountering a single shell fired at us, however, as we turned away from the target, I could see flak at a distance. Why were we spared that day? Perhaps the German war machine was suffering shortages unknown to us but one should never make assumptions about war.

The return flight was uneventful and allowed me time to give thanks for completing another safe mission and to reflect on the reply I had given my copilot when he asked if I had ever flow over Regensburg. In order to reassure him, I had nonchalantly answered that it was just another mission, never presuming that it would indeed be a "milk run". I also pondered over the groans pilots had expressed upon being informed that our target would be Regensburg at the morning briefing. Although I had a strong impulse to say to the copilot, "see, I told you so", I resisted and left him to his own reflections for I was certain that flak would be waiting at Regensburg for those unlucky crews who would be selected to bomb it the following day. Indeed, such are the fortunes of war!

The following bulletin was released the next day:

"5 February 1945
Target: Straubing, Germany
Colonel Lawhon also led the second mission of the month. The primary target was the Regensburg Winter Harbor Oil Storage, Germany. Over the Alps the formation picked up a solid undercast and flew through four-tenths cirrus approaching the target area. The bombs were dropped by the pathfinder method. The fact that no flak was encountered where the bombs were dropped and also that there was plenty of flak beyond where the bombs were dropped raised the question as to what happened. Back on the ground, it was figured out from the navigators' logs that the formation

had been approximately twenty miles east of course, had mistaken a town south of the Danube as the initial point, and actually bombed the briefed initial point, Straubing, Germany, instead of Regensburg which lay straight ahead on course."

MISSION #30

Strebersdorf Ordnance Depot, Vienna

7 February 1945

I LAY AWAKE, for what seemed an eternity, thinking about my imminent missions. My thoughts flashed, twisted, weaving my mind into an endless orbit of scenes from previous missions that prevented me from drifting off into sleep. After what seemed to be hours of tossing and turning, a harsh voice startled me from a deep sleep,

"Lieutenant Pettey, Lieutenant Thomas, wake up. Time to get ready for briefing."

As I opened my eyes I could see the head of an OD, officer of the day, protruding through our tent opening. After we had assured him that we were awake, we arose and dressed for breakfast and briefing. This would be Dave's last briefing and combat mission. Although we would be bombing the same target, he would be flying with a new and inexperienced crew, while I would be flying with my crew. I asked during breakfast how he was coping with this final mission. He replied that he was nervous and hoped the crew would not notice.

A double mission was announced at briefing. During a double mission the group bombed two targets: one or more formations release their bombs over one target while other formations from the group set off to bomb a different target. This was to be my first double mission. The group would fly together to Vienna but my target would be Zwolfaxing airdrome near Vienna while other formations would bomb Florisdorf Oil Refinery, also near Vienna. My airplane was loaded with clusters of small frag bombs designed to scatter shrapnel over a large area and destroy aircraft parked on the airfield. We were briefed to expect the famous and usual Vienna heavy flak.

The target was clear and the flak severe. We flew through what seemed to be a solid cloud of black smoke, released our bombs and safely returned to base.

During our return-flight-reflections, I subtracted one more mission, only five more to go—the dreaded final five.

MISSION #31

Vienna Central Repair Shops, Austria, Zagreb

8 February 1945

WHILE THE BRIEFING officer announced our target, I speculated that, inasmuch as we were being briefed to bomb repair
shops, the war must be near an end. This was the first time that I could
recall repair shops being bombed, even though I had heard rumors
that we were currently bombing supplies before they could be utilized
to repair damages from previous bombings. The briefing officer brought
me back to reality by announcing that heavy flak was expected over the
target and the weather officer again forecasted heavy cloud cover.

The takeoff, rendezvous, and flight to the target were routine and
uneventful but when we turned toward the target, I noticed a sky filled
with little black clouds signifying flak over the target. I thought back to
the briefing session where I momentarily had visions of an end to the
war. It occurred to me that being near the end of a war was beside the
point for anyone who might be killed that day. I swept all thoughts
from my mind and concentrated on the tasks at hand. Somehow we
flew through the flak, released our bombs and safely returned to our
base. A summary of this mission was issued the next day:

> "8 February 1945
> Target: Vienna Central Repair Shops, Austria Zagreb
> Major Phillips led Mission No. 171 on 8 February 1945.
> The target was the Central Repair Shops in Vienna. The
> Group was one of twenty in the Air Force hitting this target
> by pathfinder. Bomb strike photos show that the target area
> was completely cloud covered. Nine of the twenty-three
> planes over the target were hit by flak."

MISSION #32

Marshalling Yard Maribor, Yugoslavia

13 February 1945

WITH ONLY FOUR missions of my tour remaining, I wanted to fly every day so that I might sooner complete my combat obligation. Inexorably, each day had moved at a snail's pace until my name appeared on night orders to report for briefing the following morning. I had impatiently waited five days before being assigned another mission.

Again a double-target was announced. During briefing, I was relieved to be notified that I had been assigned to the blue force, which would bomb a marshaling yard in Yugoslavia. Targets in Yugoslavia were usually less dangerous than those in Germany; however, one could never be sure. I continued to remind myself that targets, whether Yugoslavia or other places, were defended by anti-aircraft gunners resolved to kill us.

The weather was clear and from our IP I could see the target ahead unobstructed by clouds or smoke. We would be bombing visually, but the anti-aircraft gunners would also have an unrestricted view of us, and so they did! Persistent flak exploded ubiquitously around us as we released our bombs, but we managed to evade the heavy fire and safely return to our base. During the return flight, I mentally subtracted another sortie—only three more missions to go!

A summation of the double mission appeared in a bulletin released the next day:

"13 February 1945

Target: Vienna Central Repair Shops, Austria, and Maribor Marshalling Yard, Yugoslavia

Mission No. 173 finally turned out to be another double header mission, each with a different target. A TWX which was received from the Air Force through channels, however, directed that in the future double header missions should be counted as one mission.

The target of the Red Force was the Central Repair Shops at Vienna, Austria. Major Poole led the formation on this mission. The weather was CAVU in the target area but smoke obscured the target which was completely missed by visual bombing. Under ideal defense conditions the Vienna flak lived up to its vaunted reputation. Fifteen of the seventeen planes over the target were hit, one man was wounded, and one plane was lost. The lost plane was piloted by 2nd Lt. Francis X. Fink. It lost altitude rapidly coming off the target and when last seen was being covered by the P-51 escort.

Captain Veiluva led the Blue Force in attacking the marshaling yard at Maribor, Yugoslavia. here, too, the weather was CAVU and here, too, the bombing was done visually. The mission was scored at 28.3 percent. Eight of the eighteen planes over the target were hit by flak and two men were wounded.

Upon returning to the Base, 2nd Lt. Robert M. Kelliher, 765th Squadron, entered the left hand traffic pattern with his No. 2 engine feathered. While circling the field he lost No. 1 engine and with the left wing down slipped into a crash landing in which his navigator, 2nd Lt. Donald Williams, was fatally injured."

. . .

Dave had completed his combat tour and received orders to return to the United States. The following morning while cleaning our tent, I noticed him standing beside a jeep a short distance from our tent. Instead of fatigues that we usually wore on our free days, he was dressed in full uniform and seemed to be staring at our tent while his driver waited patiently in the jeep. It suddenly occurred to me that he must be departing for his new assignment and was waiting for me to join him so that we could say goodbye. As I began walking toward him I could see his face brighten and a big grin spread across his face. He said,

"I was wondering if you were going to say goodbye".

"I didn't know you were leaving today". I replied.

We said little as we embraced, but through watery eyes I could see him wipe away a tear as he climbed into the passenger side of the jeep. As I stood motionless watching the jeep disappear from sight, I became aware of conflicting emotions within me. I had lost a good and trusted friend—one that I admired and who had taught me to be a better pilot. For those contributions, I was grateful to Dave, but at the same time, I had lost a commander who had cast a long shadow over me. I had lived in his shadow since I first joined his crew, almost since graduating as a pilot. Now for the first time, I was free of Dave's shadow! I could be my own man.

MISSION #33

Vienna Penzinger Marshalling Yard, Austria

15 February 1945

ONLY ONE FREE day had passed between my last mission and this one. I found my name again on combat orders. My copilot had been promoted to first pilot and a new copilot was assigned to my crew along with several other crewmembers who were replacing those that had completed their tour of duty or were assigned to other crews. It appeared that I would no longer be flying with the same crew for my few remaining missions; nevertheless, if given the opportunity, I would have flown a mission every day. Perhaps it was fortunate that I was unable to fly uninterrupted missions. Without some rest between missions, a pilot can experience fatigue and represent a danger to his crew. My nerves were being wound tighter each day. The thought swirled constantly in my head— "only three more to go and after this one, only two more to go."

The briefing officer announced our target would again be a marshaling yard in Vienna and another double mission. I was assigned to a group called Red Force with both Red Force and Blue Force bombing the same target. Not only did the briefing officer predict the usual heavy Vienna flak over the target, he forecasted a heavy cloud cover over the target. I was experiencing deja vu—Vienna, heavy flak, marshaling yards, bad weather, double targets! The good news for this mission was that the cloud cover would cause the anti-aircraft gunners to fire at us through a layer of clouds. The bad news was Vienna where flak was regularly heavy and accurate.

Takeoff and the flight to Vienna was uneventful and although we saw heavy bursts of anti-aircraft fire during the bomb run, it was a distance beyond our formation and we were able to release our bombs without casualties. Indeed, the clouds had not only obscured our bombing target, but it must also have obscured us from anti-aircraft gun sights as well. Because of a humdrum return flight, I was able to mentally subtract one more mission from my remaining missions, give a prayer of gratitude for another safe mission, and request two more "milk-runs".

Following is the official bulletin released the next day:

"15 February 1945
Target: Vienna Penzinger Marshalling Yard, Austria
Again, a double header mission, Vienna, and ten-tenths cloud coverage. Again pathfinder bombing and unobserved results. Again good protection against the flak by the cloud coverage.

Major Poole, who started out leading the Red Force, was forced to abort. The lead was taken over by the Deputy, Captain Cooper. Only one plane in this formation was hit by flak, but a man on that plane was wounded.

Major Mixson was the leader of the Blue Force. No flak damage was sustained, but oxygen failure cost the life of Corporal John O. Moore."

MISSION #34

Dry-docks Fiume, Italy

19 February 1945

FOLLOWING A FOUR-day reprieve from combat, I was informed at briefing that our primary target was to be South Station, again near Vienna. This was my 34th mission, and with only two remaining, I was not pleased to be informed that our target was again Vienna. It appeared that the 15th Air Force was determined to destroy Vienna. I listened intently and nervously as the commander talked about the heavy flak and possible fighters anticipated over the target. The weather officer again gave us a forecast of heavy clouds between our base and the target, but he thought the target would be clear by the time we arrived. I made a pledge to myself that I would attempt to withhold from my crew any indications that I was becoming progressively edgy as I approached the end of my combat tour. While preparing for takeoff, I pretended to be confident, carefree, and cheerful, but in retrospect, I suspect that my act was more for my benefit. The performance must have been successful, for all my apprehensions diminished and I could concentrate better on my tasks as pilot.

The weather forecast was very accurate. We were flying in clouds shortly after takeoff and despite radio contact with flight leaders, the poor visibility made it impossible for many to find their assigned formation. As we circled the rendezvous area searching for our formation, the squadron leader, finally in desperation, instructed us to join any available formation. We had consumed so much fuel, we were compelled to bomb our alternate target, the shipyards at Fiume, Italy. Although I was concerned that I had not located my flight formation, I was greatly relieved that I would not be flying through flak-alley over Vienna.

My prayer was answered—my luck held fast—my next to last mission was another "milk run"! We had released our bombs over the target and had encountered little flak. Although we had missed the target, I was unconcerned. My sole concern now was to survive one more bomb run and one more mission.

An official bulletin released the next day accurately described the mission:

"19 February 1945
Target: Vienna South Station Area, Austria
With Mission No. 178 the Group missed another opportunity to register a satisfactory visual bombing score at Vienna. The target was the South Station. North of Judenburg, engine failure forced the formation leader, Major Poole, to leave the formation. After the bomb load had been dropped on a target of opportunity at Wolfsburg, Austria, the plane staggered back to Base on two engines. Captain Thackston, who had been flying the Deputy lead position, took over the formation lead. Bad weather split up the formation and only fourteen planes bombed the primary target for a discouraging score of 3 percent. Three of the planes over Vienna were holed by flak and two men were injured. Nine airplanes which had lost the formation made a visual run on the dry-docks at Fiume, Italy, but completely overshot the target".

MY LAST MISSION #35

Bolzano Marshalling Yard, Italy

20 February 1945

HEADQUARTERS HAD SHOWN some compassion by allowing me to fly my last mission the day following my previous mission. While I was acutely aware of those who had been shot down and died on their last mission, I was grateful that I could fly the following day with little time to think about that frightening "One more mission". To contemplate the many young lives that were sacrificed in World War II is depressing—to reflect on how many of them perished during their last mission is unspeakable. An analogy might be made to the final seconds of a foot race when one leads the race and while exerting that one last ounce of energy, collapses inches from the finish line. As I tossed restlessly in bed the night before that last mission, I prayed that God would grant me one last, safe bombing mission. The old clichés, "to be so near yet so far" and "one more to go", incessantly swirled through my troubled mind as I tossed and turned. Sleep refused to draw near that night.

I sighed a breath of relief the next morning when the briefing officer announced that the Bolzono Marshalling Yards in Italy was to be our bombing destination. Although there is danger present in all bombing missions, Italy seemed to defend their military installations with fewer guns and less fervor than other targets in Europe. If given a choice of targets for my last mission, I would have chosen one in Italy. I was praying for a "milk run", and perhaps I had been granted my prayer; however, the weather officer cautioned that we could expect severe weather.

As I had the day before while preparing for take-off, I cheerfully pretended that I had few concerns or cares; nevertheless, I suspect my crew knew better. Soon after take-off, we encountered cumulus, cirrus clouds building up to over 20,000 feet. Judging that we could not safely fly around or above them, our flight leader abandoned our primary target and headed toward our second alternate target, the shipyards at Fiume, Italy. We released our bombs over the target with good results and returned without encountering flak. I could barely contain my elation—I had finished my tour of combat with a "milk run"! During my return-flight-reflections, I gave thanks for my prayers being answered and planned a celebration party at the officer's club that night. I mentally tallied the names of friends I would invite to help me celebrate my last mission—it was a tradition that those who completed their tour of combat buy drinks that night.

The following bulletin was an official summary of my last mission:

"20 February 1945
Target: Fiume Shipyards, Italy
Thick Cirrus at the head of the Adriatic with tops over 23,000 feet compelled the Group leader, Major Mixson, to abandon the Bolzano Marshalling Yard, Italy, as a primary target on 20 February 1945. The second alternate target, the shipyards at Fiume, Italy, was bombed visually for a score of 37.3 percent. The main concentration of bombs fell in the built-up area near the docks with hits on the docks, warehouses, and harbor jetty. This mission resulted in three cases of frostbite, an unusual experience for the flying personnel of this Group."

I have often said that my last mission was so dull that some were bored to sleep and awoke with frostbite!

AFTER COMBAT

WITH MY APPREHENSIONS and tensions from combat set aside temporarily, I was free to begin planning my future. The war in Europe raged as if it was never to end and rumors abounded that the American Army would soon invade Japan. The 461st Bomb Group would fly 44 additional bombing assignments before hostilities ceased. Only a few days before my last mission, the British RAF had bombed Dresden, Germany, one of the most important ports of Germany, where it is estimated that 25,000 residents were killed and 30,000 were wounded from fires created by the bombing.

I had heard rumors that some returning combat veteran pilots from the European Theater were sent to the South Pacific Theater of war. Had I been seeking a career in the Air Force and a promotion, I would have volunteered for service in the South Pacific flying B-29s, a newer and larger bomber, but my only military ambition was to be discharged and return to civilian life. From the moment I had entered the military establishment, I had detested military bureaucracy—the unthinking, unfeeling, "go by the book" mentality.

Another rumor had intrigued me. I had heard that the Mediterranean Allied Transport Service (MATS) needed additional pilots and would welcome combat veterans. One of my best friends, Larry Weimer, who had just completed his tour of duty, had heard the same rumor. We were both single, ready for adventure, and had no desire to serve another tour of combat with Japan; consequently, we thought it a good idea to visit MATS headquarters and investigate the rumor. It was a coincident that at the same time my squadron headquarters approached me and asked if I would consider flying a B-24 to Naples for the purpose of returning some personnel who had been on leave. I volunteered and requested that Larry and I fly together as pilot and copilot. This flight assured us a round trip from Cerignola to Capodichino Air Base in Naples where we could visit MATS headquarters, pick up the returning personnel, and return the same day.

Upon arriving we found that MATS indeed needed additional pilots. We were immediately offered a transfer from the 461st Bomb Group to MATS, where C-47 and C-46 transport airplanes were employed to ferry equipment and personnel between allied bases scattered over Europe, North Africa, and Middle Eastern countries. This was a very tantalizing offer for us because, more than anything, we longed for adventure and an opportunity to see the world. We wasted no time signing all the necessary papers and returning our passengers to Cerignola. During our return flight, while Larry controlled the airplane, I sat dozing in the pilot seat with my safety belt unfastened. I saw a small cumulus cloud ahead but ignored it assuming that Larry would fly around it. Most cumulus clouds contain violent air currents that can be dangerous and are best avoided if possible. I was relaxed and barely awake as we flew into the cloud. Suddenly I shot upward as the aircraft was sucked downward in a downdraft. My head crashed into the overhead radio control before I dropped back into my seat like a sack of potatoes! As I rubbed my aching head, I asked Larry why he had flow through the cloud rather than around it. He replied with a big grin,

"I just wanted to make sure you were awake."

Only very, very, good friends can remain friends after such a remark!

While I waited for my transfer to become official, events were unfolding around me that would hasten the end of the war. The Yalta Conference between Stalin, Churchill and Roosevelt had concluded only a few weeks before, 11 February, 1945, where Stalin had agreed to enter the war against Japan in exchange for territorial concessions in the Far East. In a huge effort to reach Berlin, the allied armies were

striving to cross the Ruhr and Rhine Rivers. On February 23, the U.S.
Ninth and First armies crossed the Ruhr and within a few more weeks,
the allies would cross the Rhine on March 24. In the Pacific, Japan's
position was hopeless but an early end to the war was not in sight. On
February 19 U.S. forces landed on Iwo Jima which would cost 6800
American lives before it was secured on March 16.

While awaiting my final transfer orders to report to MATS, I was
awarded a Distinguished Flying Cross and an Air Medal with three
bronze clusters. The Distinguished Flying Cross Medal was awarded
for "distinguished flying during a bombing mission over Linz, Austria
on 20 January 1945", and the Air Medal with three clusters was awarded
for completing a total of 35 combat missions.

FROM TERROR TO THE SERENE

THE MEDITERRANEAN ALLIED

TRANSPORT SERVICE

L ARRY AND I reported to MATS Headquarters on 16 March 1945, and were promptly directed to our quarters, another tent. This one, however, contained a wooden floor, four wooden walls, and a wooden screened door. The tent only served as a roof. Our living quarters appeared luxurious after living for eight months in an unfinished crude tent in Cerignola. When we first entered our quarters, a captain was sitting on one of the four beds and introduced himself as Ray Artusy from Galveston, Texas. Ray was a soft spoken, tall, smiling young man a few years older than I was. Within a short time Lawrence McGilvray appeared and introduced himself. While we introduced ourselves and searched for ways to become acquainted, McGilvray said that he was raised on a farm outside Groesbeck, Texas and requested that we call him Mac. Larry Weimer quipped,

"It looks like I 'll be the only non-Texan here. How can I put up with you guys!"

From that moment we were good friends, three Texans and a Californian. Art was about 25 years of age, the senior of the group and had completed a tour of duty flying cargo before transferring to MATS. Mac, Larry and I had each completed a tour of combat flying B-24s. Larry completed his tour of combat with the same bomb group and squadron that I had. Mac had been attached to the 485th Bomb Group and during a mission was compelled to bail out of his severely damaged B-24 over Yugoslavia. He was rescued by the Chetnik underground army and returned to his air base in Venosa, Italy. He subsequently described the incident as follows:

"McGilvray's Liberator bounced upward from the loss of weight as his bombs fell from the bomb bay floating downward toward an aircraft factor near Vienna, Austria. Barely a minute had passed when a deafening explosion jolted his plane. He and the other pilot reacted instantly struggling with the controls in a desperate effort to maintain control of the aircraft. McGilvray could see from his window that flak had damaged three of their four engines. They shut off power to the one good engine for fear that it would flip them over and were attempting to feather the other three propellers when one of the damaged engines sputtered to life. The aircraft had descended from 22,000 feet to 10,000 feet in a matter of minutes when, incredibly, the pilots found themselves with one functional engine on each side of the airplane. One engine countered the torque or rotary force produced by the other engine making it possible for the pilots to again control the ship; however, the two engines could not supply sufficient power to regain lost altitude. Indeed, the two engines could barely maintain their present altitude. The flight engineer, Donald Landrum and belly turret gunner, Kelvin Brown, had been drenched with gasoline from a ruptured fuel line that created a vapor and inundated the interior of the airplane. Fortunately, the volatile vapors soon discharged as a result of the air blasting into the airplane from the open bomb bay.

The crew began ejecting everything that could be lifted or shoved overboard in an effort to lighten the airplane and maintain altitude. The radio operator began announcing a 'mayday' or emergency call to 'Big Fence', a British air-sea rescue station located off the coast of Yugoslavia. When 'Big Fence' located the McGilvray aircraft by radar, they were advised to fly an eastern course that would take them over Lake Balaton, Hungary and then south to Baja Luka, Yugoslavia.

Flying at such a low level, it was unlikely that the McGilvray's airplane could survive an attack from the numerous anti-aircraft installations located along their flight path. If they survived the flak, they faced another huge problem of being able to maintain altitude with sufficient fuel to fly across the Adriatic Sea and to their base in southern Italy. For over an hour, McGilvray and his crew struggled to maintain altitude when 'Big Fence', advised them to abandon their airplane. While the crew bailed out, McGilvray and Tuttle made last minute adjustments, leaving the final task of activating the automatic pilot until last so that they could abandon the controls and make their way to the bomb bay and parachute from the airplane.

McGilvray sat on the edge of the bomb bay with his legs hanging into the slipstream below as he prepared to push off and drop through the opening. The air rushed by underneath the aircraft with such force, like a powerful current of water, that it lifted his feet back up into the bomb bay. He feared that when he plunged into the maelstrom beneath him, the air might impel him upward, as it had his feet, and cause his head to strike the other end of the bomb bay. He doubted that any crewmembers parachuting before had been injured but rather than take a risk, he tied a rope that lay nearby to the bomb rack. Lowering himself by the rope until he was confident that his head would not strike the bomb bay, he relaxed his grip and plunged into a world of silence. He remembered watching his cigarettes float away after being wrenched from his pocket by the force of the wind.

Upon landing in an open field and searching the landscape for sight of his crewmembers, McGilvray noticed a man leading a donkey along a nearby road. As he folded his parachute, he saw that the man had stopped and was intensely observing something in the forest. Suddenly two men in military uniform emerged from the timber and ran toward him. The soldiers withdrew chains from around their necks, which looked like military dog tags, and began pointing at them while repeating the word, "Chetnik! Chetnik! Chetnik." After a few tense moments, McGilvray then realized that the double eagle engraved on the tags was the insignia used by the Chetnik army and that two Chetnik soldiers were rescuing him.

Underground forces opposing the Nazi-fascist in Yugoslavia had emerged as two movements: the anticommunist nationalists Chetnik, which were mostly Serbs under the command of General Draja Mihajlovic, and the communist Partisans under the command of a Croat, Marshall Tito. The two Chetniks motioning McGilvray to follow were loyal to the exiled government and were under the command of General Mihajlovic. They were anti-communist and resisted both the Germans and the communist. Mac began following them through a thick forest and into the mountains—a journey that would last forty days and forty nights.

When complete darkness had descended, they walked down the mountain path to a small village where McGilvray was introduced to the Chetnik commandant of the area. Bottles of vodka were opened and a series of toasts began. Soldiers proposed a toast to the commandant, the commandant proposed a toast to General Mihajlovic, the group proposed a toast to Lieutenant McGilvray, then to President Roosevelt, then to America, until they could think of no one else to toast. Someone then proposed a toast to the commandant and the toasts began again. McGilvray was soon to learn that toasts were part of the local culture and would occur almost daily during his forty-day walk to freedom. At the conclusion of the toasts, he was hosted to a banquet provided by the village.

One morning McGilvray was in the middle of a stream washing his clothes when several Chetniks ran down a mountain path pointing their rifles in his direction shouting, "communisti Partasani, Partasani!". Wisely McGilvray froze, not daring to move while cocked rifles pointed at him, but several other Chetnik soldiers quickly moved to a position that shielded him from their rifles. It was evident that there had been a misunderstanding and because they were speaking Serbia, McGilvray could only understand some of their body language. The group, wearing puzzled expressions, continued pointing their rifles in his direction while other soldiers talked with them. A few minutes later, they lowered their rifles, turned, and with sheepish grins retreated back up the mountain. McGilvray was later informed that the young Chetniks had mistaken the silver star on his Air Force T-shirt for a communist red star, an emblem worn by Partisans, enemies of the Chetniks.

A village along the Chetnik rescue route was celebrating the arrival of McGilvray and several other rescued airmen, when they were suddenly quieted by a Chetnik soldier shouting as he ran down a mountain trail,

"Tedschi, Germans, Germans!".

In perfect English a Chetnik said, "Come with me!"

The Americans were quickly guided into a nearby building

with a window opening out onto the enclosed courtyard. Peeping through the curtains, McGilvray could see a jeep approaching the courtyard with a German officer at the wheel. He parked near the window and began talking with the residents of the village. Aware that the Americans were unarmed and unable to fight the Germans, McGilvray asked his Chetnik escort if they should consider surrendering. The soldier replied again with an almost perfect American inflection,

"Keep your shirt on, nothing will happen."

After what seemed an eternity, the German officer finally drove away leaving behind some very nervous Americans and Chetniks. McGilvray was informed later that his Chetnik interpreter was named Nick and had lived in the United States before the war. Mac then understood why a Chetnik soldier in Yugoslavia would use American colloquial speech to say, "be patient."

A column of Chetniks and Americans quietly made their way down the mountain, cautiously pausing and listening between steps. As the group neared a river crossing, a Chetnik materialized from behind a boulder silently signaling them to halt. He hurried toward the Chetnik commandant and gestured for him to vacate the area. After a hushed brief conversation, the commandant and the column began retracing their steps up the mountain. Word spread through the column that the Chetnik scout had detected hidden fortifications located on the opposite side of the river. They walked until dark and were instructed to make camp quietly and without fires. The sound of gunfire and soldiers' voices were heard throughout the night.

The next morning the group was informed that the river crossing had been cleared of the enemy during the night and that it was safe for them to resume their journey. At the river, they encountered a grim sight of German and Chetnik bodies littering both banks of the river; casualties of a battle fought the previous night. On the opposite banks of the river, they observed empty gun installations on a hill overlooking the river that had been occupied and ready to ambush them as they crossed the river.

Arriving at a mountain pass near Sarajevo forty days later, McGilvray and the other American airmen anxiously waited for U.S. military airplanes to return them to Italy. As they waited, a group of American P-38 and P-51 fighters bombed and strafed the pass to make it safe for the transport airplanes to land. The C-47s had barely landed and taxied to the end of the runway when the Chetniks ushered the Americans to the steps of the airplanes and bid them farewell. The C-47s were loaded and ready for takeoff in less than thirty minutes while the fighter planes waited overhead to escort them on their return trip to Bari, Italy and their bomb groups."

Ironically, the United States abandoned General Mihajlovic and his Chetnik army near the end of the war. Instead, the assistance previously given to him was diverted to Marshall Tito and his communist Partisans. The United States could no longer support anti-Communists Mihajlovic without offending its Russian ally, Stalin. Countless American airmen, including McGilvray and his B-24 bomb crew, owe their lives to General Mihajlovic and his Serb countrymen, yet at the conclusion of the war, we as a nation remained shamefully silent while General Mihajlovic was arrested, tried, and executed as a traitor by Marshall Tito, a communist.

. . .

I was soon checked out in the cockpit of a C-47 and C-46 and scheduled to fly cargo missions as a copilot so that I could learn more about the aircraft. While landing, I discovered that a C-47 seemed to float forever before touching down on a runway compared to a B-24 that dropped like a bucket of lead onto a runway. Indeed, it was a challenge to even coax a C-47 to remain on the runway after the wheels touched down because it had a tendency to float again into the air like a kite. On the other hand, the C-46 was a heavier aircraft with more power and when loaded with cargo, landed more like a B-24.

A few days after being checked out, I received my first orders to fly machinery to a British air base near Cairo, Egypt. We were ordered to unload the C-47, remain overnight, and return the next day. It was common knowledge among MATS pilots that to exchange Italian allied currency to English pounds in Cairo and upon returning to Italy, change the pounds again to allied currency was a profitable exchange that would double the original value of the allied currency. When U.S. forces occupied Italy, the U.S. military government issued allied script, which became the legal currency of occupied Italy. One hundred lire was equal to one dollar in U.S. currency. Anyone traveling between Italy and Cairo could officially change $100 in allied currency to an equal amount of British pounds at any official British exchange office. One could then exchange the $100 in British pounds for allied Italian script worth about $200 with any unofficial street vendor in Cairo. Egypt was at that time a colony of England and their official currency was the English pound; therefore, Egyptians had more confidence in British pounds than allied Italian script. It was also possible, but illegal, to change British gold sovereign into lire at about nine times the value. Although I observed many pilots exchanging gold with apparent impunity, I was reluctant to enter into this profitable but criminal activity. Italy, like all war ravaged countries, developed an illegal underground economy to provide commodities that were in short supply, but it also created vast wealth for criminal networks which were too enticing to be ignored by some American servicemen. I repeatedly heard rumors about American officers who had earned vast sums of money engaging in criminal activities. Some had sold food or clothing bound for American military bases to the Italian underground; nevertheless, it seemed there was less street crime than now.

"Author Relaxes in Naples 1944"

When scheduled to fly cargo to Egypt, I borrowed from every pilot that could afford to loan me money. Most MATS pilots had accumulated copious amounts of money dispersed between pages of books, in their clothing, between mattresses, and underneath their beds in preparation for their next flight to Cairo. I usually borrowed a total of about $500 and anticipated returning from Cairo with $1000. I soon filled my hidden coffers but I was cautious about sending an inordinate amount of money home to be deposited in a bank; rather, I found countless methods of spending it.

MATS only assigned a crew of two pilots, alternating them between the position of pilot and co-pilot, on short flights. For longer flights, MATS assigned two pilots, a flight engineer and a navigator. "Rookies" or recently transferred pilots were usually ordered to operate as copilots during their first few assignments so that they might learn procedures and gain experience with more experienced pilots. As expected, during my first flight in a C-47 to Cairo, I was ordered to fulfill the duties of a copilot. When I arrived at the airplane, I could see that it was loaded with heavy machinery and secured with ropes. The first pilot was inspecting the outside of the aircraft where we met for the first time.

The flight over the Mediterranean was uneventful and boring but as we approached land, I reflected over my first flight over the Sahara Desert as we flew from the U.S. to Italy. I recalled the amazement I felt as I first observed this limitless uninhabited area of shadowed valleys and corrugated ribbed sand expanding before me as we passed over the coast of Africa. Within a few minutes but still far away, I could see the City of Alexander on the horizon. A short time later, with a view of the Nile River, its phalanx of houseboats on our left and the silent pyramids with the sleeping sphinx ahead, we began our decent to the runway of the British air base. I had never observed so many houseboats and was to learn later that they were never moved from their moorings. They were stationary residences, usually weekend homes for the wealthy. I was impatient to land and visit Egypt's exotic sights.

After parking and departing our airplane, we dined and were then escorted to our quarters. I must mention British cooking at this juncture because it deserves a commentary. I had little respect for American military food, although at times I would find something tasty, but British cooking was consistently unpleasant. During my period of duty with MATS I flew into many British bases. I was astounded at the poor preparation and taste of the food at each air base. This proved to be true of the bland food in London as well, although today London boasts some of the finest restaurants in the world. Perhaps the lack of taste in the British military food was a result of England's exhaustive war efforts but whatever the reason, it seemed that U.S. military cooks produced gourmet food compared to British food.

It was shortly after midday when we had finished our tasteless lunch and were driven by jeep to our billets. I could hardly wait to change the currency I had brought with me and see the city of Cairo. I hailed an Egyptian taxi outside the base and began to marvel at sights never before witnessed or even dreamed about in Nacogdoches. Turbaned men in white flowing garments, veiled women in flowing black garments, beggars asking for alms, donkeys, horses, camels, blaring sounds of automobile horns, and the grating noise of minaret loud speakers calling Moslems to prayer—all blended altogether to form an exotic cacophony of sounds and sights. I headed directly to the Shepherd Hotel, perhaps the most famous hotel in the world at that time. It was said that if one waits a while, he is sure to see someone he knows. It was a meeting place of the British royalty, the rich, and the world famous. Sitting at the bar, I observed fierce looking black Sudanese with tribal scars on their cheeks, wearing fezzes and white robes as they served hotel guests. Most Egyptians at that time wore either robes or western business suits with a fez.

After a drink at the bar and a stroll gawking at the strange sights, I entered a restaurant. I do not remember what I ate that night but I vividly remember the flies. Restaurant doors were covered by hanging beads to discourage flies but windows were open, allowing heat and food scents to escape and attract them. The food inside restaurants attracted flies while the many horses and camels outside created them. I found it impossible to keep them away from the food or to finish my meal. I decided to leave the restaurant and seek a nightclub where I could witness an original Arabian belly dance.

The nightclub contained a stage where belly dancers performed to an audience of men sitting on the floor or in chairs smoking water pipes. Belly dancers were venerated by Egyptian men and became famous much like movie stars in the United States. Whenever a popular dancer appeared on the stage, the men would cheer and applaud the same as a famous entertainer would be cheered in the United States. Since I was not educated in the finer techniques of belly dancing, I was unable to judge their divergences; all belly dancers seemed the same to me. I was only able to understand that one dancer was better than another by the cheers of the audience. Satisfied that I had witnessed an exhibit of authentic Arabian Belly Dancers, I was ready to return to the air base.

I returned to Naples and Capodichino airfield with more money than I had borrowed before departing for Cairo. I previously had made an allotment from my monthly salary to be sent to my father so that he could regularly deposit it in a bank for me. With the future probability of several more profitable trips to Cairo, I decided to change the allotment and send my entire salary to my father. I could easily pay my expenses from the profits that would be earned from each future trip or by lending to other pilots who had been instructed to fly to Cairo. We developed a banking system and charged a fee for loaning money to those flying to Cairo.

Apart from making money from these flights to Egypt, I was able to enjoy a camel ride and a visit to the pyramids, a visit to a Nile houseboat, a visit to a famous museum displaying Egyptians mummies, and to crash a diplomatic garden party with King Farouk in attendance. Most of the trips were for three days, which allowed me two evenings and one free day for sight seeing.

As I walked past an office building bearing a British flag, I heard western music emerging from a garden behind the building. A sign on the building stated that it was the office of the British Embassy and I could see through an open door a beautiful garden filled with people. Many wore formal dress, some wore fezzes, most held drinks, and they were gathered in conversational groups while an orchestra played western dance music. The door seemed to beckon me to enter and enjoy a reception hosted by the British Embassy. As I entered the garden, I observed a few high-ranking English and American uniforms standing in the groups; nevertheless, I walked to the bar, ordered a scotch and soda, strolled to the bandstand and stood concentrating on the music. Within a few minutes I noticed across the garden a large group of people surrounding a short fat mustached man wearing a military uniform and fez. Because many of his photographs were displayed around Cairo, I instantly recognized the pudgy little man as King Farouk, the king of Egypt. He was famous for living the life-style of a young playboy debaucher and apparently died soon after exile from overindulging. I walked to the buffet, enjoyed a gourmet dinner, and then decided the time had arrived for me to depart. As I walked away, it occurred to me that I had finally discovered a tasty British meal—fit for a king!

Much like today, I found anti-western resentment among Egyptians and Arabs. A small Arab boy asked me as he held up a box for shining shoes,

"Shoe shine—Joe?"

"No, thank you" I replied.

Ignoring my answer, he followed me threatening to pour shoe polish liquid on my uniform. Despite my frustrated shouts for him to leave me, he persisted until I hailed a taxi as a place of refuge. I instructed the cab driver to deliver me to a merchant that had been recommended by another pilot. After traveling a short distance, he stopped at the entrance of a casaba and indicated by hand signals that the merchant was located inside the casaba and that he could not drive past the entrance. A casaba is a pandemonium of crowded shops and vendors on dark streets too narrow for an automobile to pass. A young Arab boy offered to lead me to the store.

Long after we should have arrived at the merchant's store, I began to suspect that I was being led deeper into the casaba to some place that I did not wish to go. I stopped walking and asked the boy if he was leading me to the correct address. He replied in the affirmative and began walking again signaling for me to follow. By that time I was certain that the Arab boy had a different agenda; nevertheless, he soon pointed to a shop and indicated that it was the merchant I had requested. I gathered the front of his shirt in my fist, pulled him near to my face, and said,

"This is not the store I wanted. You take me there now!

I shook him roughly as I spoke, but upon reflection, I should have been more aware that I was a lone American on a street crowded with Arabs. Suddenly I became aware that a group of Arabs had silently formed a circle around us. I could only release him, smile, and walk away with as much dignity as I could muster hoping they would allow me to pass through their circle. They reluctantly permitted me to walk past them but I was hopelessly lost and was forced to continue walking while searching for a well lit street that would lead me back to the Shepherd Hotel. At a great distance a small area of light began to appear indicating an end to the narrow streets of the casaba. As I walked toward the hotel, a streetcar passed with the Arab boy hanging outside the back of the car waving and smiling at me while he shouted,

"Goodbye sucker!"

. . .

McGilvray and I received orders to transport a load of equipment to London and return the next day. We were provided a flight engineer for some incomprehensible reason that we dared not question although we were disappointed. London was a desirable destination and our only hope of remaining longer was to develop engine problems, but with an engineer along to oversee maintenance of the engines, our prospects of an engine failure was substantially reduced. During the flight to London we discussed our desire to visit London and explored different scenarios that might delay our return but discarded each one as unworkable until the engineer said,

"I could foul the magnetos."

Mack and I looked at each other as the thought slowly unraveled and comprehension began to sink into our brains. Magnetos are small electrical motors that provide a spark to ignite a combustion engine. Without a spark, we would be unable to start the engines the next morning. I asked him,

"Can you really do that?" The question was intended to determine if he would—not if he could.

"Sure, nothing to it."

Mac and I nodded our heads in agreement.

Rather than remain overnight on the military air base, Mac and I found a room in a private residence nearer the center of the city. "Room for let" appeared in windows of numerous London homes during the war and created a convenient method for one to find overnight lodging. We found rooms within walking distance of Hyde Park and nearer the center of London than the air base. The room was on the third floor of the residence and could only be reached by climbing outside stairs to the main living area. To reach the bedroom it was necessary to climb two more narrow flights of stairs to the tiny room packed with a double bed, small furniture and figurines. Recognizing that we would be returning to the room late in the evening, I pondered over the noise of the creaking stairs as we climbed to our room.

Hyde Park was one of the beautiful parks in London but was notorious then for blanket covered lovers ubiquitously scattered over its well-kept lawn. One could only walk between the numerous blankets with difficulty. The conduct of those under the blankets was famous and considered titillating then, but one can find more noteworthy scenes at any local park today.

Before daybreak we hailed a taxi to the military air base where our airplane was located. In order for our deceptive layover to appear genuine, we had planned to arrive on time, file a flight plan, and attempt to start the aircraft. Only then could we report a legitimate engine failure. We followed the plan and found the engineer had indeed fouled the magnetos after our departure the day before. We radioed the British operations office to report the problem and were informed that due to a backlog of repairs, it might be several days before they could schedule our aircraft. They suggested we telephone each morning before departing our lodging and ask if they had completed repairing the magnetos. We were elated—everything worked as we had planned. It was no longer necessary for us to return each morning to the base. We could merely telephone requesting the status of our airplane and then plan another day visiting the sites of London. We hoped that the British mechanics would be unable to repair our airplane for many more days and indeed, it did require three days for the magnetos to be repaired.

We slept very little during our three-day excursion. We visited historical places during the day and pubs during the evening; we saw the city from horse-drawn buggies; we watched the changing of the guards at Buckingham Palace; we dined in some of the best restaurants (with poor food); we visited the lobby and bar of the Grovner House where attendants wore beef-eaters uniforms; we met girls; we danced and found after hours nightclubs. During our return trip we were exhausted but contented.

A short time after landing at Capodichino, I was summoned to the office of the commanding officer and asked,

"Lieutenant, where have you been? We were about to call out the search patrol thinking you had crashed in the sea!"

I replied, "I am sorry, sir, I thought the British had notified you that we had engine troubles and that we were grounded until they could repair the engines."

"No, lieutenant, they did not notify us. It is your responsibility, as pilot, to make certain that we are informed if it is necessary for you to change your flight plan. Do you understand?"

"Yes, sir!"

"Very well—dismissed!"

I was only twice reprimanded for minor infractions, both times by a major. I did and still do believe that the rank of major is just barely sufficient to make a major feel important but not high ranking enough to make him important.

While I was enjoying visiting unique countries and places that I never before dreamed I would visit, other events were taking place that would soon have a significant effect on my life. During the early weeks of April 1945 American forces had crossed the Elba River placing them within striking distance of Berlin, believed by the British to be the most important target of the war. General Eisenhower, however, believed that Berlin was not worth the cost of taking it and Russia began a whirlwind offensive toward Berlin the first week of April. President Roosevelt died April 12, 1945 reviving a faint hope for Hitler that his death and the disagreement of the allies would benefit Germany. While the battle for Berlin raged, another simple event unrelated to the war was developing in Italy that would change my life forever.

While visiting Rome, Mac McGilvray had met a girl who informed him that she and her sister would visit Naples soon. She and her sister had accepted a job with an Italian variety show that was scheduled to open during the month of April in a Naples theater.

. . .

"Jess, I have a date tonight with the girl from Rome and she has a younger sister. Want to come along and meet the sister?" McGilvray asked me.

"Mac, you know I have a date with Maria. In fact, You said that you would date her friend and we would go together to the Orange Club."

He stated that he wanted to forget the date with Maria's friend, that he liked the girl from Rome better, and described the sisters as "good lookers" with class. He continued to try to persuade me to join them by informing me that they were appearing as dancers in a variety show, much like the old U.S. vaudeville shows. His description of the sisters had attracted my attention and after more urging, my curiosity eventually overcame my hesitancy. I reluctantly agreed to meet them at the Orange Club that night.

While we sat on the patio of the club, I found it difficult to take my eyes from the girl I had just met. Both sisters were pretty but when introduced to Carla, I was thunder-struck. She was the most beautiful person I had ever met. I was captivated by her smile, a tiny gap between her teeth fascinated me, and her stature intrigued me. She was above average height with strong legs and pearly white teeth; I was hooked, enslaved, indentured and instantly forgot poor Maria who I had rudely deserted that night. Carla was 17 years old and a ward of her older sister, Piera. Carla had been offered a job dancing with a variety show but her mother would not approve until Piera also joined the company and could chaperone Carla. I was to discover later that she was indeed Carla's chaperone and regarded her responsibility as fervently as though Carla was her daughter rather than a sister.

Suddenly my magic moment was shattered—from behind me came a loud voice,

"Why you no be with Maria tonight?"

Startled—every head within hearing distance turned toward us as I twisted around to see who was standing behind me.

"Why you no with Maria?"

It was Maria's girlfriend. I was dumbfounded, unable to think of anything intelligent to say. I stammered,

"Do I know you?

Tenaciously she replied,

"Si, si, you know me—why you no with Maria?"

If it were possible, I would have crawled under the table. I was doing my best to impress my new acquaintances when Maria's friend suddenly appeared and implied that I had humiliated Maria. Desperately I arose, grasped her arm, and ushered her into the adjoining bar where I admonished her for interrupting our party and threatened to call the military police. An introduction of the word "military police" was usually sufficient to attract the attention of most Italian civilians for they feared the military police. Without a word, she turned and walked out of the club.

I dreaded returning to our table for fear that the sisters had formed an unfavorable impression of me, but the subject was never mentioned again that evening, nor was it ever brought up again during the next 44 years.

. . .

MATS not only transported equipment, we occasionally transported passengers to various destinations. Most flights were filled with regular military personnel or an occasional athletic team but on two occasions, I recall ferrying two outstanding and famous people. British General Smit was my lone passenger during a flight from Naples to Udine in Northern Italy. He was one of the British representatives who signed the surrender agreement with Germany. I also flew Primo Carnera (1906-1967), a former Italian world champion boxer and his wife to a military base where he appeared in a show sponsored by the USO. Carnera, was idolized during the 1930s although he was a world heavyweight champion for only a short time, 1933-34. He was a huge man with the largest hands I had ever seen. At 6.5 feet he was known for his knockout victories. He later took up wrestling and acted in the film "On the Waterfront" (1954). For a portion of the flight, I invited Carnera to visit the cockpit and occupy the copilot seat, which he found almost too small for him. While saying good bye at the end of the flight, the copilot almost disappeared when Carnera placed his hand on his shoulder.

. . .

Between flights, Mac and I would often entertain the Bernardi sisters by taking them to dine and dance at the Orange Club. The club was located in the hills of Posilipo above Naples with a delightful view of Naples below. At other times we hosted them at the downtown Naples Officers Club which had once been a royal palace. We attempted to impress the sisters with exclusive clubs and expensive restaurants while we pretended to be dashing brave young American heroes. This seemed to be working well, for Mac and Piera soon fell in love and began making plans for their wedding. The responsibility of entertaining the younger sister, Carla, was then delegated to me. I did not mind— I found the whole thing rather pleasant.

. . .

While I flew cargo to exotic places, the war in Europe had set in motion a dissonant crescendo of kaleidoscopic horrors that climaxed and began to diminish with the fall of Berlin and the suicide of Hitler. On April 24th, the Russians closed a circle around Berlin. The following week resistance almost ceased, although, the Germans continued to fight desperately in an effort to reach allied lines to surrender rather than being taken prisoners by the Russians. On the afternoon of April 30 Hitler committed suicide in his Berlin bunker. The following week, May 7, General Jodl signed an unconditional surrender agreement at General Eisenhower's headquarters in Reims. The U.S. and British governments declared May 8 1945, VE (Victory in Europe) day despite Japan's resistance for several more months. At Capodichino air base celebrations began early on VE day but after celebrating the liberation of Naples from Nazi occupation, Neapolitans had little remaining enthusiasm to celebrate the surrender of Germany to the allies. As a consequence, downtown Naples was quiet and only military clubs held any sort of festivity. The Stars and Stripes, a military newspaper, published a famous photograph of a sailor kissing a girl in New York and various other photographs of celebrations in the United States but our celebration in Naples seemed feeble in comparison. On VE day officers clubs offered special menus with champagne and we drank toasts throughout the day.

. . .

I flew a load of machinery to Tirana, Albania eager to visit the backward communist city; however, upon landing we were immediately surrounded by soldiers and instructed to remain in the airplane. My only view of Tirana was from the pilot's seat in the cockpit of a C-47. Flights with brief visits were also made to Sofia, Bulgaria where I found only enough time to purchase two beautiful Balkan blouses for Carla and Benghazi, Libya, a depressing city that offered nothing of interest for me. Despite these few disappointments, my decision to volunteer for duty with MATS proved to be the most desirable commitment I could have possibly made. I enjoyed living in Italy, I found the destinations of our flights intriguing and I discovered the girl that would improve my life.

The Bernardi sisters had departed Naples with their company for an appearance in another city. They were scheduled to again appear in Naples in a few weeks. In the meantime, I flew only a few days each week, which allowed me time to visit the Naples area where I discovered many attractions, both cultural and historical. I also found Naples, its inhabitants and its music fascinating. The streets were a labyrinth of narrow dark passageways filled with overhanging laundry and with sounds of frenzied activity as the citizens scurried about like hyperactive ants. With animated gestures they hailed each other in their musical dialect and were answered from distant balconies overhanging the street. Neapolitans seem to develop the loudest voices anywhere from conversing with others at great distances. It was routine to witness a conversation between a Neapolitan on a fifth story balcony and another standing on the sidewalk, both competing with traffic noises. Who needed telephones? Their songs, interspersed with fiery Arabic sounds from past conquerors, usually proclaimed a sad passionate love of something or someone, but in the next moment the mood might change to one of untamed exuberant joy. Every fiber of their being vibrated with emotion—they loved with passion, spoke with fervor, sang with ardor, gestured with enthusiasm, and most of all, ate with gusto. As I walked the streets in awe of the emotions surrounding me, I thought how pleasant it would be to live every moment with such excitement and enthusiasm.

· · ·

For the first time, I discovered opera at the Neapolitan Opera House. I had only hear bits of opera broadcast by radio but had never attended a complete opera. I was unsure that I would enjoy it but the opera house looked interesting and it was an opportunity to see a complete opera for the first time.

Thoughts of Carla cascaded through my head as I sat in a soft red cushioned seat surrounded by magnificent opulence. Mounted on velvet walls, baroque cherubs hovered like golden angels, while overhead, magnificent twinkling chandeliers radiated soft reflections on massive red curtains. As I anxiously waited for the curtains to open I vowed that I would invite Carla to witness these splendors when she returned. Suddenly the lights dimmed and the orchestra began the overture to Boito's MEFISTOFELES. I gasped as the curtain slowly parted revealing Mefistofeles in satanic costume standing atop a huge earth-like sphere. Fanfares from seven brass choirs opened the scene as invisible choruses of saints and angels sang AVE. In the following intermezzo the devil, Mefistofeles, represented by a chorus of bass voices, tells God in sarcasm that it is no longer a challenge to tempt mankind because they have become too fatuous and worthless. With ear-splitting brass, crashing cymbals, and soft heavenly music sung by a female chorus, the conversation between God and the Devil was unlike anything I had ever before experienced. I was stunned—my skin tingled. At that moment I knew that it marked the beginning of my love and appreciation for opera.

I returned to the base resolved to describe the magnificent evening to my tent mates the following morning. I wanted to share with them the elegance of the opera house and the splendid performance of the opera company; instead, my description was countered with their humorous skepticism about how anyone could endure such singing and noise. I was determined, nonetheless, to continue enjoying opera at every opportunity, even if I must attend alone. Much to my delight, I later discovered that Carla was taught to appreciate opera almost from birth by her mother and would not only accompany me but would teach me many operatic arias in the future.

I was privileged to attend a rare performance of Beniamino Gigli who prior to the war had been acclaimed the successor of Caruso by the New York Metropolitan Opera Comapany. He had returned to Italy during the 1930s and, according to his critics, supported Mussolini's fascist regime. When the war ended, the allies banned his appearances for a time because of his alleged fascist sympathies, but ultimately he was allowed to perform. I witnessed one of his last few appearances at the Neapolitan Opera House before he retired. I also had the good fortune to hear and see Ferruccio Tagliavini, another famous Italian tenor, at the Neapolitan Opera House in Naples. Several years later, while finishing my university studies, Tagliavini appeared in a concert at Nacogdoches. At the end of his performance, I had the pleasure of paying my respect for him backstage and said to him that I had enjoyed several of his appearances at the Neapolitan Opera Theater in Naples. I suspect that he was surprised to meet anyone from East Texas who had ever witnessed an opera, let alone attended several of his performances at the Neapolitan Opera Theater in Naples.

Newspaper and radio announced that an atomic bomb had been detonated in a test at Alamogordo, New Mexico, on July 16, 1945. Two more bombs were built and used in quick succession—one over Hiroshima on August 6, the other over Nagasaki on August 9. U.S. estimates put the number killed or missing as a result of the bomb in Hiroshima at 60,000 to 70,000 and in Nagasaki at 40,000. The USSR declared war on Japan on August 8 and Japan announced its surrender on August 14. For me, the war was over when Germany surrendered and even though Japan finally had surrendered, there was little celebration of VJ day in Italy. The war with Japan had seemed too far away, nevertheless, I felt a great sense of relief to know that I would not be called to bomb Japan. I could continue my pleasant tour flying cargo with MATS, and seeing parts of the world that I might never see again.

. . .

Northern Italy was the destination of many MATS flights, only a few hours from Naples. On days that I was ordered to fly, I would takeoff during the early morning, land, unload and reload the airplane before returning to Capodichino the same day. Since we did not fly every day, I also had leisure time between flights. After the sisters returned to a theater near Naples, Mac and I would meet them after their last appearance and dine together at the officers club or the Orange Club. It was only a brief time after their return that Mac and Piera announced their intention to marry. Upon investigating their requirements for marriage, they discovered that although Catholic, a Catholic Bishop, the Catholic Church, the Italian government, and the U.S. military headquarters must approve their marriage. It was very complicated, requiring government stamps to be attached to many official papers; however, love always wins in the end and they were able to fulfill the requirements and set a date to marry on 29 September 1945. Carla was to be their Brides Maid and I was to be their Best Man.

While Mac and Piera were feverishly preparing government and military applications for marriage, I asked for Carla's hand in marriage. We were standing on an outside balcony of the Officer's club one evening during a dance intermission when I impulsively asked her to marry me. Although I had been in love with her since we first met, I had not seriously contemplated marriage before that moment. The question just seemed to burst forth from my lips surprising both of us but, fortunately for me, she accepted. I could not possibly foresee at the time how profoundly blessed I would be.

ITALIAN MARRIAGE: SOME OBSTACLES
AND REWARDS

THE ANNOUNCEMENT THAT I was engaged to an Italian girl produced an avalanche of advice from friends and acquaintances. My best friend almost became my least liked friend when he voiced an opinion that I was about to commit a mistake. He implored me to give up the idea of marrying Carla founding his argument on the growing number of Italian War Brides who only seek marriage as means of transportation to a better life in America. I understand now that as a friend, he was sincerely concerned about my welfare, but at that time I resented his opposition to my decision. After a time, when he became better acquainted with her, he became one of Carla's staunchest supporters.

While seeking information about procedures I must follow in order to marry, I was informed that I must seek advice from a captain who counseled military members. After receiving lecturers and advice from friends, I must yet endure another lecture from a personnel officer. I was also to discover that to be granted permission to marry Carla, like Mac and Piera had before, it would be necessary to enter the deepest layers of a bureaucracy that Italy had painstakingly built over the centuries. Thus, I began my quest—one of the most difficult and frustrating periods of my life.

The captain who interviewed me was a nice fellow but it was soon evident that he was convinced that American soldiers who requested permission to marry Italian girls were committing grave mistakes. Furthermore, he was committed to save them from making such errors in judgment. He began our interview by exhibiting statistics from a study of marriages between foreign women and servicemen that revealed

T

a high ratio of divorce and separation. He pointed to the differences in culture and religions as the reason for the poor results and stated that most foreign women could not adjust easily to the customs of the United States. For some time he continued to pursue this argument until he was certain that his advice had fallen on deaf ears. He then dismissed me and signed a statement that he had explained the consequences of my marriage request and directed me to another military office where I obtained more papers to be completed. Among the papers was a set of instructions directing me to a number of Italian government offices that were required to approve and record all request made by an Italian citizen to marry an American citizen.

It was a revelation to me to find Italian bureaucrats so demanding. My previous experience had been limited to small town friendly bureaucrats who were acquainted with almost all citizens of Nacogdoches. I found that Italian bureaucrats customarily refused almost every paper submitted to them. They seem to enjoy finding errors or insufficient information and would often inform us that additional information and signatures were required from an office on the opposite side of the city. I was convinced that bureaucrats who were offended by American soldiers marrying Italian women created some of the problems I encountered. I also found there had been little improvements made in government efficiency since the ancient Roman government first devised the forms and procedures 2000 years ago that were still in usage. I remain convinced that Italian bureaucrats alter requirements and procedures in order to gratify their needs at the moment; they rarely favor the victim. It is a method of demonstrating power derived from offices that they would occupy for the remainder of their lives.

Finally the day arrived when all requirements were satisfied—when all permissions were granted and we could concentrate on where, who, and when our wedding could be held. Although I had grown up in a Protestant environment that had tolerated marriages between different faiths, I was aware that the Italian Catholic Church was most intolerant of such marriages. I suggested to Carla, who was Catholic, that in order to comply with the beliefs of the Catholic Church, we should be married by a Catholic Priest in a Catholic Church. Not feeling certain that she wanted a Catholic wedding, she suggested that we talk with both a Catholic Priest and a Protestant Minister before deciding. We therefore promptly made an appointment with a very disagreeable Priest who proceeded to lecture us about the sins of marrying outside the church. He also declared emphatically that we must promise that our children would be raised as Catholics or risk excommunication from the church. Carla was angered over his arrogant manner and convinced that she desired a protestant marriage. Our appointment then with a military Lutheran Chaplain was a pleasant experience. He was undemanding and courteous, even reminding us that in order to prevent Carla from having later regrets, we should consider a Catholic marriage. His considerate manner convinced Carla that she preferred to have him marry us. I reserved the Capodichino chapel for 3 October 1945, and arranged for Captain Tilford Junkins, a Lutheran chaplain, to marry us at 4 PM. While sitting at a cafe sidewalk table in Naples before our wedding, I hired a brilliant street violinist to play "Ave Maria" for our wedding ceremony. We asked Piera to serve as Carla's bride's maid and Mac as my best man. Their wedding was scheduled to be held at a Catholic Church in Naples September 29th, only a few days before our wedding October 3, 1945.

We had finalized our wedding plans except for the purchase of a wedding dress for Carla. Italy was devastated from the war and clothing store display windows were virtually empty. Although there were many highly skilled seamstress and tailors desperately in need of work, there was a scarcity of materials for them to fashion into clothing. The military PX offered only bulk materials for military uniforms. We laughed as we thought about how unusual it would be for Carla to wear a military uniform to her wedding, unless____! Heavy olive drab or dark green wool materials were too dark to dye and unless their colors were changed, they would be identified immediately as military uniform material, but light wool-worsted material was another matter. It was intended for

T

summer uniforms and was a light beige color; could it be successfully dyed? I immediately found a dye shop and asked the question. The answer was yes, for the material was not only lightweight, but also light in color. With the problem of finding material to make a dress solved, the only obstacle remaining was to decide on the color and find a seamstress to tailor the dress. After consulting with several persons, including the seamstress we had selected, we decided to dye the material a maroon color and fashion it into a skirt and jacket. At the same time, I purchased an army wool blanket that could be dyed and fashioned into a topcoat for her. Because there was no material available to make her a hat, she found a tailor who could modify a worn and out-of-fashion hat into a new one. She was then the best-dressed and most lovely Italian girl that could be found in the land. It is difficult to imagine today, in our affluent nation, just how drab Italian women were obliged to dress at that time. New dresses were nonexistent and old ones were passed from sister to sister, friend to friend, or mother to daughter until they could no longer be worn. Make-up, perfumes, stockings and all unessential items had not been manufactured for several years and were nonexistent. Italy had diverted all of her available raw materials and efforts into the war.

The morning of 3 October 1945 finally arrived. I awoke from a restless night with a list of things I must do before the wedding—deliver flowers to decorate the chapel, make certain the violinist had transportation to the chapel and would arrive on time, drop Carla off at the seamstress for a final fitting, deliver and pick her up from the hair dresser, make final arrangements with the chaplain and other endless small last minute problems that seem to always occur. We were late, perspiring, and exhausted by the time Mac, who was our best man and designated driver, drove us in a jeep to the chapel.

The wedding ceremony was informal, simple and pleasant. The violinist, an excellent musician, performed "Ave Maria" and other renditions beyond all expectations. When the marriage vows were finished, a group of friends began throwing rice and attaching "just married" signs with tin cans to our jeep. Mac drove us, followed by a motorcade of military jeeps with horns blaring, through the streets of Naples to a hotel where I had reserved a room for our first wedding night.

"Wedding Day LtoR—Piera, McGilvray, Bride and Author"

While I continued flying cargo missions and waiting for approval for a leave, we were hosted by Mac and Piera at their apartment. I had been unable to locate an apartment for rent; consequently, we had no place to stay even though I had applied for a wedding vacation on the Island of Capri and for off-base housing. In order to qualify for off base housing, Mac had transferred from flight duty to another one supervising a motor pool. He had been fortunate to locate a nice apartment within a short time. I was in a dilemma, however. I also was compelled to change my status from flying to one that permitted me to live off base but had not had sufficient time to locate different duty and housing. While searching for such a position and living with the McGilvrays, my application for a one week leave was approved. I immediately requested and was granted a conference with a colonel who was responsible for military housing on Capri. As we discussed hotel rooms he informed me that a villa was vacant and advised me that we could occupy it but we would be required to move if a senior officer requested the use of the villa. My pulse began racing with excitement and my heart beat a flamenco as I stammered, "yes sir". It was almost too good to be true that we would stay in a luxurious villa that had been confiscated by the U.S. military.

Capri sits above an aquamarine sea, a kaleidoscope of hills and rocky cliffs splattered with whitewashed houses. It is located in the Bay of Naples overlooking a background of purple mountains standing guard around cloud haloed mount Vesuvius. A funicular extends from colorful beached boats below to the top of a cliff near a villa once owned by one of the wealthy families that had lived on the island. Until the war arrived, the island had been a playground for the famous and best know names of Europe, but with the advance of the American Army, most of the homes had been temporarily appropriated for the use of senior military officers. Carla and I were astounded that we would be the sole inhabitants of this opulent honeymoon villa. We discovered that we need only telephone the PX for any item we desired and it would be delivered to our door. Also to our delight, we learned that a maid would arrive each day to cook and clean. We drifted into sleep each night with our fingers crossed hoping that we would not be asked to move. Each day we roamed the countryside exploring trails and beaches; we dined, we danced at the best hotels, and even adopted an abandoned puppy. It was an enchanting romantic week that provided us a taste of luxury and created a memory for us to cherish the rest of our lives.

"Honeymoon Isle of Capri"

The day after we departed Capri, events unfolded so rapidly that I found myself reacting to them almost hourly. In one day I located a job, which allowed me to live off base, and was granted permission to transfer from MATS. The following day, I found a furnished apartment downtown Naples and completed all necessary papers. At the time I was reassigned, I was advised to make an appointment with a major in response to my request for off-base housing. During our meeting I informed the major that I had just married and that I was desperately in need of an apartment. He unfolded a list of a few available apartments that were reserved for senior officers and informed me that officially there was nothing available for my rank of lieutenant. As he continued to look over the list, he said,

"Lieutenant, I'll tell you what I'm going to do. This apartment is vacant and although it's reserved for rank of a major or above, I think I will let you have it. Will you promise to not reveal who approved it?"

T

With a big grin, I answered, "YES SIR."

It was located in a large villa surrounding a courtyard which had once been occupied by a wealthy family but was divided into a number of smaller apartments during the war. In order to drive into the courtyard, it was necessary to first enter through massive arched wooden doors, located a few feet from the street. In response to a doorbell, a portiere would open the doors from inside. During the day, the doors usually remained open while the portiere sat in a glass enclosed office where he could observe those who entered the courtyard. The portiere eventually became an important part of our life, serving as a security guard, providing directions and information about the city, washing and ironing our laundry, repairing items, and buying Carla's ration of cigarettes each week for $20.00. Carla did not smoke but nevertheless, we bought her allotted cigarettes for $2.00 at the PX and sold them to him for $20.00. He then sold them to a black market contact for another profit of $20.00. The average price of American cigarettes on the Italian economy was $40.00 a carton. The government furnished our rent and meals at the officers club. We could then pay our entire monthly expenses from the sale of Carla's cigarettes.

With the transfer from flying status with MATS to the European Air Transport, 305th Troop Carrier Squadron, I became a supervisor of a warehouse at Capodichino airfield where flight cargo was unloaded and stored by Italian civilian workers. I found the duties to be dull and uninteresting after I had experienced the excitement of piloting airplanes to exotic and interesting destinations. About the time that I transferred, another lieutenant had been assigned the identical duty of supervising the same warehouse that I was to supervise. We found it amusing that we shared a duty requiring so little time and attention to detail—so undemanding that only one of us would find it difficult to stay busy. We agreed that we should alternate our workdays by each working a weekly three-day schedule. It would prove to be an excellent decision— we enjoyed three free days each week with few responsibilities and the salary of an officer. I was about to add yet another diminution to our idealistic circumstances. Soon after transferring to my new duties, I was offered an illegal Fiat by an officer who was ordered to return to the U.S.

Military personnel were being returned to the U.S. in increasingly large numbers; consequently, one could buy many things from them including undocumented military automobiles. In the confusion following the German surrender, German equipment was often not recorded by the conquering allies. Much equipment, particularly vehicles, was impounded by unauthorized military personnel and sold to other military individuals. I purchased a 1939 Fiat coupe, a German officer vehicle, for $200.00. Mac, who had changed his duty in order to live off base, supervised a motor pool of military vehicles. A motor pool contains a parking lot of stored military vehicles and a garage where they are serviced. Because he supervised a garage as part of the motor pool, he authorized papers that assigned my Fiat to his motor pool and ordered the bumpers to be painted with authorized numbers and the insignia of his motor pool. As an officer, I could authorize orders for trips with the Fiat and fill it with gasoline from any military petrol station. Carla and I enjoyed a private automobile, free gasoline, free rent, income from Carla's cigarettes, and all the other privileges accorded a military officer. Life was indeed a piece of cake.

Our apartment opened into a foyer that led into a large living room, dining room, kitchen, and a bedroom. The living and dining room contained the largest furniture I had ever seen. Two sofa chairs were so huge that when we sat in them we appeared to be reduced in size to that of a midget sitting in an adult chair. There was a balcony outside the kitchen and bedroom overlooking a street three stories below, although the hallway leading into our apartment was on the first floor. The ground beneath the apartments gave way to a steep decline making it possible for us to walk into our first floor apartment to the back balcony and find ourselves three stories above a street. There I could stand and observe loud and fiery Neapolitans on the street below. I witnessed noisy children playing, laborers working, housewives

T

shopping, vendors trading, and funeral processions led by black plumed horses drawing ancient hearses followed by a cortege of mourners slowly making their way to the cemetery. It was a dramatization of man's ephemeral voyage from birth to death—a drama of humanity performed daily on the street below our apartment.

. . .

"Alla saluti d'noi pardre?" Nonno shouted as he stood and raised his glass of wine.

"Si!" The group responded as they raised their glasses.

"Alla saluti d'noi madre?" He repeated!

"SI!" The group again responded and began to sing,

> "E noi che filiaiamo, beviam, beviam, beviamo
> E noi che filiaiamo, beviam, beviam, beviam.
> Alla salute de nostri padre, alla———."

My father-in-law (Nono is "grandfather" in Italian) had proposed a toast to all our fathers, mothers, ancestors, and even St. Jovani in an ancient Italian drinking song. Carla and I sat at a dining table with her family and relatives at my new mother-in-law's apartment in Rome. Attending our reception were father-in-law Pietro Bernardi, mother-in-law Gina, Carla's brother Regolo age 16, and her sister Marisa age 14. There were also several aunts, uncles and cousins present. I had been rapidly introduced to so many that a blurred image of faces and names flashed through my head. We had driven from Naples to Rome the previous day where I had reserved a room in a hotel to maintain our privacy and avoid being crowed into her mother's small apartment. In addition to a shortage of housing caused by the war, Italian families have traditionally been accustomed to living in small apartments.

During our drive to Rome three vivid scenes remain embedded in my memory:

I recall driving over congested and narrow roads behind charcoal-burning trucks. Italy had produced these trucks during the war to conserve oil and gasoline. They produced a thick cloud of smoke for those following to breathe and were not only slow, but also lacked sufficient power to climb steep hills. Several times during the drive we were forced to wait while passengers stepped out of the charcoal truck and physically pushed them over the crest of a hill. Some were constructed with only three wheels, yet they were used for several years after the war due to a shortage of gasoline.

Our route from Naples to Rome required that we pass through the small town of Cassino that lies adjacent to a monastery perched on the crest of a steep hill. The monastery was used by Germans as an observatory and lay in the path of the allied forces as they advanced toward Rome. I had seen movies of destroyed cities and observed the explosion of bombs from airplanes but I had never personally witnessed such destruction from close proximity. Not a single building remained upright. The allies believed, rightly or wrongly, that the monastery had been converted into a fort and must be destroyed; consequently, airplanes, artillery, and soldiers were employed in an all-out effort to destroy the monastery. The cost in terms of destruction and human lives was frightening. I experienced such a shock that I found it necessary to stop the car and silently observe the debris before continuing our drive.

As we approached a curve in the road, suddenly before us appeared a panorama of the city of Rome and surrounding country set in a background of the distant Mediterranean Sea. It is a sight rarely seen by travelers and is only accessible to those observing from one of the hills overlooking Rome on a rare crystal-clear day. I have visited Rome many times since then but I have never again witnessed such a sight. We stopped and gazed at the magnificent view for several minutes while I thought about the stark contrast between Cassino and Rome. I think I understood for the first time the aphorism, "See Rome and die"—there has never been since, a sight so beautiful.

"Author and new Captain bars"

. . .

A military policeman attracted my attention by blowing his whistle and signaling for me to stop. He saluted as he approached and said,

"Sir, I have orders to confiscate all former German military vehicles that have not been turned it. Did you not know that you were ordered to turn in your vehicle a week ago? Please follow me and talk with my captain."

My heart sank as I contemplated the trouble in which I suddenly found myself. I was near the end of my military career and indeed did not wish to have a record of arrest placed in my file. The MP captain asked me why I continued to drive the Fiat past the date they were to be relinquished. I attempted to make up some clumsy story about the vehicle being attached to Mac's motor pool and loaned to me before the date of recall. I am sure now that he was only following orders and had no desire to punish me. He suggested that I collect my personal items from the car before they drove it away and then promptly dismissed me. There was surely another "Guardian Angel" somewhere in the neighborhood of Mac's motor pool; however, within a few weeks I bought another vehicle and assigned it to Mac's motor pool. I was able to use this jeep for almost six months, until I sold it before departing for the United States.

. . .

While delivering our laundry, the portiere's wife said to Carla,

"Signora, siete incinti?" (Madam, are you pregnant?)

Her statement at the time was a shock to both of us but indeed, she proved to be prophetic, a military doctor declared Carla pregnant a short time later. This new information presented a sudden need for me to begin preparations for our return to the United States. Military ships would not allow passengers to be more than six month pregnant and there were no other means of transportation for military wives at that time. Carla was scheduled to leave Italy carrying our first born, Lana, on the ALGONQUIN, a U. S. Navy hospital ship that had been converted from a cargo ship and equipped to care for pregnant war brides. She departed Naples 7 March 1946 with 800 other pregnant military wives and arrived 12 days later at New York. During the passage to New York she was asked by one of the seasick Italian pregnant war brides why they could not travel to New York by train. Upon arriving at New York, Carla traveled by train from New York to Houston and

T

by bus to Nacogdoches where she arrived on the 21st of March. My train from New York pulled into Camp Chaffee, Arkansas the 28th of March, where I was processed and placed on leave. I finally arrived in Nacogdoches 3 April 1946, 13 days after my mother, father and brother had met Carla at the bus station—all strangers welcoming a foreign bride to an unfamiliar new world.

EPILOGUE

ON THE 3RD of April 1946, my journey from childhood to war was complete. I had departed home as a boy and returned three years later as a seasoned war veteran, husband, and expectant father. I had literally grown up in those three years and experienced a lifetime of excitement, as had many others of my generation. I hold no bitterness for being sent by my government to face the dangers of war; to the contrary, I believe it was my duty to serve my country and believe that I gained both physically and emotionally from the experience. I cannot remember the dreadful emotions of fear but I do recall pleasant memories of happy times and good friends. I have many tender and affectionate memories of Dave Thomas who was my B-24 commander, tent mate, friend, and surrogate older brother. With an incessant smile, patience, and a fierce concentration on details, he taught me to fly a B-24 and helped me survive the war. After finishing our tour of combat and separating, we would not meet again until 1988 at a crew reunion at Las Vegas, 42 years later. It would also be our last meeting. He died a short time later and only four of our ten crewmembers remain.

Each time I reflect on the young men I have know who never returned and the 50 million lives from many nations that were lost in this tragic war, I am compelled to ask,

"Why was I spared?"

Why did I survive the same combat missions that many did not? Why were other airplanes destroyed within a few short yards of my airplane? Why did enemy shells kill those around me, yet allow me to escape unscathed? I have poised these questions for many years but I have never received a satisfactory answer. With the passing of time, I

T

am now certain that I will neither discover the answer to these questions nor will I ever receive a divine message decreeing which challenges I must overcome in exchange for my life. I can only accept my survival, be humbled by it, and consider it one of many blessings that have been bestowed on me.

The only certainty that came from my war experiences is that I learned several things about fear: I became aware that fear is manageable, that it can be controlled. It can be deal with when we accept and acknowledge that we are not always in charge of every situation—that only a greater power controls events. When I finally acknowledged this fact, I discovered that I was no longer paralyzed with fear and could concentrate on other necessary actions that might save me from destruction. I also became aware that although my memory may recall a frightful event, it cannot recreate the horrifying emotions that accompany it — I can only experience each frightening situation one time. Finally, based on my familiarity with fear, I came to the conclusion that it would be almost impossible to ever again encounter anything as frightful as war. Although I may encounter scary moments in the future, I was certain then that it would pale in comparison to air combat. At twenty years of age I had faced death 35 times—nothing in the future could ever be more frightening.

Finally, I salute my fallen comrades who believed as we all did then, that this great nation is worth fighting and dying for.

May they remain forever at peace on the battlefield, never again to fear ONE MORE MISSION.

Index

by Lana Pettey

T

T

T